THE ESSENTIAL SMALL BUSINESS HANDBOOK

By
John A Ockert
Retired CPA

Mission Statement

THE ESSENTIAL SMALL BUSINESS HANDBOOK
**The best and most complete handbook for the Small Business Entrepreneur.
Essential information for starting, buying, operating and succeeding.**

The Essential Small Business Handbook is designed for the Small or Micro Business Owner with ten or fewer employees. Although there are over four and half million Small Businesses with less than ten employees, they are subject to laws and regulation that stretch their financial ability to understand. Micro Businesses are required to navagate over 72,000 pages of tax codes without the financial resources of a large company. We understand that these laws are applied equally, we just don't understand why we need a team of Tax Lawyers and Certified Public Accountants to do business. I created this handbook in an attempt to level the playing field.

Micro Business Owners require basic knowledge on business entities, finance, tax, marketing and a whole host of operating information. Understanding bookkeeping, Financial Statements and tax information are also essential tools in managing your company and obtaining this information has been elusive. Many new entrepreneurs are frustrated that they cannot get straight answers from attorneys and accountants without putting a large dent in their budget. This handbook will provide you with basic business, accounting, tax, operating and even IRS information and at the very minimum, you will gain the knowledge to ask the right questions.

The mission of this Handbook is to provide Small Businesses Owners the tools and information for creating success when buying a franchise, purchasing a business or starting a business. This Handbook also provides Small Businesses the essential information needed to understand Financial Statements and how they can prepare their companies bookkeeping using an innovative three-step approach. I understand the confusion the tax code has create and I have included a comprehensive list of Small Business tax deductions available to the Micro Business, and tips on how to use them.

From the Author

My degree is in Industrial Administration at Iowa State University in Ames Iowa. I opened my first tax and accounting office in 1968. At one time, my office prepared 7,000 tax returns a year, and we provided monthly bookkeeping and consulting services for 150 small businesses. I have tried and failed in business, and although it is easy to blame the government for my failures, I was overextended in real estate during the last economic turndown. I always returned to my first love, tax and accounting services. I sold my CPA practice several years ago and retired in Texas; this handbook is a labor of love, and I have enjoyed every page. The tax tips alone could save you thousands but the operating advice will secure you future.

INTRODUCTION
THE ESSENTIAL SMALL BUSINESS HANDBOOK
**The best and most complete handbook for the Small Business Entrepreneur.
Essential information for starting, buying, operating and succeeding.**

Small Business Handbook Chapter Summaries and Out-Lines

Page 1 to 20

Chapter 1
Follow Your Passion – Start Your Own Business

The initial chapter explains the benefits of being Self-employed including tax benefits, job security and freedom. Since over 50% of businesses fail the first year, I cover many of the reasons for business failures and present you with a brief explanation of the steps you can initiate to insure success. Many successful entrepreneurs have been able to create a business by developing their passion into a product or service. I cannot create passion but I can help you discover your passion and guide you through the maze of problems you will encounter converting this passion into a success business.

Being Self-Employed

Benefits of Being Self-Employed:
- ➢ Control Your Own Destiny
- ➢ Earn What Your Worth
- ➢ Weather the Economy
- ➢ Pick Your Own Passion
- ➢ Tax Benefits
- ➢ Give Order, Don't Take Them
- ➢ Self-Employment Can Offer Job Security
- ➢ Felling of Accomplish
- ➢ Part Time or Full Time
- ➢ Other Reasons to Become Self-Employed

Prepare To Be Self-Employed

Are You Ready to Become Entrepreneur?
- ➢ Discover Your Hidden Talents and Skills
- ➢ Match your Abilities and Skills to an Opportunity

Business Failures and How to Avoid Them

Causes of Businesses Fails:
- ➢ Inside Competition

I

Convert Your Passion into a Business

Types of Businesses

✳✳

Page 21 to 34

Chapter 2
Guidelines for Buying a Franchise

In the past 20 years thousands of franchises have been created and sold. For years clients engaged me to analysis different franchises and I discovered many were outstanding and created an opportunity and many made exaggerated promises, took deposits and even franchise investments without delivering on these promises. The abuses were so numerous that the federal government and all states have laws regulating franchise marketing. This manual spells out the due-diligence requirements you need to undertake when selecting a franchise. Over all I like franchises because they force you to become successful by providing an operational blue-print and a business plan you are required to follow. However never forget that you may be giving up the very thing which created your entrepreneurs spirit – freedom and independence.

Franchise Advantages

➢ Brand Name
➢ Systems and Internal control
➢ Business Environment
➢ Training and Education
➢ Buying Power
➢ Negative Side of Franchise

Finding Franchises

➢ Franchisor Web Sites
➢ Franchise Expositions
➢ Franchise Broker

Investigation and Due Diligence

➢ Franchisor Investigation, Information and Prospectus
➢ Franchisor Disclosure Statement
➢ Franchisor's Business History
➢ History Of Legal Actions
➢ Franchisor Bankruptcy
➢ Startup And Operation Cost
➢ Franchise Restrictions
➢ Location Approval And Construction
➢ Design and Appearance
➢ Sales Area
➢ Goods And Services Restrictions
➢ Operational Controls
➢ Franchise Termination
➢ Franchise Education And Training Available
➢ Advertising Cost
➢ Terminated Franchisee Information

Franchise Documents

➢ Franchise Documents and Provisions are Extensive

III

- ➢ Provisions In The Contract You Need To Consider
- ➢ Projected Earnings Information
- ➢ Attorney Advice
- ➢ Government Regulations

Franchise Fees – Royalties - Hidden Cost

- ➢ Franchisor Cost of Buying and Operating a Franchise
- ➢ Franchise Fees
- ➢ Royalties
- ➢ Other Hidden Cost Of Owning A Franchise
  - ✓ Product Cost
  - ✓ Franchisors Owned Facility
  - ✓ Improvement Requirements
  - ✓ Training, Conferences And In-House Education Requirements
  - ✓ Franchise Volunteer Requirements

Leasehold Improvements and Building Construction

- ➢ Franchisor Building and Construction Requirements
- ➢ Pre-Construction Due-Diligence
- ➢ Picking A Contractor
- ➢ Never Pre-Pay
- ➢ Protect The Builder

Final Answer - Should I Purchase a Franchise

****

Page 35 to 54

Chapter 3
Strategies for Purchasing a Business

Is the business worth the asking price? Is the profit real? Can I qualify for a loan to purchase a business? How much business can I afford? These four questions and many other questions concern entrepreneurs when purchasing a business. I answer the question of how much business can you afford, how to calculate collateral values to secure a loan, what information you need to request from the seller and I provide you with a simple business valuation procedure. I cover why you should purchase the business from the seller's business entity and not purchase the seller's business entity. Finally I review why and how you should assign a cost to each asset included in the purchase price to maximize your tax benefits.

Questions - Buying a Business

Investment Objectives

Provide the reasonable wage for your work.
Service the business loan. (New Business Loan)
Provide a fair return on your investment.
Create sufficient profit for growth and retirement.

Will the Business Support Your Lifestyle?

Steps for Purchasing a Business

How Do I Calculate Loan-Asset Value for Collateral
- ➢ Estate Loans
- ➢ Inventory Loan
- ➢ Equipment, Fixtures and Machinery Loans
- ➢ Loans Based Upon the Value of Goodwill
- ➢ Consider Working Capital

Estimated Loan Needed for the Business You Want

Estimates of Loan Requirements for Three Business
- ➢ Retail Store
- ➢ Doctors Office
- ➢ Restaurant

Conclusion: Equity, Asset Loan Value and Working Capital

DUE-DILIGENCE STEPS

What to Request from the Seller
- ➢ Meet With the Seller
- ➢ Sign A Non-Disclosure Agreement
- ➢ Financial Statements
- ➢ Bank Statements
- ➢ General Ledger
- ➢ Be Prepared With Operational Questions

Analyze the Sellers Information

Determine the Value of the Business

Calculate Fair Market Value of Business
- ➢ Asset based approach
- ➢ Comparable businesses
- ➢ Gross income approach
- ➢ Multiple of discretionary earnings approach
- ➢ Appraised value approach

> ➤ Other considerations that influence value

Small Business Valuation Approach
> ➤ Establish the income
> ➤ Establish the cost of goods sold
> ➤ Establish the operating expenses
> ➤ Computing the profit
> ➤ Does the net profit meet your goals?
> ➤ Determine the fair market value of the assets
> ➤ Other considerations which may affect the business value
> ➤ The final value

Complete the Purchase

Purchase the Business Not the Company

Split-Out the Total Purchase Price

Non-Completive Provisions

Review the HR System

✳✳✳✳✳✳✳✳✳✳✳✳✳✳✳✳✳✳✳✳✳✳✳✳✳✳✳✳✳✳✳✳✳✳✳✳✳✳

Page 55 to 96

Chapter 4
Start-Up Business

This is the most written about subject in the business world. There are hundreds of books, internet articles and even magazines on becoming an entrepreneur. However most this information is directed toward starting a million dollar business. There is very little information for starting a small business with ten or fewer employees. Even the SBA Web Site is geared to businesses requiring a huge investment. Have you noticed that much of this advice is from government bureaucrats, college professors, five hundred dollar an hour CPAs or attorneys in white shirts and red ties? None of these professionals have been on the front lines of any small business start-up operation and why take advice from anyone who has never been in your shoes?

You are not McDonalds yet and you sure can't afford a $50,000.00 business plan or an extensive marketing plan which cost as much as you planned on spending for advertising in your first year of operation. This chapter will guide you through the steps necessary start your own business and how to do it on a budget. Write your own business plan and prepare your bank loan information.

Preliminary Approach - Starting a Business

Phase 1: Is Your Business Idea Feasible - Initial Proposal
- ✓ Ready to become Self-employed.
- ✓ Business summary - Reduce your Idea to Writing.

Phase 2: The Preliminary Business Blueprint
- ➢ What are my Products and Services?
- ➢ Basic Requirements
- ➢ Market for Your Products and Services?
- ➢ Preliminary Market Strategy.
- ➢ Business Idea Profitable?
- ➢ Preliminary Financial Projections.
  - ✓ Provide a fair Return on Your Investment
  - ✓ Service the business loan
  - ✓ Provide a reasonable income for your labors
  - ✓ Create a profit for growth and Retirement

Phase 3: Presentation of your Business Idea.

Comprehensive Business Plan

Step 1: Management and Owner Introductions.

Step 2: Company Description.

Step 3: Organization.

Step 4: Service and Product Lines.

Step 5: Marketing and Sales.

Step 6: Funding Request.

Step 7: Financial Projections.

Comprehensive Requirements

Understand your Market - Marketing plan.
- ✓ Who are your customers?
- ✓ How are you planning to market your products and/or services?
- ✓ Adverting – yellow pages, print media and/or coupon specials.
- ✓ Do I need a web site?
- ✓ What is your marketing budget?

Protect your Butt – Insurance and Bonds.
- ➢ Vehicle Insurance

- ➢ Health Insurance
- ➢ Workers Compensation
- ➢ Errors and Omissions
- ➢ Liability Insurance
- ➢ Performance Bonds

Pick a Name - Protect your name.
- ➢ Name that Reflects your Business.
- ➢ Business Name or Your Name
- ➢ Catchy name
- ➢ Is the name Available
- ➢ What does the name Look-like on a Sign.

Managing Business Risk
- ➢ Human Risk
- ➢ Criminal Acts
- ➢ Technology Risk
- ➢ Investment Risk
- ➢ Loan Risk
- ➢ Operating Risk
- ➢ Government Liabilities
- ➢ General Operational Risk
- ➢ Leasing Risk

Financial Projections
- ✓ Comprehensive sales estimates.
- ✓ Income statement projections.
- ✓ Cash flow projections.
- ✓ Balance sheet projections.
- ✓ Capital asset requirements.
- ✓ Personal living projections review personal finances.
- ✓ Personal finance statement.
- ✓ Personal budget plan.
- ✓ SBA Application.

Legal Entity – Protection & Tax Benefits
- ✓ Determine your business legal structure
- ✓ Sole Proprietorship
- ✓ Limited Liability Company
- ✓ Corporations – S or C

Licensing and Registration
- ✓ Federal tax identification number
- ✓ State & local registration requirements
- ✓ license & sales tax

Hire Attorney and Accountant

Complete Basic Operation Systems

- ➢ Hiring and Out-sourcing
- ➢ Consultants

Start-up Recourses

Final Funding Requirements
- ✓ Personal living expense
- ✓ Start-up cost – facilities, equipment and inventory.
- ✓ Working capital
- ✓ Total money needed to finance your dream

Financing Your Dream
- ➢ Where do I go for financing
- ➢ What lenders require
- ➢ Personal financial statements
- ➢ Two-years of tax returns
- ➢ Credit report
- ➢ Letter of intent from lessors
- ➢ SBA lenders
- ➢ Investors, friends and relatives
- ➢ Venture capital

Summary

✹✹✹

Page 97 to 124

Chapter 5
Understanding Financial Statements

I created this chapter because so many of my small business clients never looked at their monthly financial statements prepared by my office. As with any other discipline understanding Financial Statements takes time and training. I discovered early on in my career the importance of using financials to make business decisions so within this chapter I tackle the job of explaining financial statements. Every number on a financial statement provides information on your business operation. The Assets show your available cash and your investment into inventory, accounts receivable and even equipment. The liability section details the amounts you owe and comparing assets to liabilities clearly demonstrates if your company is in financial trouble or the future looks rosy. Everyone checks sales but most clients do not realize the importance of expenses as a percent of sales. I can tell within a couple of minutes if a restaurant is in trouble by comparing cost of sales (food) with sales and I can look at other percent's and quickly determine problem areas. Understanding financial statements can save your business from failure and allow you to grow into the successful company you desire.

Financial Statements
IX

Three financial Statements
Complicated Financial Statements

The Standard Financial Statement

Balance Sheet
Statement of Profit And Loss
Statement of Cash Flows
- ➢ Monthly Budgets
- ➢ Contra Accounts
- ➢ Financial Statement Categories – Name or Assigned Number
- ➢ Account Categories
- ➢ Contra Accounts
- ➢ Financial Accounting
- ➢ Tax Accounting

Cash, Accrual and Hybrid Accounting Methods
- ➢ Cash Method of Accounting
- ➢ Accrual Method of Accounting
- ➢ Hybrid Method of Accounting

Tax Accounting – Income Tax Reporting
- ➢ Self-Employed or proprietorships
- ➢ Limited Liability Company and Partnerships
- ➢ "C" Corporation
- ➢ "S" Corporation

Understanding the Balance Sheet

Assets
- ➢ Current
- ➢ Non-Current
- ➢ Recording Loss in Value
- ➢ Purchase and Expense or Asset

Liabilities
- ➢ Current
- ➢ Non-Current
- ➢ Current Ratio

Net Worth or Equity
- ➢ Sample Financial Statement

Understanding the Statement of Income & Expense

Revenue – Sales Income

X

Cost of Goods Sold

Disbursements or Expenses
➢ Chart of Accounts

Sample Financial Statements

Financial Statements: John Smith Plumbing Inc.
- Cover sheet
- Accountants compilation report
- Balance sheet
- Statement of income
- Cash flow statement

****

Page 125 to 162

Chapter 6
Bookkeeping –Prepare Your Own Books

Not only do I think you "can" prepare your own books, I believe you "should" prepare your own books. However you need to consider two important aspect of bookkeeping: 1) Get help setting up your bookkeeping procedures and internal operating systems and obtaining basic training from a qualified bookkeeper or accountant and 2) always be involved in your bookkeeping even after your growth demands hiring an out-side bookkeeper or hiring a full time staff bookkeeper. Financial statements that reflect true and accurate information will help guide you through your entire business career. This chapter guides your through my three step approach to preparing your books. I cover bookkeeping concepts and procedures from filing your receipts to posting financial transaction. I tackle problem bookkeeping procedures including recording business use of your personal vehicle, how to post a petty cash fund and the complicated posting of personal and business credit cards. Remember correct books cut tax liability, limit employee thief, prepare for a future business sale and provides your lenders or investors with poof you are ready for growth.

Basic Bookkeeping Knowledge

Understanding Bookkeeping
- Establish a chart of accounts
- One business bank checking account
- What the hell is double entry bookkeeping

Four Bookkeeping Concepts

First Concept: Understand the basic financial statements.
- Assets
- Liabilities
- Net Worth
- Sales Income
- Expenses - Disbursements

Second Concept: Walk through transactions in your minds-eye.
- General Ledger
- Bookkeeping Financial Transactions
- Account
- Double Entry
- Examples

Third Concept: Tunnel vision.
- Consider the easy-side of a transaction
- Do not follow the money

Forth Concept: All financial transactions have equal pluses (+) and minuses (-)

Minds-Eye Walk Through Coupled With Actual Transactions

Nine Basic Bookkeeping Examples
- Minds-eye walk through
- Journal Entry for Bookkeeping System
- Balance sheet
- Income Statement

Inventory and Cost of Goods Sold

Accounting Operating Procedures

Three Step Approach to Your Business Bookkeeping

First Step: Prepare Your Own Books with Professional Training
- Bookkeeping training
- Very small business
- Mid-size and larger businesses
- Software programs
- The bookkeeping profession

Second Step: Hire an outside Bookkeeping service.
- Preferred Booking Procedure
- Independent Bookkeeping Service

Third Step: Hire a full-time Bookkeeping service
- Hire a Bookkeeper
- Test Potential Bookkeepers
- Bookkeepers Test

"For years, we've been playing by old rules and the results have been dismal. It's time for a bold new direction!"

****

Page 163 to 200

Chapter 7
Income and Deductions
Income Tax Tips For Your Business

This is my favorite chapter. For me Tax Preparation is not a job but a passion that I turned into a career. It is difficult listening to anyone discuss their business or income taxes without butting in with tax tips and advice. My passion has become increasingly more complicated since the tax code is totally out of control with over 72,000 pages and maybe a million regulations and court decisions. Every business deduction has exceptions and many times conflicting conclusions by CPAs, tax preparers and even IRS agents. Special interest groups have high-jacked our tax codes by convincing congress to establish laws which benefit their industry or sometimes a single tax payer. Many of my clients want a flat tax however for most Americans we already have a flat tax. Usually a 1040 Long Form requires only a few entries for most tax payers and I have read estimates that up to 80% of tax returns filed are short forms. We simply have a progressive flat tax. The more you make the higher the percent of your income goes to government programs. The perceived inequality with our tax codes exist because we live in a complex

Copyright ©

environment. If I open a tax guide and turn to any page there are hundreds of exceptions for each topic.

However business deductions and expenses probably will be with us until congress creates a national sales tax or a tax based upon Gross Receipts with no deductions and no exceptions. After preparing 25,000 tax returns over 30 years I see no congressional majority with the guts to establish a simpler tax code. Just too much money involved for special interest groups. You need to review those business deductions that affect your business and at the minimum operate so you can take advantage of our confusing tax laws.

Income

Income Constructively Received
- Sales – Cash and Credit
- Money-In
- Non-Cash Income

Tax Deductible Business Expense

Cost of Goods Sold

Expense versus Capital Asset

Business Operating Expenses

Operational Business Expense

When Can You Deduct Expenses
- Cash Method of Accounting
- Accrual Method of Accounting
- Hybrid method of Accounting

Type of Business Expenses - Business Expenses and Tax Tips
- Accounting and Bookkeeping Service
- Advertising Cost
- Attorney Fees
- Answering Service
- Bad Debt Expense
- Bank & Merchant Fees
- Capital Expense
  - Cost
  - Useful Life
  - Listed property
  - 179 Depreciation

- Casualty Losses
- Cell Telephone
- Charitable Business Contributions
- Club Dues
- Commissions and Fees
- Cleaning, Cleaning Supplies and Janitorial Cost
- Contract Services
- Dues and Subscriptions
- Educational Expenses
- Employee Benefit Plans
- Entertainment – Business
- Home Office Expense
- Insurance – Liability, Medical, Officer Medical and Workers Compensation
- Interest Expense
- Internet Fees
- Lease Expense
  - Office
  - Warehouse
  - Storage Facilities
- Lease – Equipment and Tools
- Miscellaneous Expense
- Office Supplies
- Operational Supplies
- Pest Control Expense
- Postage, UPS and Freight Cost
- Printing and Reproduction
- Repairs and Maintenance
- Sanitation and Trash Removal
- Salaries – Officers
- Salaries – Staff
- Security Systems
- Taxes
  - Employer Taxes
  - Federal Unemployment
  - State Unemployment
  - Property
  - Telephone – Business
- Travel – Transportation and Meals
- Vehicle Cost
  - Actual Vehicle
    - Gas & Oil
    - General Repairs
    - Vehicle Insurance
    - Vehicle Repairs

****

Page 201 to 222
XV   Copyright ©

Chapter 8
General Business Information
Business Observations
Rules of Success

For yeaars I have observed small business operations as a consumer and a Small Business Consultant. Some entreprenuers simply have a nack for making money no matter the business. They are organized, hard working and pay attention to the smallest details. They arrive at work early and stay late, always keeping their eye on the botton line. Many do not maintian the financial records the IRS or the accounting profession believes are necessary to succeed, however, they pay attention to customer service and provide a product or service at a competitive price. You need to observe and minick the successful operations.

Business Information, Observations and Rules For Success
- Business Rule for Success 1 – Sales
- Business Rule for Success 2 – Cost Of Sales
- Marketing Plan
- Take A Salary or Fixed Draw
- Money Management
- Checking Account
- Time Management
- Make Lunch Productive
- The Importance of A Budget
- Pay Your Federal Withholding Tax
- How Long To Keep Records
- Property Basis – Keep Records
- Basis Of Property, Gift Verus Interheritence
- Don't Work For Money
- Open The Doors On Time
- Negative Advertising
- Dumb Business Moves
- Treat Your Employees Right
- What Motivies Your Employees
- Dress Code
- Nepotism
- Inside Competition
- Employ Your Child
- Chosing A Tax Preparer
- IRS Audits
     Tracking Self-Employed Income

Chapter 1
FOLLOW YOUR PASSION-
START YOUR OWN BUSINESS
THE ESSENTIAL SMALL BUSINESS HANDBOOK
**The best and most complete handbook for the Small Business Entrepreneur.
Essential information for starting, buying, operating and succeeding.**

For thirty years, my father owned and operated a neighborhood tavern in a small Iowa town. When I started writing this book, I realized the influence his entrepreneur spirit had upon my life. He may not have understood his limitations or his weaknesses, but he developed a core set of business management skills without any formal business education or experience. He purchased his business with a small down payment and a large loan and within a few short years he achieved success. I don't know if owning and operating a tavern was his passion, but I do know he was passionate about his independence and his ability to succeed.

There are hundreds of books and articles written on the subject of discovering your passion. Passion develops when you have been exposed to an opportunity or a profession and an unwavering desire for success is created. Passion for creating a successful business is a common trait of most entrepreneurs. The desire to achieve creates a genuine confidence and commitment to become successful. Don't wait for lighting to strike. An entrepreneur recognizes a business opportunity, produces a business plan and seizes the moment. The imagination of an entrepreneur creates a conceptual idea and then the company is born.

Being Self-Employed

Have I waited too long to become Self-employed? In any economy, thousands of people are unemployed and finding work that uses their talents and abilities for a fair wage is difficult and maybe impossible. Many industries are just making a comeback and are reluctant to hire because of the financial losses they incurred when the economy folded. Currently, thousands of employed individuals are sending out resumes because their job may be cut, or they are genuinely dissatisfied with their employer. Even in an economy that is booming the prospect of becoming self-employed, can be an unrealized dream. We all believe that job security is a by-product of being employed, and it is hard changing that perception. You always waited for the right time, enough money or the right business. Stop making excuses! I have heard the statement "Someday I'll start my own business" too many times. Look at the benefits of being self-employed below and take action. Don't let anything stop you!

Benefits of Being Self-Employed

Pick Your Profession: Many employees are thrust into jobs that they hate. Employees fill positions within companies without the ability or talent for the job. We have all witness employees promoted to their level of incompetence.' As a self- employed individual, you can choose your industry and develop the knowledge, skills and ability to succeed. No one is forcing you to drive a square peg into a round hole. Few self-employed individuals roll out of bed each morning dreading the thought of going to work and mustering up the effort to drive to work. Calling in "sick" is not considered.

Tax Benefits: There are many tax benefits available to self-employed individuals and small companies. The tax laws are applied equally to mega companies and to mom and pop businesses. The problem exists because small businesses do not have the resources to research all the tax laws applicable to their small business. Chapter 7 in this handbook details the many tax benefits available to a small businesses. Understanding tax law can be complicated; the tax law has thousands of exceptions and regulations. Use Chapter 7 as a guide when setting up your accounting and internal procedures. Contact your Tax Accountant for assistance.

Things like office in the home, business use of your personal vehicle and even ways to pay your children non-taxable wages are available for self-employed entrepreneurs. Sounds too good to be true, but sole proprietors can employ their children, pay them an acceptable wage and the child can create a college savings account using tax-free money. In Chapter 7 are many tax tips for the different expense disbursement categories.

Control Your Own Destiny: What are your expectations? Most nine-to-five jobs limit your potential and opportunities. The company controls your income, promotions and work product. If that control resulted in job security, you might hang in there, but in any economy, businesses and government agencies are terminating jobs by the hundreds. Being self-employed allows you to be in control of your future. Is it your destiny to become an entrepreneur? Don't bestow your fate upon company that shows little regard to your future.

Earn What Your Worth: Self-employed people earn an average of five times more than individuals employed in traditional jobs. You are in control of your income and the business decisions you make will determine your success. Most if the time being self-employed is not about the money. Time and again it has been proven to me that entrepreneurs don't work for money. Individuals respond to different challenges. Self-employed people want to create something from scratch, be independent and reap the benefits of hard work. They desire the freedom and opportunity to succeed. If that success creates wealth, then that usually is a by-product of being an entrepreneur.

Survive the Economy: In periods of recession, entrepreneurs develop plans and undertake actions that protect their income. Changing products, offering discounts or even reducing your overhead is a business decision that you can make in an instant. Large companies seem unable to make necessary business decisions in a timely fashion. The blame-game is usually the only decision made in a timely manner. As a small business, you can react in a few days or even a few hours, not a few months. Self-employed individuals can always be ready for a down economy by relying on themselves.

The Feeling of Accomplishment: Sometimes, I would sit in my office basking in the feeling of accomplishment. Not that the world knew or cared about my little tax and accounting business, I knew. Over the years, I helped hundreds of people start a business. I provided bookkeeping and tax preparation to thousands of companies and individuals, and I gave business advice that created jobs and income for families. You can have that feeling of accomplishment.

Give Orders, Don't Take Them: Nothing makes me more upset than having an incompetent boss. Just like you, I have been subjected to supervisors that were unable to manage and who generate very little respect. Many managers control employees by the use of fear, belittling, criticism, poor salary and unfair evaluation. Becoming the boss changes this equation, and it is refreshing and makes working worthwhile. Years of psychological abuse can disappear. Becoming the boss does not give you the right to abuse your employees. Treat your staff as you would want to be treated. Once again, money usually is not an employee motivator. Most employees can be motivated by an understanding boss who treats his employees with respect.

Self-Employment Can Offer You Job Security: There is little job security working for most companies or even working at a government agency. Thousands of people are unemployed because of the outsourcing, technology advancements, and many companies still are recovering from the recession. We all believe we are necessary. However, no one is indispensable, your job can be terminated at any time and for any reason. Early retirement has been a reality for many long-term employees. If you believe you are so important to your company that they would never lay you off, I have some land in Florida to sell you. Today, I have many self-employed clients who are currently the only employee remaining because of the recession. However, they are surviving.

Part Time or Full Time: Starting a part time business requires the same devotion and research as starting a full-time business. Many times a part-time operations can be financed over a period of years while you are developing the company. You have an income from your full-time job which can alleviate worry and concern about meeting your financial obligations. One problem with working two jobs is that it is easy to get burned out by working too many hours. Your personal life may suffer, and although you may be able to become successful, it may be at a high price. Many entrepreneurs convert their part time business into full-time employment. One such enterprising entrepreneur ordered jewelry from Malaysia and after a few years marketing at flea markets; she opened a jewelry store at a local mall. Part-time ventures can and do work.

Other Reasons to Become Self-employed: Suits and ties are out. Since you establish the dress code, you can wear whatever you want. However, one rule of success is to dress professionally. You also can set the hours your business is open. Flexible hours are one benefit of being self-employed. However, fixed business hours are necessary if customers visit your business.

Prepare To Be Self-Employed

Are you ready to become an entrepreneur? Start where you are today and look inward. You must learn to recognize your talents and abilities and acquire the necessary skills you lack by attending a business school or college. Change jobs to gain experience, even if it is for less money. Being self-employed requires that you must wear many hats. You need to develop business and personal skills to become proficient in many disciplines. Obtaining the knowledge of accounting, bookkeeping, budgeting, customer service, marketing, advertising, legal and regulatory requirements can be very useful in operating any small business. Successful owners today must also have an understanding of Social Media and technology, including twitter and the internet.

My high school counselor determined my future was in construction, specifically as a carpenter. My brother believed I should follow in his footsteps and become an engineer. No one, including myself realized that I had a talent for accounting and tax preparation. For many years, I worked for a large corporation hating everything about the job. I was unhappy, underpaid and despised going to work. I answered a newspaper ad from an in-home tax preparation company. I attended three months of training, acquiring an essential knowledge of tax return preparation and within a few short years I converted a part-time business into a full-time career. I discovered I loved preparing tax returns and client interaction. My natural ability in using numbers and in customer communication has developed into a set of skills organizing and managing businesses.

Discover Hidden Talents and Skills: Many of us have hobbies that consume hours of our time. We are so engrossed in this activity that time passes without notice. Hobbies create and develop skills. You have acquired talents and skills without realizing it. Thinking back, I have known many individuals who have converted their hobbies into a successful opportunity by recognizing the talents necessary for their hobby. Make a complete list of aptitude needed to accomplish this activity. Do not discount a particular skill such as communication, problem-solving, imagination or industry skills such as internet talents and computer abilities. Ask a trusted friend to help you discover your abilities. Many people today spend most of their off hours on the internet without realizing they are developing computer skills that are in demand by thousands of companies. A few credit hours at a local college can enhance these skills into a small business opportunity.

Consider your job duties, responsibilities and obligations in every position you have held. Prepare a complete and detailed list of those skills and talents required for past or current employment.

Match your Abilities and Skills to an Opportunity: Match your abilities and skills to business opportunities requiring these talents is your first step. By matching your expertise and capabilities to a business opportunity, you may recognize an activity you can convert into a small business. Detailed below are many business possibilities for you to review. Compare these business opportunities with your two lists, and maybe you will develop a business idea which will take advantage of your talents and your skills leading to success.

Business Failures and How to Avoid Them

The Small Business Administration's statistics reflects that 50% of small businesses fail within the first five years. Don't let the failure rate scare you. Before you create your company plan review why businesses fail and learn from their mistakes. Plan for success, but understand and study why business fail. Being optimistic is a requirement for all entrepreneurs, however, sticking your head in the sand and ignoring reality will result in tragedy. Quoting Albert Einstein, Insanity is doing the same thing over and over expecting different results. Many companies keep doing the same thing over and over and continue down the path of failure. Consider the major causes of business failure and plan for success.

Inside Competition: When I checked on Google, I could not find any reference to the term <u>Inside Competition</u>. Years ago I coined this phrase to describe the all-inclusive requirements owners need to control when creating and building a successful business. It amazes me of the vast amount of attention paid to competitors. Business failures occur because owners fail to manage. Entrepreneurs must wear many different hats. Grasping the basic knowledge of marketing, advertising, accounting, financing, benefits, employee supervision and interior design is a formable undertaking. These professions are only a few of the disciplines required for a successful operation.

Blaming others has become a national theme and a disgrace. I had a client who was relating to me a story about his foreman and crew installing concrete curbs incorrectly. His foreman would not take the blame and insisted 'Those guys did it'. It is not those guys; it is you and your systems, procedures, products, services and failure to change that creates failure. Details and more details create success. In the movie Casino, Robert De Niro was the manager of a large Casino. He pointed to a burned-out light bulb on the marquee and directed his staff to fix a light bulb. The bulb did not make the business successful, but paying attention to a thousand 'light bulb' type problems, leads to success.

McDonald's spends millions on <u>Inside Competition</u>. Every detail is checked. The appearance inside and outside is the result of studding customer needs and wants. Mickey Ds did not become the fast food leader because they worried about outside competition, they paid attention to Outside Competition, but they focused on <u>Inside Competition</u>. They created a total enjoyable buying experience which induces customer visits and maximizes purchases. Entering the restaurant, ordering, paying, eating and leaving is a rewarding experience. People often criticize McDonald's but guess what? Customers still wait in line. Does that tell you anything? They are not inexpensive; they have convinced us their prices are reasonable. It is all about perception.

Consider 7-11 stores. Can you imagine the difficulty of convincing a lender that you need a loan to open a store that all the products are 30% to 100% higher priced than the competition? They studied the market and developed a retail model and business plan that few business gurus understood. Why did Blockbuster fail? Management was more worried about continuing an outdated marketing concept than innovations. It is all about <u>Inside Competition</u>. In this case Blockbuster did not pay attention to new technology in the marketplace. Netflix established a new business model, and Blockbuster continued expecting customers to drive to a retail store. The pathetic thing about the demise of Blockbuster is they had the money and the ability to change and management chose to continue down the path to bankruptcy.

Insufficient Capitalization: Insufficient capitalization is the result of poor planning. Financial Projections are an essential tool necessary to project capital requirements. Using well thought out cash flow projections will pinpoint the capital necessary for your operation. Use money-in and money-out projections for the three budgets necessary to correctly predict the capital needs for one or two years of survival. Projections required are:

> ➢ A Household Budget of personal expenditures
> ➢ A Start-up cost budget
> ➢ Statement of Cash Flow - Income and Expense projections.

Merge the three budget projections into Money-in and Money-out two-year cash requirements forecast. By starting with your investment, adding sales income and subtracting business expenses the loan or additional investment needed will become apparent.

Usually, the household budget and the Start-up Cost are accurate. Fixed business expenses also are estimated correctly. Other costs such as wages and operating supplies are a little harder to project, and many of these expenditures are directly related to sales volume. The biggest problem is projecting sales income. Because entrepreneurs are blessed and cursed with the 'glass is Half Full' viewpoint, many times sales income is over estimated.

A variance of a few percent can be devastating to your cash flow, and a 20% error could result in inadequate operating capital. Unrealized sales projections can cause cash flow problems within a few weeks of opening. Cut your income projections in half and then consider reducing them further. Over and over entrepreneurs create income projections without a marketing plan or enough dollars devoted to advertising. When sales projections do not materialize additional capital investment is need to continue operations. It is simple to conclude that you opened your business without sufficient capital, but the real problem was rose colored glasses when projection income.

It is interesting to note that too much of a good thing can also create a cash flow problem. For a small manufacturing facility or a retail store, an overwhelming increase in sales can create serious cash flow problems equality as devastating as poor sales. When we initially generate our cash flow projections we anticipate a dollar level of inventory, either in raw materials or retail merchandise. A surge in sales can quickly result in a shortage of merchandise or a storage of raw materials. Additional capital is necessary to replenish materials or merchandise. Many times entrepreneurs believed that this is a 'good' problem. However, if the money is not available, your competitors may step in and fill a customer need before you can obtain required capital to take advantage of the opportunity. If you are financing your accounts receivable you have an additional cash flow problem.

Cash Flow Projections are tools necessary for success. As a new business, it is a tool that could make the difference between success and failure.

Lack of a Marketing Plan: The first rule of business is sales. Sales are the result of a reliable marketing plan. In a later chapter, I detail the information necessary for preparing a business plan including a marketing plan. Base your sales volume projections on your conviction and belief in your marketing plan. The old marketing approach of 'My business will spread word to mouth' just does not cut it. By the time word spreads about you and your business you will be out of money. A marketing Plan is essential for success. A marketing plan must detail your dollars and time you intend to commit to promoting your products and services.

Lack of Budgets: I recommend a 12 month moving budget. Each month you update the next month's projections. Delete the expired month and create a new 12th month. Review each month and make corrections. However, the next month's projection is the most significant forecast you can make. An accurate prediction of next months income and disbursements is your short-term guide to success. Make your staff a part of your budget process.

Review the last month's actuals with your budget and request ideas and input from your employees. If your actuals are greater than a 10% variance to your budget, you have a problem that needs attention. By making your staff a part of the budget process, you build a team striving for success. Many times employees know what is happening with your customer base and business before you do. You do not have all the answers. Don't let your ego override common sense.

You need to monitor your income daily if not hourly and make changes in minutes not months. Operating expenses also need regular monitoring. It 's hard to change fixed cost such as rent and utilities so concentrate on those expenditures you can change. Many fast food outlets call in staff or send employees home early as needed.

Poor or No Bookkeeping: Bookkeeping is the procedure invented for businesses that allow entrepreneurs the ability to compare actuals against budgets. Although Bookkeeping provides many other benefits, comparing your budgets against your actual income and expenses can be an eye-opener. What you do with that information is completely your responsibility. OK, I know I'm an Accountant, and I emphasize bookkeeping, but you must realize the importance of accurate financial statements. How can your obtain loans or investors without financials? Giving your Tax Accountant a shoebox full of receipts and believing that is funny is just plain dumb. Tax Accountants can save you thousands with tax planning and tax preparation based upon correct financial statements.

Many of my clients did not review their financials with the intensity I believe is necessary. However, on a daily basis they used current information, consider their income and expense and make changes to save money or take advantage of the opportunity. They did not make changes at the end of the month; they made changes daily.

Study History: As Gus said in the TV saga Lonesome Dove, Yesterday is gone, you can't get it back. I don't want yesterday back, but we need to study business current business operations to prevent making the same mistakes. Analyzing business failures and successes is equally important. A significant benefit, when purchasing a franchise, is their history of achievement. I have always said that if I were starting a hamburger business I would review and copy McDonald's or Burger King's Operation. Mimicking successful companies can be the key to your success. When visiting any store, observe the operation and facility. Make notes for future reference. Assess every business you enter and chat with the owner or staff. You may be surprised at the amount of information available asking questions.

Personal Use of Business Funds: I was sitting with a client in his small retail store and I was amazed when his wife came in, opened the cash register and took out a wad of money. I have also seen restaurants feed their family and any other family member who happens to stop in. Of course, the owner always justifies the act of converting business assets to personal use as a way to beat the IRS. Taking company money and goods without accountability can result in spending without controls. Put yourself on a fixed salary and live within your budget just as you did when you were and employee.

Nepotism can be a Disaster: Thousands of businesses fail because of nepotism. It sounds wonderful when planning a future for your son or daughter; however, there can be disagreements over money, control, work assignments and hundreds of other things. Problems and conflicts within your home also may end up affecting your business. Nepotism can have an adverse effect on other employees. Decisions concerning layoffs, salary cuts, and promotions affect other employees and create additional pressures on business decisions when objectivity should be the standard. Don't do it! You will be sorry. How do you lay off your son or daughter? They will stay until the bankruptcy.

I have seen many husband and wife teams become successful. However, I have also seen businesses create additional friction in relationships already strained. I believe it takes a special couple to tread the waters of a business operation. Adding to your relationship dynamics with other problems can affect any marriage. Carefully review your business model to limit conflicts.

Partnerships and 50-50 Ownership: In 30 years as a small business consultant and Tax Accountant I have seen few partnership survive success or failure. This lesson was learned very early in my business career. Two very capable individuals operated a service station. One individual was the mechanic, and the other handled the sales. This arrangement resulted in a very successful business. However, it wasn't long before each partner begrudged and even belittled the abilities of the other partner. It did not take long before one partner demanded control and of course a larger percent of the profits. It was incredible that a successful business would fail because of egos.

I could give you two dozen examples, but the result is the same. When success or failure is realized, fingers are pointed, and a messy breakup soon follows. I hate partnerships. If you and a friend decide to organization a company because additional financing is needed, or the company requires a specialize expertise, own over 51% of the business. If two partners each own 50% of the company, nothing gets decided. At the very minimum, request that your attorney prepare a buy-sell agreement in case of a split. Most buy-sell agreements favor the partner with the most money simply because that partner has the resources to buy out the other partner.

Probably the easiest way to obtain a business divorce is using the Net Worth of the company to determine the fair market value of the enterprise. However, many times the value of a company is not easily computed. Just because the partners have a buy-sell agreement does not allow a partner to force the other into selling. The break-up of any business creates hard feelings. Talk to your attorney before entering into any business with partners and protect your position.

The Wrong Reason: Don't start your business for the wrong reason. An obsession with money or an overwhelming desire to please another, usually, leads to failure, not success. It is your passion for succeeding which leads to success.

Lack of Experience or Education: Your success requires experience, training or education. Most franchisors require several weeks or months of on the job training. If you are buying a business, I suggest you require the seller to provide in-house training for a period of not less than four weeks. Starting from scratch or purchasing a business requires experience concerning the product, procedures and specialized knowledge of that business. Of course professions such as plumbers, attorneys, electricians, accountants and MDs are needed to obtain a state license. In some occupations, on-the-job training is required. Education and experience are necessary for any business endeavor.

Poor Management: The function of a manager in a small business is to develop plans of action, implement these plans and evaluate each plan taking corrective measures to ensure success. The management is in control of Inside Competition. As a company grows the manager's responsibilities grow. He must become a leader by motivating and encouraging employees. Managers are in charge or all aspects of the operation. As an example Microsoft founder, Bill Gates hired a CEO within a short period after forming a company. He realized he did not have the tools to take his company to the next level.

There are many skills necessary to become a good manager. Financial Planning, bookkeeping, purchasing, employee management, marketing, and production are all specialized occupations which require considerable knowledge. You must realize that you do not possess all of these disciplines and seek outside help. As a one man operation, you need to study and listen to the experts. The Small Business Administration can provide you free business mentors who will help you succeed. A counselor can make the difference between success and failure.

Procrastination and Disorganized: Develop a do-it-now attitude. When you combine procrastination with disorganization, you have a roadmap for failure. Take steps today to overcome these disabilities. We all have heard the phrase: Plan your work and work your plan, but I have lived it for 40 years. Every day I spend a half-hour planning my work and developing a schedule to complete the work that needs my attention. Write it down and check your progress. If a task is distasteful, I always attempt to complete that task first. Does it always work? It never works the way I planned, but every day I accomplish many goals because I had a plan, and I worked my plan.

Sell All The Time: Everyone is a potential customer. Ask for their business. Every waking minute you need to be selling your product or service. Standing in an elevator is a waste of time, waiting for your car to be repaired is a waste of time and waiting at the doctor's office is a waste of time. You need to convert these downtimes to productive marketing/sales opportunities. Make sales calls. If you have a staff ask them to talk about your business and invite potential customers to patronize your business.

Location, Location and Location: From all the information available, every businessman should understand the importance of the business location. However, clients still drag me to a building site or a strip mall with reduced customer accessibility. Locating behind another outlet or leasing office space where parking is a premium is just another obstacle for customers to navigate.

Pick stores with adequate parking and accessibility. Is your place easy to see and find, is the parking sufficient to support your business and any other business close by and will the facility support signage which quickly identifies your company? Malls can demand high rents because hundreds of people a day walk-by your store. Visibility and accessibility are similar to creating an expensive marketing plan. When customers can see your business and can access your facility, customer traffic follows. A good location is better than spending advertising dollars, and high rent may be the cheapest bang for your buck.

Most cities require sufficient parking when approving new construction. However, planning departments still approve office buildings without adequate parking. Currently in the town of Bee Cave Texas a new office building is being built with over fifty thousand square feet of rental space and too few parking places. Architects maximize rental space without considering customer parking. A primary consideration when leasing office space should be accessibility for your clients. Retail businesses depend upon on customer visits. Why make it difficult for a potential customer to find you?

A good location coupled with excellent signage creates business. When customers can easily see your company, identify your products and services the savings in advertising dollars can be considerable. Increased rental cost is easily justified by the increase in business.

Industrial and manufacturing firms require a different set of rules when considering their location. When your business does not rely on direct customer access, a different set of criteria is necessary. Square footage cost, high ceilings, large rooms and receiving and shipping bays are necessary.

Poor Inventory Management: Inventory problems can be extensive. Buying a product that does not sale is only one of your concerns. A flawed business plan can result in purchasing excessive inventory because sales income projections were not realized and on the other end of the scale, shortages because you underestimated sales. Cash flow problems occur when needed operating capital is tied up in unnecessary inventory and of course without sales you can have an asset that is difficult to convert to needed Gross Profit. Most retail stores have the problem of obsolescence, spoilage or outdated inventory.

Inventory problems associated with managing raw material inventories for a manufacturing facility are also considerable. Manufactures have a two-fold problem, raw materials and finished products.

Point of Sale (POS) systems can and will eliminate many inventory problems for small retail stores. However, POS systems are expensive and require considerable time and effort to record purchases and prices. With bar codes on every product, the labor for recording inventory has been reduced. A computerized cash registered will record sales of stock, and the program will provide management an actual inventory at cost almost at any time. No matter how you control your inventory every business needs an actual inventory count at the end of their fiscal year.

If your business involves inventory of any kind the need for expert help should may be necessary. The problems associated with inventory management are time-consuming and can be expensive.

Know Your Competition: Do not miss understand me. <u>Inside Competition</u> is more important than <u>Outside Completion</u>, however researching your competitors and taking completive actions is necessary to ensure your share of the market. Do not be forced into changes by your competition. However, knowledge of competitor's pricing, products, operating procedures, and services should guide you, not control you. Unless your products and services are unique and demand a higher price, being competitively priced is a requirement. The simplest example of direct competition is the pricing of gasoline by convenience stores. The product is essentially the same and competitive pricing is necessary to compete. However, even in that cut-throat business, companies have established convenience stores as a way to induce customer visits.

You cannot control your outside competition and other than meeting or exceed sales discounts or special offers, it is not worth the effort it takes to track a competitor in detail. Service, cleanness, merchandising, product mix, marketing, competitive pricing and knowledgeable staff are all business aspect under your control. Many companies fail or cease to exist because of the price. A low or competitive price without the benefit of high volume can be just as devastating as over-pricing.

The Big-Box Store: It is not the end of the world. Consider focusing on a narrow but lucrative niche making your store the place to go. On the other hand, new products may appeal to a wider range of customers. Many customers are attracted to independent shops and the specialty items they stock.   Be prepared to haggle over prices. Customers do realize an independent businessman can and will haggle over the price or maybe a service. Loss leaders have proven very successful and profitable for these retailers. Competition with a big-box store requires renewed customer personal attention along with renewed concentration on small details. Many small businesses have concentrated on increasing their purchasing power by joining co-op buying groups thus competitive pricing is possible. Not all consumers shop for price alone. Combining excellent service and other competitive pricing many small companies can compete.

- ➤ Keep your relationship with consumers personal.
- ➤ Move your business to the 21st century by attracting customers using the internet.
- ➤ Offer a better quality line of merchandise.
- ➤ Visit your competition and understand that price is not the only attraction.
- ➤ Offer specialize products coupled with outstanding service.

Poor Credit Policy: In this day and age of easy credit, I find it difficult to believe a small business needs to extend credit. Many wholesalers still offer credit but unless you have a credit service company on retainer, extending credit can be a crap shoot. If your customers are unable to obtain bank loans, lines of credit, credit cards or inventory loans you should not become their lender. If you are extending credit make sure your customer understands your credit policy.

I always found it interesting that when a small business cuts-off credit and request cash only purchases, the customer takes his business to another supplier. Not only have you lost the customer, you have little chance of collecting the amount he owes. Set credit limits both in amount and time. Call your customer and ask for his cash only business and for a small monthly payment. The key is continued contact.

Rent, Labor Cost, and Materials: Stop thinking rent, labor cost and materials are fixed expenses. In today's commercial market, rent is negotiable. Talk to your landlord and impress upon him the necessity of reducing your rent. Cutting salaries and wages can make you an evil person but if cutting my wages by 20% results in continued employment without layoff, you could be a hero. Review your material cost and shop around for the best deal. Ask your supplier for bulk discounts and specials. Pay particular attention to all disbursements.

Failure is not an option. You now have the knowledge of a few potholes on your road to success. Reading and understanding the above ideas and problems can create two reactions. The first is total horror. I can't do it and why should I take the risk. The glass is half empty. If you are a real entrepreneur, your second reaction is to read and study all the reasons for failure. Once you have a handle on the causes of failure you can take a different path. Do not let any problem defeat you. You will review the information above and use this knowledge to succeed. Building on past failures, either your own or analyzing other business mistakes can and will provide a learning process which will guide you. Your drive and termination coupled with knowledge should make you more determined than ever.

Convert Your Passion into a Business

Steve Jobs said, "Do what you love." The first principle of working is to love the work you do, and it will not be work. How many times have you said; "I've got to go to work today" when you should be saying 'I get to go to work today. For over 25 years, I could not wait to get to my office. My job was my love. I have a client who owns and manages a small restaurant and bar. He goes to work two hours before opening because he can't wait to get the restaurant and tavern ready for his customers.

Clients have quit high-paying professions to open the business that turned their crank. Lawyers have become contractors, and engineers have opened restaurants. One client told me she decided to spend eight hours a day doing what she hated wasn't worth the thousands of dollars she earned. She gave everything up and bought a bed and breakfast in Colorado. Last time I spoke with her I couldn't get her to stop talking about her business. Her passion for her business bubbled over with enthusiasm.

Discover a Business Niche: Many small businesses have become successful by identifying a niche in the market. It would be great if we knew a niche when we see one, but most of time entrepreneurs wouldn't know a market niche if it hit them in the face. Use some common sense. Don't compete with Wall Mart, however, many of their products lines can be duplicated with unique products available from specialized wholesalers. Plumbers and electricians can undertake specialized contracting jobs. One plumber became an expert in Fire Sprinkler Systems. An electrician specialized in installing power lines for a rural electric co-op. Travel to other cities and review companies that that are unique. I just returned from Denver where I discovered a small deli that specialized in different specialty meat products and a line of sauces. The line of customers stretched ten deep while I was there. I'm not in the market to open a deli, but I can recognize an opportunity when it hits me in the face.

Look at Yourself: What are your talents and what makes you different? Different people have different skills and interest. I determined early on that managing employees was not one of my strengths but my real ability was face to face meetings with clients where I controlled the subject discussed. I had one client that could sell ice to an Eskimo and another client who had exceptional abilities repairing cars. I don't care what you do just strive to be the best.

There are steak houses where the chef cannot cook a rare steak. I have been to a Chiropractor, who was more interested in signing me up for 25 adjustments than easing my back pain. We all have employed plumbers or electricians that can't seem to stop a faucet leak or repair a plug-in, but are always on time with their invoice. Many entrepreneurs just don't give a damn about anything except money. Look within yourself and be the best. I just don't understand striving for mediocrity.

Research the Market: Once you have identified your abilities and hopefully discovered your niche, you must do market research. A market study is where many entrepreneurs fail. I had two talented clients who were expert knitters. They had all the skills necessary to operate knitting retail store. The market for teaching knitting and selling knitting products was small, and the competition from the big box stores such as Michaels and Hobby Lobby wiped out their dreams. They found their niche, applied their considerable talents, and the result was failure. You must conduct market research before you leap into an expensive mistake.

My ex-brother-in-law, who has a doctorate in business but no practical business experience in the real-world, would suggest you hire an expert to undertake an expensive and extensive market study. I agree with him, so venture out into your backyard and visit your money tree. If you are McDonalds, you can afford this study, but in the actual world of Small Businesses the market study needs to be you. You need to review companies that offer similar products and services. Talk with owners and operators about their businesses and how they got started. Go to different cities and meet entrepreneurs and tell them your plan to open a similar business out of their marketing area. Ask if you can work for free for a couple of days or even weeks to help you understand their operation. You will be surprised how many businessmen are willing to help and mentor new businesses.

When visiting different companies you need to record all your observations. Start with the outside of the company by checking the access, parking and review the location. When you enter a business, check the floors and counter tops for cleanness, review the signage and basic customer flow. Some businesses do not unlock both sides of a double door and are so lazy they hand-write a sign telling customers to use the door on the left. I have seen store clerks laugh at customers attempting to negotiate the locked door. As a side observation: One business I frequent has double sliding doors. Every time I visit this store the sliding doors seem to welcome me. Once inside any store, restaurant, retail outlet or a business office check the employee's attire. Casual Friday has turned into casual every-day. Fast food stores require uniforms and some staff must pass inspections before they are allowed to serve customers. Secretaries in blue jeans or an inappropriate clothing will deliver the wrong message to customers or clients.

Franchise operations are covered in Chapter 2. Most franchisors have considerable information concerning acceptable markets for their operation. That is one significant positive benefit of purchasing a franchise.

Offending Your Customers: It is surprising to me that businesses will go out of their way to offend paying clients and customers. I call it the 'Dixie Chick Syndrome.' In 2003, The Dixie Chicks went out of their way to voice their political views concerning the President of the USA. Their personal opinions had nothing to do with their business. I respect their opinions and defend their right to express them, however offending your customer base can result in devastating losses. Many of my readers will be offended that I chastise anyone for expressing their opinion. That is not what this information is about. Clearly the Dixie Chicks have the right to express their opinion however, insulting your customers was foolish. I will give them credit; they have not back down.

No matter what you do there will be a few customers who will be offended by the simplest things. Your job is to root out as many offensive subjects, decorations or even staff attire as reasonable. Getting new customers and keeping old customers is difficult enough without going out of you way to offend them. My mother always told me there are no winners when discussing politics and religion. Both can be informative and even challenging, but neither has a place in most business operations.

Operate as a Big Business: A small pharmacy in my area specializes in mixing individual medications prescribed by doctors. CVA and Wal-Mart are not competition since neither can offer this specialized service. Look at particular products and services. Review foreign product lines on the internet. Thousands of products are available from overseas manufacturers. Learn how to import these specialty items. You can also operate as a manufacturers' representative and drop-ship products. On a smaller scale, there are hundreds of products manufactured throughout the world that would require a small investment for a flea market operation. Large box stores such as Wal-Mart, Home Goods, and Michael's import large quantities but thousands of small producers are looking for sales outlets. Many of these companies products that you can import for a little investment and you can compete with large business.

15 Seconds to Impress: When customers visit your store or company for the first time you have one opportunity for a first impression. When I meet tax clients for the first time, I know I have less than 15 seconds to make an impression. Before a personal greeting, I would say: "I'm going to save you money on your taxes." Wow, you talk about the opening line! You and your staff must be professional and courteous to every customer, but it is the opening line that sets the tone for the customer visit. When you visit Waffle House, you are always greeted with a hello from the staff on ever visit. The greeting is standard operating procedure.

Businesses

There are so many different businesses it would be impossible to cover each type. This Step is a guide for you to discover what turns your crank. If a new idea jumps from the page follow through and research this idea in detail. Go on the internet or visit an operating facility for more information. Contact franchisors or experts in the industry. Start writing a list of contingency ideas related to the business idea. As an example in the computer industry, there are hundreds of things you could do such as starting a computer repair & installation business or start an in-home computer training business. There are hundreds of software programs such as accounting programs or windows software which require instructors.

There are hundreds of products you could sell over the internet or from your home. Become a manufacturing representative and make sales calls to different professions such as physicians or auto part stores. Manufacturers are always looking for sales representatives. Many of these opportunities are overseas where you could travel and see the world

Business Ideas by Industry:

Advertising
Arts and crafts
Auto/transportation
Beauty and Personal Products
Business Services
Children's Businesses
Computers
Education and Instruction
Entertainment
Financial Services
Food Services - Manufacture

Maintenance
Manufactures
Media/Publishing
Online Business
Pet Business
Plants-Agriculture
Real Estate
Recreation
Retail Business
Security
Sports

Health Care and Services
Import/exported Business

Technology
Travel

Business Ideas by Profession:

Accountant
Advertising Agent
Beautician

Employment Agent
Entertainer
Event Planner

Mechanic
Painter
Pet Groomer

Carpenter
Chef
   Photographer
Childcare Professional
Cleaning professional
Clothes Designer
   Restaurateur
Coach/instructor
Computer Technician
Decorator

Financial Services
Fitness Provider

Florist
Gardner
Graphic Designer

Handyman
HealthCare
Importer/Exporter

Pet Trainer

Publisher
Real-estate

Retailer
Security
Technology

Delivery Specialist
E-Retailer
Educator

Manufacturer
Marketer – Products
Message Therapist

Web Design
Writer

Business Ideas by Interest:

Antiques
Arts and Crafts
Autos – Transportation

Fashion
Finance/Investing
Fitness

Non-profit
Organizing
Outdoors

17

Beauty	Floral/Gardening	Pets
Carpentry	Food and Dining	Photography
Children's Business	Games	Real Estate
Computers	Graphic Design	Recycling
Construction	Health Care/Medical	Shopping
Consulting	Home Improvement	Sports
Equipment		
Cooking	Interior Design	Technology
Customer Service	Internet & E-bay	Travel
Education	Luxury Goods	Wine/Sprits
Entertainment	Manufacturing	Writing
Environmental	Movies	

Retail Business: Below are details concerning Retail Business, Wholesale Business, featured ideas, low-cost Startups and Home-based Ideas?

Retail businesses sell goods directly to consumers. We could spend hundreds of pages talking about different retail businesses from a small Donut Shop to a large box store such as IKEA or Best Buy. No matter what type of a retail store you undertake you have the same business problems and operational procedures. You wear every hat such as purchasing agent, stock boy, advertising specialist, customer sales, bookkeeper, and employer. When you visit a small shop, please notice the enormous chore the entrepreneur undertook organizing, producing and operating his store. Retail stores can be very profitable for the right individual and if this is your passion I suggest you follow your heart.

In today's electronic world hundreds of people have made a business of marketing without a store. The internet is being used for every type of product there is. There are info commercials selling all types of products by using TV home shopping. Retailing can be done using mail order from catalogs that sell gift baskets or just about any other product. Using e-bay or Amazon or your Web-site can be very profitable. Don't forget about retailing through vending machines. This old retailing concept has made many people a good living without the curse of a boss.

Consider selling stable goods such as bags, brushes, grooming products, toothpaste, milk, bread and even some hardware items. These items are used and replaced on a regular basis by consumers. Sales of Staple Goods can be predictable because consumers purchase these items consistently. Many convenience goods such as bottled water, magazines and other items found in convenience stores, grocery stores or gas stations can be sold at concerts or sporting events.

Fashion products that are popular for a short period and items classified as Fashion Goods can go in and out of style in a period of less than a week. Such items as clothes, shoes or specialty items can make an excellent internet or catalog business. Also consider selling seasonal products that are only popular for a short period of the year such as ski equipment, swimsuits or specialty candy for Halloween or Valentine's Day.

Wholesale Business: There are many different wholesalers, but Merchant Wholesalers are the most common. Most small businesses purchase products from wholesalers. In the simplest terms wholesalers purchases goods from manufacturers or producers, usually in large lots and then sell these products to companies. Before the consumer buys the product several companies may be involved in the distribution. Small retailers and restaurants rely on many different wholesalers. A Bar/restaurant may buy several different products from a single wholesaler or many times a particular product such as Coors Beer is delivered directly from a franchise distributor.

Merchant Wholesalers	General Wholesalers
Single-line Wholesalers	Specialty Wholesalers
Cash-and-Carry Wholesalers	Drop-Shipper Wholesalers
Truck Wholesalers	Mail-order Wholesalers
Producers' Cooperatives Wholesalers	Rack Jobber Wholesalers

Brokers are middleman between the manufacturer and a retailer or restaurant. The broker does not take procession of any products and only acts as a salesman for one, or more manufacturers or producers. A Broker usually has an existing contract with the manufacturer for a set commission depending on volume. They may also have a prearranged price agreement with the manufacturer and can wheel and deal for the most profit possible.

Manufacturer's Agents may be an employee or a contract agent. Many times Manufacturer's Agents have contracts with several different companies producing related or unrelated products. Most operate from their office, pay all expenses directly including office and travel expense, and work on commission. Sometimes a Manufacturer's Agent may sell directly to the consumer such as the sales of large construction equipment to major road contractors. Another type of Manufacturer's Agents will sell a product or service to the end user and then contacts the manufacturer or construction company to fill their contractual obligation. One client I had would prepare a detailed construction bid for government road work, win the bid and then fulfill the construction contract with a principal road construction contractor.

Many Wholesalers' Agents have a limited potential. In the age of the internet and increasing global communication, technology and global completion wholesalers have been forced to change with the times. More and more businesses are selling products using the internet and having that produced drop shipped to the customer. Some resourceful Wholesalers are using the internet for advertising hundreds of products and drop shipping the product from the manufacturer. Many times products are advertised without the knowledge of the manufacturer. Consumers pay the Wholesaler who in turn pays the manufacturer, receiving the difference between the retail price and the wholesale price. The product is shipped directly to the consumer from the manufacturer or maybe a wholesaler who stocks the product.

There are hundreds of different arrangements between manufacturers and producers. Many enterprising entrepreneurs have and will start new business directly marketing using the internet or by direct contact with consumers.

Buying Activities: Where to purchase inventory or products is one of the first jobs the owners of a retail store or restaurant has to accomplish. Many times your inventory, or products will be determined by your ability to obtain agreements with manufacturers or wholesalers. Determining your product line or merchandise mix is a tremendous responsibility and may determine your success or failure. Now you must discover where to purchase this inventory. Wholesalers in your area are more than willing to offer their expertise however when considering price you should plan, research and evaluate. Many specialty retail stores operators travel to Merchandise Marts throughout the country before they finalize their product line. In this day of the internet shopping, a new retail company can research different manufacturers and vendors throughout the world. A small costume jewelry store imports all it inventory from Indonesia and Malaysia. Other products can are purchased or manufactured from many various countries, and supplies can be researched online.

Act like a wholesaler when possible. Large Box Stores such as Wal-Mart and Costco can obtain their inventory and wholesale prices because of their purchasing power. Depending on your product line, you may be able to exercise the same purchasing power. Look to the internet; call other similar business not in your marketing area. Although many Big Box Stores can secure favorable pricing and delivery, you may be able to do the same thing on a limited basis. As an example, there are many independent hardware stores which could co-op their purchases.

Organize similar stores to make large purchases and have the manufacturer drop ship the product. I believe there is considerable future for Co-op purchasing by similar stores. The Wholesalers is currently fulfilling this market, but I think the future looks bright for co-op purchasing and warehousing to grow larger. Just like independent motels are banding together to advertize and market, retailers and even wholesalers must learn new and efficient methods to fight stores like Wal-Mart. It can be done without becoming a multi-store retailer. Organize and co-op purchasing, warehousing and distribution.

CHAPTER 2
GUIDE FOR BUYING A FRANCHISE
THE ESSENTIAL SMALL BUSINESS HANDBOOK
The best and most complete handbook for the Small Business Entrepreneur.
Essential information for starting, buying, operating and succeeding.

Sorting through hundreds of franchise opportunities can be overwhelming. A Franchise operation can offer entrepreneurs a tested and proven business model, operating systems, internal control systems, basic training, accounting systems and much more. Many franchisors will also provide assistance in determining a business location and facility planning. With all this support, success seems within your grasp. However, statistics indicates franchise operations have a higher failure rate than business start-ups. As with any business opportunity you must conduct an extensive due-diligence. Although it is in the best interest of every franchisor for you to succeed, you need to conduct a review of the contracts, operating financials and franchisor projections to insecure your investment.

Hundreds of franchises are available costing a few thousand to well over a million dollars. It is nice to dream big, but you better have very deep pockets, experience and connections to purchase a franchise similar to Mac Donald's or Krispy Kreme Donuts. On the hand, I just reviewed a Web Site called Franchise.com, and there are many franchise operations available for less than $50,000 and some as low as $3,000.00.

Advantages of Franchises

Franchising in the past 25 years has grown by leaps and bounds. It is very attractive because of several factors.

Brand Name: An established brand name clearly is the main attraction when buying a franchise. Many franchisors have spent millions of dollars to establish their Brand name, and many brand names mean quality and consumer trust. With a recognized name, you start your business a step ahead of a generic named competitor or a startup company. Customers know franchise companies and the quality products and services being offered. You indeed may be purchasing success before opening the door.

A new or a developing franchisor may not have established a recognized name; of course, the initial franchise fee will indicate this fact. If you are going to be a guinea-pig for a new franchise in your area, consider not only the name but review the following information.

Systems and Internal Control: Most franchise operations have established business systems, techniques, marketing plans and internal operating procedures. Start-ups fail because of poor management, namely <u>Inside Competition</u>. Start-ups must commit considerable capital and time reinventing the wheel creating internal operating procedures and systems. A franchisor has already invented the wheel. A proven system will enable you to avoid the costly mistakes new business makes, and many franchisors provide operations manuals that will guide new entrepreneurs in day to day operations.

Business Environment: One benefit of a franchise operation is a tested business environment. Everything from the building layout, colors, designs, internal marketing designs, equipment and location is tested and proven effective. Unless you have an unlimited budget, mistakes in developing a customer environment can absorb operating capital that needed for marketing or other more pressing business requirements. Casinos in Las Vegas have spent millions establishing an environment that creates a gamblers atmosphere. The interior design seduces gamblers to gamble longer and therefore lose more money. The millions of dollars many franchisors have devoted to interior design is available to franchisees.

In the past couple of years, several TV reality shows have been started concerning business turnarounds. As a small business consultant, I have watched these shows with great interest. One the first business elements tackled by a professional business consult is customer environment. Customers need to feel comfortable when entering and patronizing any business. Again colors, designs, and sounds all become part of a successful buying experience.

Training and Education: Most franchise opportunities require education and on the job training. If the internal operating procedures and systems are going to function correctly, employees must be trained. Usually, the franchisor will provide training for a reasonable number of workers as part of the franchise fee. Also, most franchisors have a staff of employees that can travel to new locations and provide hands-on assistance for a short period during pre-opening and even for several weeks after opening.

Buying Power: Franchisees have buying power. A large franchise chain has purchasing power for materials, equipment, and products. Vendors are willing to reduce their margins when large quantities are purchased. Of course, the purchasing power gives you a competitive advantage. Although your buying power may exist for the acquisition of equipment, furniture, fixtures and tools, many franchisors have not established lines of supply for daily operations. Such products as food and daily operating supplies may need to be purchased locally without the franchisor's influence. Larger franchise operators have successfully mastered the problem of providing raw materials and products to their franchise operations because it is another source of profit for their operation.

Negative Sides of a Franchise: Not everything concerning a franchise is positive. They are in control. A franchisor can take away your entrepreneur spirit. Almost every aspect of your franchise business is controlled by the franchisor. Because franchisors have a vested interest in your company, the contracts you sign will protect their position. It is good due-diligence to hire an attorney to review the franchise agreement. However, similar to having your attorney review a mortgage loan; you can read, and you can understand the requirements, but you will be unable to change the contract to your benefit. Hire an attorney to understand your legal obligations. However, don't waste your money trying to change the contract unless it is a franchisor is attempting to increase his market share and appears willing to make exceptions. If a franchisor wants outlets in a particular city or he is striving to grow his franchise operation into new markets, he may be willing to grant contract concessions.

Do your due-diligence. Ask questions and make a list of problem areas. Get everything in writing. Verbal agreements are not binding so reduce all agreements to paper. Your best source of information is from current franchisees. Even those franchises that have failed can be an excellent source of information. All franchise operation has failures. These failures may or may not be the fault of the franchise organization, and you need to speak with successful operators and a few operators who have failed.

Finding a Franchise

Franchisor Web Sites: Websites such as "franchise opportunties.com" and 'franchise.com' review hundreds of franchise operations from advertising businesses to video services. Franchisors provide information regarding their franchise on these sites including the investment needed. Once you have picked out several interesting franchises, you can then review the franchisor's website for detailed information.

Franchise Expositions: There are franchise exhibitions in many cities throughout the year. Hundreds of franchisors set up elaborate booths and provide information concerning their business. Be prepared with your questions. Sometimes exhibitors will offer you incentives at an exposition. Ever pay a front-end fee before you have completed your due-diligence. Any time a front-end fee is requested you need to walk away from that company.

Franchise Brokers: A franchise broker could call himself a business coach, advisor or a referral source consultant. They often advertise on the internet or in trade magazines, and they will help you select a suitable franchise. Two problems exist with franchise brokers. First, many of them work directly for a franchisor, so they do not have your best interest in mind. Secondly, many brokers receive a commission from the franchisor, so question their objectively. If you do use a franchise broker, I suggest you interface with an independent CPA or a small business consultant to review the franchise documents for hidden problems. Remember my model: I like consultants who do not have a dog in the fight – if his income depends upon you buying, he may not be objective. If you contact a franchisor directly, you know up front he is not objective with your money, and you can act accordingly.

I'm not a fan of franchise brokers. I prefer dealing directly with the franchisor and making use of an experienced business CPA or an experienced business consultant to complete your due diligence. However, franchise brokers can provide you a service, namely information. If you are convinced a franchise broker is necessary to weed through hundreds of franchisors, consider the following:

> Can you get enough information shopping online or from the franchisor?
> Does the franchisor pay the broker?
> Are you paying the broker?
> Is the broker's commission depended upon the price of the franchise?
> How many franchisors does the broker represent?
> If he represents a small number franchise, is his markup excessive.
> How does the broker select a franchisor to represent?
> How does the broker choose a franchisor?
> Verify any projected earnings provided by the broker with the Franchisor.
> Who provide the projections?
> Do his claims seem reasonable? Remember, if the forecast seems too good to be true, then they probably are too good to be true. (When reviewing Profit and Loss projections – usually the only number overstated is sales.)
> Contact current franchisees and confirm the broker's information.

Investigation and Due Diligence

Franchisors Investigation, Information, and Prospectus: Franchisors are required to furnish a considerable amount of information to each prospective buyer. Historically many unsavory individuals fleeced potential franchisees, and the State and Federal agencies have developed many laws controlling franchise agreements. Over the years, I have seen many clients become the victim of illegal activities, and I'm very cynical when dealing with anyone who wants my money. Statements such as "Sign today" or "for the best deal buy today" increase my cynical nature and many times I'm simply out the door. Complete your Due-diligence. Any request for front-end money from a contractor, a car dealer or a Franchisor should put you on guard to protect your pocket book.

That being said there is another side of every business. Most Franchisors are honest and bring a vast amount of business knowledge and skill to the table. These companies realize that a good franchise business complements their overall operation and developing a successful franchise creates profit and success for them. It is in the best interest of the franchisor for his franchise operations to succeed. However, we have all hear about franchise companies who are being sued because they are unable to keep their side of the franchise contract, or they are just bad business operators. Remember a franchisor is just another business. Many seek success but either do not understand their obligations or they are unable to operate a successful business. Protect your operation for incompetent franchisors.

The Franchisor's Disclosure Document: The FTC requires all franchisors to provide a disclosure document 14 days before you are asked to sign any contract or pay any money to the franchisor or his representative. Disclosure are sent after the franchisor has received the application. I find it interesting that because there are so much franchisor abuse and illegal actions, the Federal government stepped in and set-up regulations. Below is the information the franchisor is required to include in the disclosure document.

Franchisor's Business History: You need to know how long the franchisor has been in business and the laws controlling the industry. Included in the disclosure document are any Special technical requirements. As an example, the state of Colorado requires pest control company employees to be licensed and certified. This provision requires education and training and of course additional cost.

The franchisor's disclosure document or prospectus describes management experience in managing a franchise systems and their general business background.

History of Legal Action: Franchisors are required to disclose felony convictions, violations of franchise law and unfair or deceptive practices of any executive. The discloser must cover both Federal and State violations. Also included are any civil legal actions if they involve franchise relationships. There is a requirement to disclose legal actions brought by franchisees the past year. Carefully review any legal action concerning payment of royalties or other franchise contractual obligations. These legal actions may be an indication of a deeper franchisor's problems.

Franchisor Bankruptcy: Has the franchisor, or any of its executives declared bankruptcy? This information is in the FTC franchisor's disclosure document. A bankruptcy may or may not indicate a problem; however, this information is necessary to complete your due-diligence. Many times a past bankruptcy is not a sound indicator of the current problem. A little research is required to determine if the disclosed information is applicable to the franchise being investigated.

Startup and Operating Cost: The following are some of the costs that you may incur starting and running a franchise. When preparing your financial projections for startup cost and operating cost make sure you include these costs within your numbers. I strongly suggest that when you meet other franchisees, review these costs with them and confirm the amounts. Review all non-refundable fees, deposits and cost. These costs could be extensive.

> ➤ Check for Non-Refundable Deposits.
> ➤ Initial inventory cost.
> ➤ Signs and other advertising fixtures.
> ➤ Real Estate purchase or rental cost.
> ➤ Remodeling for rental property.
> ➤ Operating equipment, office equipment, software cost, and fixtures.
> ➤ Royalties and advertising cost.

➢ Grand opening cost including initial business promotions.
➢ Operating license and city, state fees.
➢ Training cost or educational cost.
➢ Legal and accounting fees.
➢ Liability insurance cost.
➢ Another standard is operating cost.

Franchisor Restrictions: Many times franchise outlets are required to purchase operational supplies, products and services from the franchisor. One problem is competitive pricing of items the franchisee is not allowed to buy locally. Check your local suppliers before you commit since "Cost of Goods Sold" and "Operating Cost" can affect your bottom line. Once your sign the franchise documents, you lose all ability to negotiate this cost.

Location Approval & Construction: Many franchise contracts allow the franchisor to pre-approve your location. If you had selected a site, the franchisor might not approve your location. Some contracts require the franchisee to use the franchisor's construction company. Of course, the franchisor receives a fee for this service. At the very minimum, I would hold out for competitive bids.

Design and Appearance: The franchisor dictates the inside and outside appearance. For the original design, the franchisor controls the final design plans and maybe the franchisor requires a fee for the architectural drawings. Some franchisors required seasonal design changes or even remodeling can be demanded by the mother company. All these controls cost money and eat into your profits.

Sales Area: You probably will be limited to a geography area which could be beneficial provided other franchisees also have territory restrictions. You need to protect your area by contract. If all franchisees are allowed to market and sell in your area, you could be competing against a competitor selling the same products and who may have considerably more financial backing. Also, some Franchisors market the identical goods and services on the internet or in company operate outlets. Check your agreement for conditions that may create unfair competition.

Goods and Services Restrictions: Most franchisors regulate the products and services you are allowed to sell. If you own a restaurant or retail store, the franchisor can prevent you from changing the menu or they may be able to stop you from selling a local product. Some service franchise operations limit the type of service you can perform. An Oil Change Franchise could restrict you from doing brake repairs.

Operational Controls: Franchise contracts may allow the franchisor the right to control hours of operation, signage, and uniforms, in-house advertising and in some cases the Franchisor can control your prices or product discounts. One of the largest areas of profit for the franchisor is that the franchise contract will require you to purchase 100% of your supplies and product through them, even if the price is lower somewhere else. Because of this restriction your profit margins could be cut two to five percent. If you have gross sales of a million dollars, this could cost you twenty thousand to fifty thousand dollars.

Franchise Termination: Franchise contracts contain specific information concerning termination of the agreement. Review this section carefully because you need to remember the grounds that allow a franchisor the right to terminate your contract. Many franchisors agreements enforce their operating restrictions and controls with contractual threats of termination.

Franchisor Education and Training Available: You need to know who is eligible for training and at what cost. The disclosure document should detail the length of training for operations, management, and employees. You will want to know who does the training and what their qualifications are. After the initial training is complete does the franchisor offer continued education and for what price? Of course, the training you will need will depend upon your past education, knowledge, and experience. Do not be too proud to ask for help. You are buying a franchise because of the franchisor's experience.

Advertising Cost: Some franchise agreements require the franchisee to spend a certain amount on advertising, promotions or in product discounts or giveaways. Sometimes the advertising fee is shared between you and other franchisees, usually, the franchise contract requires the franchisee to pay into a central advertising coop and the franchisor determines where the money goes. Your advertising money could be spent by the mother company for advertising to attract new franchisees. Every new business needs an advertising budget, and I do not disagree with an imposed advertising budget. However, consider each item below when reviewing the advertising requirements in the franchise contract:

> What percent of the advertising fund goes to national advertising?
> Who manages the fund and at what cost?
> What are the expenses paid?
> Do you receive any amounts from the fund for your advertising?
> Is there a limit on local advertising?
> Is any amount spent on obtaining additional franchisees?
> Do all franchisees contribute equally to the fund?
> Do you need the franchisor's consent to spend additional funds for advertising?
> What advertising does the franchisor currently do?
> Will you have any control over the fund?
> Is there a 'franchise board' appointed to advise where to spend advertising money is spent?

Terminated Franchisee Information: Review terminated or canceled franchise information in detail. A high number may indicate a problem. Is the franchisor purchasing failed outlets and recording them as company-owned outlets? Any franchisees that have left the program within the last few years can provide you with reliable information concerning the franchisor's operations. I suggest you visit these people before you sign any agreements. Sometimes in legal proceedings the two parties may sign confidentiality agreements in order to reach a settlement. If a disgruntled franchisee is unable to detail the facts surrounding a termination, you need to request this information from the franchisor.

We all have heard of a legal truth, 'any contract can be broken.' Contracts can be broken, but I assure you the legal language in the franchise agreement is written in favor of the franchisor. They can terminate your contract for many infractions such as failure to pay royalties, lower standards of service or sales restrictions. Losing a franchise could result in losing your investment.

Many franchise agreements are for a period of fifteen years of more. Check your contract concerning your right to renew your franchise. Some contracts contain provisions for royalty increases or new design standards.

Franchise Documents

Franchise Documents and Provisions are Extensive: Review the franchise legal provisions before you sign. You are making a big financial and personal commitment when opening a new business. A Franchise operation will demand strict adherence to their business methods, pricing, product lines and many other requirements. Read the Agreement! Have an attorney and a CPA review the contract. You may not be able to change one-line item, but you need to know what your legal commitments are.

Provisions in the Contract You Need to Consider: It's important for you to read the franchise document before you sign. Your attorney does not have the same goals or concerns you have, and there could be provisions that you are not able to follow. Years of heartbreak and difficulties could result. Look for some of the following clauses:

> ➢ How much is the franchise fee?
> ➢ What is the length of the franchise period?
> ➢ Is there a provision for a franchise period extension? For what fee?
> ➢ Does the franchisor provide training? Where, how and how much?
> ➢ Will the franchisor train my employees? What cost?
> ➢ Are there training guides for particular jobs?
> ➢ Is there a specific requirement such as previous franchise ownership?
> ➢ Is there technical experience required?
> ➢ Is a there a royalty fee on sales? How much?
> ➢ Do you need special training outside of the franchise?
> ➢ Can I purchase operating supplies from a different vendor?
> ➢ What is the estimated cost for franchise outlet?
> ➢ What is the estimated cost of capital equipment?
> ➢ Who sells the equipment?
> ➢ Do I have to build a free-standing building?
> ➢ Who do I use for a contractor?

> ➢ Does the franchisor furnish the plans? At what price?
> ➢ Can I sell other products or services in my franchised outlet?
> ➢ Can I purchase fresh products locally?
> ➢ What are the hours of operation?
> ➢ Are there provisions for reinstatement if I lose my franchise?
> ➢ What is the length of the franchise? Can I renew?

A franchise is an investment, and you need to do your homework, i.e. due-diligence. Ask the franchisor for references and conduct an interview with other franchisees. Investing thousands of dollars of your money, leaving your job and changing your life requires' that you check every detail of the franchise agreement. After you sign, franchise problems are resolved by attorneys. Business then gets messy and expensive. Never pay the franchisor before signing the contract. If the franchisor requires a commitment fee or a down payment, it should be small. Many times I have required up-front payments held by an attorney in his trust account with specific instruction for the release.

Franchisee Associations: There are many franchise organizations. These organizations will provide considerable information concerning the history of a particular franchise. The organization will be able to provide you information franchisees are having with the franchisor.

Projected Earnings Information: The bottom line for any franchise investment is the potential profit. Purchasing a franchise is buying an opportunity with an income stream. The FTC does not require a franchisor to disclose earnings statements. Each franchise profit picture may vary because of management and location. Completing your due diligence requires you to visit established franchises and request their Profit and Loss Statements. Although the franchise may refuse, it is necessary and imperative you know the income stream. Preparing financial projections for lenders or investors need accurate income estimates. Chapter 5 - Understanding Financial Statements will help guide you. Actual income statements demonstrate a franchise potential. As I related in Chapter 1, the revenue projections need to be accurate when making your projections.

Sales income is necessary; however, sales without an adequate gross profit margin, Sales minus Cost of Sales, is an essential ingredient for success. You can accurately estimate expenses. Income stream is a problem. I consider sales and cost of sales as number 1 and 2 Rules of Success. Expenses do matter, but number one rule for success is sales. Obtain gross sales information from several similar outlets if possible. Lending institutions are much easier to deal with when you provide hard evidence of sales volume from other franchises.

You need financial statements from current outlet operations. Take those financials to your accountant or business consultant for his/her review. Ask questions.

Attorney Advice: Problem existing with the franchise contract needs to be solved before you sign on the dotted line. However, if it is a popular franchise with many outlets, changing the contract will be impossible. It is something like changing a Mortgage Lenders document. It is not going to happen. The most pressing reason for an attorney is to give me a legal review of what the contract provisions that I must follow. If it is a small franchisor operation, you may be able to change some of the contract provisions. Your attorney should provide you with an explanation of your legal obligations under the contract. I would not spend thousands of dollars on legal fees expecting him to reinvent the contract. Be very detailed in the information you expect from your attorney and of course obtain fee schedule first.

Government Regulations: Many states regulate franchise sales. I suggest you contact your state government to see if your state has regulations.

Franchise Fees – Royalties – Hidden Cost

Franchisors Cost of Buying and Operating a Franchise: Usually there are only two direct franchisors fees, and they are the initial purchase fee and royalties based upon sales. However, many franchises have additional cost. Buying a Franchise and royalties may not be your only cost. Many franchises agreements detail the costly control a franchisor has over your operation. Make sure you check the contact for hidden cost.

Franchise Fees: Initial franchise fees can be considerable. Usually, this fee is non-refundable and paid directly to the franchisor. Other than basic training, proprietary software and business systems many franchisors do not provide any other startup cost such as construction of the outlet, rent, equipment, business insurance or local license requirements. You need to analyze all this initial cost against the benefits received. Compare all cost with other franchises and against the startup cost without a franchise.

Royalties: Usually a franchisor requires a monthly fee based on a percent of gross revenues. Fees are based upon sales and do not consider operational cost and many times the fee is payable even if the franchisor does not complete his contractual commitments in the franchise agreement. The fee is also due if you lose money in your franchise operation. You could be liable for these royalties even if you cancel you franchise agreement, change your business name and move your business.

Other Hidden Cost of Owning a Franchise: Consider several hidden cost of owning a franchise that may affect your bottom line. Review the contract agreement for all charges.

> **Product Cost:** Franchisors may require the purchase of goods and materials at a non-competitive price or you may be required to buy products, not sellable in your marketing area. Franchisors want to control quality and therefore insist that you buy goods directly from them. This requirement limits competition and can place an undue burden on your

bottom line. You need to check national averages Cost of Goods versus Gross Receipts.

Franchisors Owned Facility: Some franchisors love playing the Real estate market. They buy or build your facility and require a long term contract at excessive lease rates. For most businesses, rental expense should not be greater than 8% of your gross revenues. Franchisors may demand a compulsory build-lease program attempting to control construction standards. However, all buildings plans include detail materials and construction specifications. Therefore, competitive bids should be requested.

Improvement Requirements: Since you have to operate to the standards defined by the franchise contract, legally they may be able to insist on improvements, new systems and services that they developed for the franchise. As an example, my Gym just discovered that their franchisor can require expensive improvements even though these improvements did not make any sense in the overall operation. Moving plumbing and electrical systems can be very expensive, and the cost versus benefit may be unnecessary.

Training, Conferences, and In-House Education Requirements: Many Franchisors required that you and many of your staff attend quarterly or annual conferences or training seminars. If they charge for these required lessons, you may want to confirm the charges. If the franchisor charges for their time and travel expense may be, their expenses are out of your control.

Franchisors Volunteer Requirements: You may be required to train, participate in grand openings or even conduct tours or your operation for free. Check the contract for these conditions.

Leasehold Improvements and Building Construction

Franchisor Building and Construction Requirements: You may be required to erect a building or undertake extensive improvements in a leased facility. This front end cost can be considerable, and many franchises do not participate in the construction or in the management required to complete a finished facility. If you do not have development expertise, overseeing the building project may require hiring an engineering firm for inspections. Even with a Completion Bond many contractors cut corners costing you thousands of dollars. I have hired many inspectors who visit the building site several times a week and report their findings.

Pre-Construction: Detailed design and architect plans are the first step in the construction process. One inexpensive way to obtain detailed plans is to hire a local designer who works with a civil engineer or architect. The designer or planner can prepare the detailed structural, electrical, framing, and heating, air conditioning and plumbing plans and the engineer can review building codes and stamp the plans. Detailed drawings and complete materials list will save you thousands of dollars. Contractors can detail their cost estimates from the building plans and the bids are detailed. Do not start any construction job unless you have detailed plans and specifications for several contractors to bid. Receiving several proposals based on identical plans allows you to compare apples to apples. Plans should detail all furniture and fixtures as well as equipment including names, descriptions, and model numbers.

Many franchisors have plans, and some even require you to use their architects and contractors. All plans and specification must consider the building site and be submitted to the local building department for approval and a building permit.

Picking a Contractor: I believe the only one way to select a contractor is by referral. Construction is going on everywhere so just introduce yourself to the contractor at a construction site and tell him you noticed the construction and may want him to bid your work. I ask the contractor for five references, name, address and phone numbers. Call all references and set up a meeting with each. Review the contractor's work and obtain as much information about the build as possible.

Never Pre-Pay: Never pre-pay a contractor for any construction work. There are thousands of stories of contractors who receive down-payments, material and supply payments or pre-payments and disappear. Also, you could be financially responsible for unpaid completed construction work or outstanding materials cost delivered to the job site. Make payments using a restrictive endorsement only for completed work. I have made payments weekly if necessary, or you can make payments based upon completion of different phases. If the contractor purchases materials and they are delivered to the job site make the check payable to the contractor and the supplier or sub-contractor. If the contractor fails to pay for materials or sub-contractors, you can provide proof in the form of a canceled check, which demonstrates that the vendor or sub-contractor had an opportunity to receive their money.

Protect The Builder: Deposit funds with an attorney or a local bank using specific requirements for the release of funds. Contractors need assurance that the funds are available this will protect the contractor. Of course, if you are using a lender he will only make contractor payments based upon completed work. Never pay deposits to any contractor! Some contractors will not start work unless they have received a pre-payment. When faced with that problem, I can come to some agreement for periodic payments. I have even paid contractors before the foundation is complete by paying every three days. In this weak economy, many contractors need front end fees to pay for work completed on prior jobs. The contractor's inability to manage his finances should not become your problem.

© Randy Glasbergen
glasbergen.com

"I got in trouble at school today.
I got an A on my test and they said it was
unfair to the kids who didn't study as hard."

Buy a Franchise or Start from Scratch

Not a simple answer. Yes, with a "but". If you have done your homework and are satisfied with your conclusions, I recommend that you purchase a franchise. I like franchises simply because they force you to be successful. Have you done your due-diligence? Don't say yes unless you truly have checked everything. Sign the bottom line when the franchisor proves they are a worthwhile investment.

Notes

Chapter 3
STRATEGIES FOR BUYING A BUSINESS
THE ESSENTIAL SMALL BUSINESS HANDBOOK
The best and most complete handbook for the Micro Business Entrepreneur.
Essential information for starting, buying, operating and succeeding.

Although this manual contains the steps necessary to start a business from scratch, one of the easiest ways of becoming self-employed is to buy an existing business operation. Purchasing a doctor's office, a one-man plumbing service or a concrete foundation company can provide instant cash flow, a customer base and many times the business is already profitable with a positive cash flow. Established businesses have the fundamentals in place. Location, name recognition, inventory, equipment, operational staff and a decent sales record will provide you with a jump-start to becoming a successful entrepreneur.

The due-diligence required for purchasing a business is different than the due-diligence needed for a start-up business. Finding a company that meets your requirements can be difficult, and the steps necessary to ensure the sales price reflects the fair market value requires careful deliberation.

Questions when Buying a Business.

What type of businesses satisfies my passion?
What category of business suits your skills and abilities?
How much business can I afford?
How do I find a business that I can afford?
How do I determine the value of the business I want to buy?
What steps are necessary when buying a business?
Will the business profit
Will the business meet my personal and investment goals?

Before we investigate the answers to the above questions, we need to review General Investment objectives.

Investment Objectives

Do not lose sight of your goals. Your goals when buying a business are the same as starting a business from scratch. You are attempting to determine that your business entity will provide sufficient Net Profit to:

Provide the reasonable wage for your work.
Service the business loan. (New Business Loan)
Provide a fair return on your investment.
Create sufficient profit for growth and retirement.

1. **Providing a Fair Return on Your Investment:** Money has 'Earning Power.' Your Invest goal into a business, the stock market of even in a

savings account is to create a capital return based upon the dollars (amount) you have at risk. Earning Power is 'Earnings an asset can produce.'

2. **Servicing your Business Loan:** Similar to a car payment, business loan payments repay the principal borrowed and the use of the money, which is called 'Interest.' Interest is a business expense and comparable to your earning from your personal investment. In this case the lender requires a return on his asset, namely his money invested in your business. Interest is deductible as a company expense; however, the principal payment amount must be generated from profit.

3. **Provide a Reasonable Income for your labors:** Of course, we all want to earn millions and many of you will. As an employee, you received a salary. Your labors, knowledge, ability and education has value. However, when considering a start-up business or business purchase your earnings come from profit. Will there be enough profit available to provide an acceptable wage or salary? Online you can review income averages for different industries, but in reality you are not interested working for a salary. Every entrepreneur aspires to produce sufficient profit to create a higher standard of living. Pride and self-worth are other measures of success.

4. **Establish a profit for Growth and Retirement:** Not much to add to that statement. Not every entrepreneur wishes to grow, but all businessman need to generate sufficient earnings for retirement. Retirement funding may be tax deductible for a Proprietorship, Corporation, Partnership or an LLC. However, there are many rules and regulations.

Will the Business Support your Lifestyle?

You're first indicator when reviewing a potential business must be Net Profit. I realize that all entrepreneurs believe their abilities will create sales growth and therefore increased Net Profit. However, many companies have reached maximum profit potential and unless your vision includes a significant restructuring and overhaul of the current operation, use the current Net Profit when determining if the company can support your lifestyle. You may want to work this formula backward. Start with your current salary and calculate the Net Profit needed to support your take-home amount.

As discussed above, Business Start-ups and Business Purchases are saddled with the same core problem. Will the company produce sufficient profit to realize your personal and business goals? Your first goal is buying or starting a business that will support your adjusted or current lifestyle. The two examples below analyzes Net Profit of $80,000.00 and $120,000.00 per year.

Many entrepreneurs fail to consider the effect of the business loan payment and employers share of Social Security (FICA) and Medicare taxes have on their net take-home pay. As an employee, you are required to pay 7.65% FICA and Medicare Tax on your wages. Your employer must match that amount. As a self-employed individual, you are both the employee and employer. Therefore, your net profit is subject to FICA and Medicare in the amount of 15.3%, double the employee amount.

Your profit may equal the salary you received as an employee, but the two additional drains on self-employed income will reduce your net take home pay. Unless anticipated, the net amount may not be sufficient to support your lifestyle. Net profit and wages are subject to the same Income Tax rates. The Income tax on a salary of $80,000 is the same as the Income Tax on Self-employment income of $80,000.00. The business loan and the amount of matching Social Security Tax are an additional expense reducing the take-home amount. Your new business must support the loan payment, payroll taxes, income tax, and your lifestyle.

Example 1: We determine that the company has a profit of $80,000.00 a year or $6,670.00 per month before loan interest or principle payment. First deduct the estimated Social Security Tax burden on Self-employment income at 15.3% or $1,020.00 per month. Next view the Federal and State Income tax burden of a minimum of 10% or $667.00 per month. Next, deduct the business loan amount of $2,500.00 monthly.

Monthly gross profit Before Interest Expense	6,670.00 (Profit = Salary)
Payroll Taxes – Employee FICA & Medicare (7.65%)	510.00
Payroll Taxes – Employer FICA & Medicare (7.65%)	510.00 (Extra Expense)
Federal and State Income Tax	667.00
Loan payment	<u>2,500.00</u> (Extra Expense)
Net take home amount	2,483.00

Example 2: The business profit is $120,000.00 a year or $10,000.00 per month before loan interest or principle payment. First deduct the estimated Social Security Tax burden on Self-employment income at 15.3% or $1,530.00 per month. Next project the Federal and State Income tax burden of a minimum at 14% or $1,400.00 per month. Deduct the business loan amount of $2,500.00 to arrive at net monthly take-home pay

Monthly gross profit Before Interest Expense	10,000.00 (Profit = Salary)
Payroll Taxes – Employee FICA & Medicare	765.00
Payroll Taxes – Employer FICA & Medicare	765.00 (Extra Expense)
Federal and State Income Tax	1,400.00
Loan payment	<u>2,500.00</u> (Extra Expense)
Net take home amount	4,570.00

Note: The current Social Security Wage Base for 2014 is $115,500. Medicare Wage Base is $200,000.00, and the Medicare rate increases .9% over $200,000.00.

It is important for you prepare a personal budget including all your expenses before you plunge into a purchase or even a start-up. Buying a business requires some sacrifices, but if you're current take home pay or current personal expenses exceed the projected and realized profit, you may be on the road to failure. Our government seems to create unlimited debt; however, I doubt your lenders will approve of an endless debt increase.

Word of Caution: When preparing your business projections it is easy to increase your sales income to fit your personal lifestyle. I'm convinced that every number of your predictions will come true except for sales revenue. Plan for the worse and you can be surprised when your sales exceed your estimates.

© Randy Glasbergen / glasbergen.com

"When we pay women less, that's discrimination.
To make it fair, we should pay everyone less."

Steps for Purchasing a Business

Step 1: Buying a Business You Can Operate: Not all available companies will fit your passion, skills or abilities. I would not buy a restaurant and bar because I do not excel at employee management and restaurants and bars demand constant supervision. Purchase a business that has your same basic core values. Passion is essential, but you also need the ability and skills to manage the businesses day to day operation. Understand your capabilities.

Step 2: Finding a Business to Buy: In any market there are many companies for sale. Unlike the housing market which has rebounded in most markets, the market for business opportunities is still a buyer's market in most cities. If you have cash, equity in hard assets and outstanding credit, this is the time for you to act. Historically the market for companies lags well behind the housing market. Businesses are for sale because of a wide variety of reasons. Profitability, retirement, family problems such as divorce or maybe the owner simply wants a change. Focus your concerns on sales income and how to sustain the sales at a profit.

Contact a local business broker, review internet ads and most importantly contract local companies in your area. Many businessmen may not be actively soliciting buyers but because of many factors they will entertain an offer. Also, business owners are aware of other opportunities and will be more than happy to direct you to a company that is available. I sold my first business because I initiated a conversation in a grocery store. This person had a friend who was looking to purchase a business and within a month we concluded a deal.

Step 3: How Much Business Can I Afford? Experienced realtors will require that you are pre-qualified for a mortgage before you start looking at homes to purchase. Pre-qualifying you for a business loan can be more difficult than pre-qualifying for a home. Buyers realize the amount they have available for investment, however, the amount you can borrow is dictated by the available collateral included in the purchase price. You may also want to consider a business where the owner is willing to finance all or part. You may have co-signers and equity in personal assets which you are prepared to pledge, but a significant problem is the collateral available to you in the business selected for purchase. Commercial realtors are very competent at finding companies available, but many times they do not understand the relationship between your available investment and the companies you wish to buy.

There is little information available to the public concerning the ratios and requirements lenders use to qualify you for a business loan. Sometimes the bank's commercial loan officers have no clue what loans will be approved or rejected by their mysterious Loan Review Board. For 30 years I have interfaced with bankers and other lenders, and I have established a few guidelines for pre-qualifying you for a commercial loan, even an SBA Loan.

A. Liquid Assets: You need to determine the amount of liquid assets you have available for a down payment. Liquid assets include savings accounts, stocks, and bonds or any asset readily converted to cash. A retirement fund is also considered a liquid asset, however, cashing in your retirement fund may incur a tax as high as 45% to 50%. You also may have access to other funds from relatives. Borrowing part of the down payment from a relative or friend may not be allowed by the lender and of course, you must consider the repayment amount when calculating profit. The lender may allow you to borrow funds from a relative; however do not forget that the relative's loan is always in second position. A first mortgage on business equipment, real estate, and even personal property must be satisfied first if your company fails.

B. Equity Assets: Consider the equity you have available in assets you are willing to pledge as loan collateral. A second mortgage on your real estate is subject to a first mortgage in case of failure. Business lenders will use personal assets as collateral however a second mortgage is subordinate to the first mortgage. Your home may have an FMV of $300,000.00 with a first mortgage of $200,000.00 thus creating equity of $100,000.00; however, lenders will not make a loan based upon this equity. If you fail to make your payments, they may be forced to satisfy the first mortgage in order to protect their position. The bank would need to pay off the first mortgage, and then the bank would have a total of $300,000.00 at risk and a sale may not satisfy the entire debt.

Because the second mortgage holder gets paid after the first mortgage is satisfied, the second mortgage holder may receive nothing. Therefore, many times a lender will not consider a second mortgage as collateral. A denial may have nothing to do with your credit rating, and a denial is because the available equity is insufficient.

As a guide only consider 50% of your asset equity, Fair Market Value minus outstanding loans, when estimating credit available. The example above would result in a loan of $50,000.00.

Knowing your investment amount is half the equation, the other half is determining the value of the assets in the business you have identified for purchase. Review companies that have a sales price of five (5) or six (6) times the amount of equity you have available. Calculate the equity on hard assets and the equity on any assets you are willing to use for collateral. Then multiply this amount times 5 or 6 to create an estimated purchase price of the business you can afford.

C. Business Assets: A & B above created what I term as 'Purchase Equity.' and it is considered a down payment amount. Again every deal is different. The 'Purchase Equity' is the basis for determining business opportunities within your price range. Similar rules exist when purchasing a home; lenders will not consider you for a house costing $600,000.00 if you only have $20,000.00 down payment. Step A and Step B do not consider several variables. We are only starting our search for a business we can afford.

D. Calculate Loan-to-Value for Collateral Requirements: Lenders have established loan-to-value percentages for most assets. I have suggested that you will need 20% to 25% down payment of the total purchase price however this percent depends on the loan-to-value of the assets acquired. The down payment, interest rate, and other terms can be negotiated depending on Loan-to-Value calculations. Your credit rating, the business history, projected income and expenses and the lenders perceived ability that you will repay the debt are all considerations.

Real Estate Loans: Commercial property requires a greater down payment than a residence. Many times the required down payment is 30% to 50%, depending if the Real Estate is considered a 'Special Use' building such as a Hotel or Health Club. Lenders consider Special Use Real Estate difficult to resale and therefore require a larger down payment and maybe a higher interest rate.

Use 80% of Real Estate value.
As the collateral amount. (Unless Special Use Building)

Inventory Loans: Many lenders simply will not lend money on stock. Inventory loans are risky because inventory can disappear through sales without replacing. Before a lender realizes there is a problem; his borrower is in trouble. Stock can be sold or even worse the inventory becomes outdated and worthless. Retailers, merchandise wholesalers or manufacturing operations have difficulty financing their inventory. Some lenders are more liberal concerning inventory loans, but a general rule is not to expect more than 50% loan to cost or Fair Market Value. The lender is not interested in your markup. Inventory lenders will analysis and appraise the inventory value to determine the loan value based on a fire sale.

Use 50% of Inventory fair market value.
As the Collateral amount.

Equipment, Fixtures, and Machinery Loans: These assets can be mortgage or even leased. The resale of most equipment is well established and therefore bankers will make loans up to 80% of the fair market value. Loans on trucks, vehicles, and other marketable equipment are made up to 90% of fair market value. I suggest you use the 80% loan to value figure to determine the amount a lender will consider lending on equipment. You need to determine if a particular piece of equipment has a resale value. I had a client finance equipment at 75% loan to current market value in 2007 and within one year the fair market value decreased 80%. A $60,000 piece of equipment was so specialized that when the economy tanked, the value was less than $12,000.00.

Use 80% of the hard asset fair market value.
As the Collateral amount.

Goodwill Loans: The definition of Goodwill (Blue-Sky) is: an element or item of value in the business sales price. It is the value of the company's profit generated yearly. Profit is similar to any other asset; it has value. The second definition is that Goodwill is the cost of purchasing a business over and above the value of its assets. When accountants record a business purchase price in the company's books, hard assets are registered at the purchase price which cannot be greater than fair market value. Goodwill is the amount of the purchase price exceeding the fair market value of the hard assets. A lender may finance a limited amount of Goodwill; however, SBA lenders are only allowed to loan a maximum of 50% of Goodwill up to a maximum of $250,000.

Use 50% of Goodwill value.
As the Collateral amount.

Working Capital: Working capital is the amount of money necessary to operate a business. Until profits are realized, a company needs money, hard cash, for the day-to-day operations. Working capital is not part of the purchase price. However, money-in and money-out (cash) projections will dictate the amount of working capital needed for your operation. For this section, working capital is not counted as part of the equation for purchasing a business.

E. Calculate estimated loan obtainable for the enterprise you want: The SBA does not make loans. (Some exceptions) SBA guarantees a percent of the loan and the lender bank assumes the liability for the balance. Once you have established the asset value you can now apply the estimated collateral value for the assets acquired. You have determined the amount of money and equity you have available for purchasing a business and using the collateral value of the property being acquired will create a target market value for you to review. Companies that have extensive hard assets including real estate, equipment and furniture and fixtures are easier to finance. Hard assets provide acceptable loan collateral.

Below are three examples of businesses available for purchase and a simple breakdown of the sales price:

The Retail Store: The total purchase price is $150,000.00

1. FMV of Inventory = $80,000.00   50% Loan Collateral = 40,000.00
2. FMV of Equipment = $15,000.00   80% Loan Collateral = 12,000.00
3. FMV of Goodwill = $55,000.00   50% Loan Collateral = 27,500.00

Available collateral from assets purchased = $79,500.00. Cash or hard equity required for the purchase/loan= $70,500.00

Banks, lenders and the SBA are reluctant to make loans using goodwill as collateral, and it will be necessary for you to finance 50% of the seller's value of goodwill. The amount of mortgage available using the business assets as collateral would be $79,500.00 of the total purchase price of $150,000.00.

The Doctors Office: The total purchase price is $300,000.00

1. FMV of Inventory = $10,000.00   50% Loan Collateral =   5,000.00
2. FMV of Equipment = $150,000.00   80% Loan Collateral = 120,000.00
3. FMV of Goodwill = $140,000.00   50% Loan Collateral = 70,000.00

Available collateral from assets purchased = $195,000.00. Cash or hard equity required for the purchase/loan= $105,000.00

The bank may make a loan without requesting the SBA to provide a guarantee. Although there are considerable risk and a large amount of goodwill, doctors usually are a good credit risk and many times can secure 100% financing. The SBA guarantee would be for a maximum of $195,000.00.

The Restaurant: The total purchase price is $380,000.00

1. FMV of Inventory = $15,000.00   50% Loan Collateral =   7,500.00
2. FMV of Equipment = $85,000.00   80% Loan Collateral = 68,000.00
3. FMV of Real Estate = $280,000.00   80% Loan Collateral = 224,000.00

Available collateral from assets purchased = $299,500.00. Cash or hard equity required for the purchase/loan= $80,500.00.

The sales price of a restaurant only includes hard assets such as inventory, equipment and real estate. It appears that the business has no Goodwill, and that alone could make this company a good buy. Why this business is for sale, should be determined before dismissing the company as a potential acquisition. Although lenders will escalate their review of the current financials, your abilities to produce a profit sufficient to cover the business loan will be a critical factor in obtaining financing. A down payment of 20% of the fair market value of the assets should be sufficient to secure a business loan providing you bring experience to the table.

This analysis of the business sales price being able to generate a business loan is not set in stone. It is a guide. If you have additional assets such as equity in your home or land or even another business, lenders will consider these assets as collateral. Even with all the hype and advertising about the availability of commercial loans, banks, and the SBA can be difficult. Remember the Golden Rule: He who has the gold makes the rules. Lenders are not in the business to lose money, and you are just a "risk" which needs to be computed. Make you lender your advocate.

Equity, Asset Loan Value, and Working Capital Summary

Once you have established the collateral available you can then compute the loan available. However, additional funds will be needed as Working Capital. The investment required needs to include the down payment necessary and the working capital needed to operate a business. This exercise can be reduced to a simple formula.

Business Purchase Price
Minus (-)   Loan Value of Assets
Plus (+)   Working Capital Required
\---------------------------------
Equals (=) Your Investment Needed

Due Diligence Steps - What to Request from the Seller

Many buyers approach sellers expecting a seller to divulge every detail of the business up front. Sellers are contacted many times, and they may be hesitant or unwilling to provide information. Sellers may want to keep a sale secret from employees or their competition. A buyer's deposit may be necessary, or the seller may require a letter of intent or even a letter of non-disclosure. Realtors understand customer requirements and usually the needed documents are available without jumping through hurdles. Request the following information:

Step 1 Meeting with the Realtor: Realtors have most of the necessary information regarding the seller's business operation. A good broker guides the seller through the listing process by recommending the price and terms. They also gather the business information and prepare a Sales Boucher for potential buyers. Problems, if known by the realtor, must be disclosed. Pertinent information will not be disclosed unless the purchaser has been pre-qualify.

Step 2 Review the Financials: You will need a Balance Sheets and Statements of Income for a two-year period. If there are no Financial Statements request two years of the Business Tax Returns. However, as pointed out in Chapter 5, Financial Statements for internal control will be different than the information on tax returns. The IRS code does not mirror General Accepted Accounting Principles. Understanding financial statements is crucial when analyzing the information presented. If you are uncomfortable wading through the financials, you should contact a CPA or Tax Consultant for a comprehensive review.

Step 3 Business Deductions Related to the Owner: Many business expenses not associated with normal operations may be recorded in the Financial Statements. Owners may include a deduction for home office, health insurance or some other personal cost that will not be an expense of the buyer. When analyzing the profit or creating projected profit scenarios the seller's personal expenses should be ignored. Do not include the seller's interest expense when calculating Net Profit. Interest expense is incurred because the owner needs a loan, and you may be paying cash. Of course, the salary or wages paid to the owner should be considered profit. Check the financials for any amounts not directly related to the business operation.

Step 4 Non-Disclosure Agreement: If requested, do not hesitate to sign a non-disclosure statement. Sellers are very concerned about confidential information and need to feel protected.

Step 5 Bank Statements: Request twelve months of Bank Statements directly from the bank. It is important to obtain bank statements directly from the bank unopened. I have seen two cases of altered Bank Statements, and because the Sales Income is the most important factor when analyzing financial statements, an analysis should be completed using original documents.

Some Small Businesses fail to keep business receipts and adequate records. I have had more than a handful of clients request a business valuation, but express concern because the seller   has 'hidden income' from the IRS. The seller is on the horns of a dilemma; he has hidden sales that he wants you to count, but he is unable to verify these sales. Walk away unless the purchase price is computed using the confirmed revenues or the purchase price is adjusted for future receipts for the next year or longer. To establish a business value sometimes the only ingredient is an income analysis. If records do not substantiate the income, it is impossible to make a correct appraisal.

Step 6 General Ledger: Check the historical entries in the *Cash in the Bank Account*. Deposits and disbursements are all included in the General Ledger. You can compare the deposits against the Accounts Receivable ledger. As you will learn in the future chapter, a General Ledger is a recap of Income and Expense Accounts over a period. When printed, a General Ledger could be over a hundred pages but if you are going to complete a thorough analysis you need to see the General Ledger. Review each transaction within the Accounts.

Step 7 Meeting with the Seller: First off you need to remember that employees may not know about a pending sale. The owner may wish to keep that information confidential, and you need to respect his position. Your meeting with the owner should accomplish several things.

Why is the owner selling the business?

Discuss the customer base. I reviewed a business several years ago that had only three customers. Although the business income was in the $800,000 range, the risk of losing just one customer could be devastating.

Does the business have key employees and do they know about a pending sale? If so are they willing to stay with the new owner?

Request the owner to participate in the conversion of the business operation to a new management team. Does the owner want a salary or consulting fee for this consulting period?

Walk around and inspect the facility, equipment, and inventory. Make notes for problem areas and estimate the general cost of correcting these issues.

Is the inventory obsolete or damaged? What is the current cost basis of the stock? What is the inventory Turn-Over Ratio? (The number of times the inventory is turned over and replaced in a given period).

Can the building lease be transferred? Obtain a copy of the rental agreement. If the seller owns the facility, is the building included in the price? If not what are the terms of the rent? Is the building available?

What about any Accounts Receivable? If the Trade Accounts Receivable are included in the price, request a customer aging Schedule? Two important concepts: First the AR changes daily and usually the acceptable AR amount is finalized at or close to closing. Secondly, is the owner willing to discount the AR due to projected bad debts? For many small business sales, the outstanding Accounts Receivable are collected by the seller and are not included in the selling price.

Another point of discussion is the Accounts Payable. If the Accounts Payable are included in the purchase price do not forget that this is no different than paying off the seller's mortgage. If the purchase price is $200,000 and you are assuming AP debt of $25,000 the real purchase price is $225,000. Be careful signing any documents assuming all debt. If you are paying the seller's debts complete a detailed list and include a disclaimer for any debts you refuse to pay. Contact your attorney to protect your position.

All hard assets such as Equipment and fixtures need to be inspected to determine the value and condition. Many times a professional appraiser is hired, and he determines the Fair Market Value.

Use the Financial Statement to determine assets and liabilities you need to consider. Review each line-item on the financials and ask questions. Financials have many different Accounts for Assets and Liabilities. Check Account balances and conduct an inspection of the backup information. Some of the Accounts are hard assets you can touch, feel and observe, and some are only an accounting entry which requires reviewing the paper trail.

Step 8 Closing Agreement: Review the closing documemt for all the agreed upon terms and conditions. Pay particular attention to the purchase of inventory, accounts payable and accounts receivable if included in the acquisition. An attorney is necessary to ensure that the title to the equipment is transferable. Make sure that your attorney understands the items you want in the contract have been included.

Establishing the Business Value

There are many reasons entrepreneurs sell their businesses. Sellers may have financial problems; personal problems, retirement or they need a change and selling their business is a way to secure their future. I was involved in purchases where the owner had died, and the business is for sale by the heirs. The price reflects the death of the owner and usually the price is based upon hard assets only.

One of the easiest valuations is a bankruptcy. Again the price probably is based upon hard assets. A going operation, even one in bankruptcy can demand a higher sales price unless the owner has hidden material facts. As a buyer, you must identify all the aspects concerning why a business is for sale.

There are also many reasons to buy a business. The new owner may want an ongoing concern, limit competition, secure cheap equipment, or reorganize and sell at a profit. Sort of like buying a house, making improvements and selling at a profit. Whatever the reason for purchasing a business, your goal is to the buy a company for the lowest price possible.

Below I have listed and explained in summary different valuation approaches. I have also developed a simpler, and easier method to evaluate a business by using a combination of Net Profit plus Asset Value. Sellers will be able to apply the same calculations when determining a suitable sales price.

Asset Based Approach: Obtain a complete list of each asset and determine its Fair Market Value. Include every item on the Balance Sheet such as inventory, accounts receivable, equipment, vehicles, fixtures and other items. An appraiser may be necessary. Also consider real estate and leasehold improvements. Many times the value of the assets is so extensive that computing the value of a business using the Asset Based approach with the Income approach is not reasonable. The total value of the assets could be more than a reasonable profit will support. The current owner may not have a mortgage and a loan payment; therefore, the current profit is sufficient for his lifestyle.

For example, the assets could be worth $300,000.00, and the profit is only $50,000.00. Clearly 50K is an excellent return on your 300K, however, 50K is not sufficient to satisfy your self-employment goals.

Buying a company based only on the asset value is also acceptable if you are planning on buying cheap and selling the assets for a profit. I have clients buy only assets, restructure the business and earn a tidy profit by selling.

Compare Other Businesses: Usually does not make sense because no two businesses are the same. However, you could be buying a business where the owner has financial problems, and you have determined a similar business has a higher value and therefore you can steal this business. Again there are many factors you need to review before plunking down your money.

Income Approach: I like the Income Approach because it focuses on sales income. It is reverent when combined with an analysis of Gross Profit. (Sales - Cost of Sales = Gross Profit) There may not be any net profit; however, an excellent income flow coupled with an acceptable sales margin may make the business an outstanding buy. The Gross Income is one of my strongest indicators of the value of any company. However, if the Cost of Goods Sold and the Fixed Expenses are unreasonable compared to the income, this sign may need some review to determine its importance.

Computing Net Profit: The Income minus Cost of Goods Sold minus the Operating Expenses equals the Net Profit. The Net Profit is the basic number you must deal with it. As I stated above; it is what it is! There may be other things to consider, and your perceived value of the business may be different than just a calculation of the Net Profit. This exercise only considers Net Profit as a way to determine the actual value. I cover other items below and although several of these items are subjective they must be considered before you finalize your purchase.

Multiplier Approach: There are many industry averages used to calculate the value of a business. Simply stated an industry standard can be applied to Net Profit, Gross Sales or Gross Profit. Using several years of actuals calculate an average. Multiply this average by some magic number as determines by the government or industry trade association. This multiplier approach does not consider your objectives. The business needs to produce sufficient after tax profit to provide a fair return on your investment and service the business loan. Also, you must have a reasonable income for your labors and be able to create a profit for growth and retirement. Applying a magic multiplier may or may not achieve these goals.

Appraised Value: Hire a professional business appraiser. Determining the value of your company can be a complicated process. You can find a local appraiser by selecting the link, "Find an Appraisal Expert" at the website for the American Society of Appraisers. Many lenders will require an appraisal of the business of the business assets before approving a loan.

Intangible Valuation: Do not buy a business using q 'Feel Good' or "Touchy-feely' procedure. Start with Profit or even Project Profit based on the market study. You may want to analysis intangibles as a part of your study, but stick to facts if possible. Many times a business opportunity is easy to spot. Visiting a retail store or a fast food restaurant that is poorly operated may be an opportunity. However, the business may be poorly managed because the public does not demand the services or products and the owner is hanging on with a prayer.

Return on Investment: Acceptable valuation method but only part of the equation. You still need a return on your labor, sufficient profit to service your loan and adequate profit for capital improvements (growth) and retirement.

Business Valuation that Meets
Personal and Business Goals

I wish I could provide you with a unique valuation method that magically concludes the price is fair and equitable, and the purchase of the business will meet your business and personal goals. Determining the value of any business takes time and information, and the final result ends up being a subjective decision. In other words after your investigation and number crunching is complete, the decision to buy or not, is based upon your informed instinct. Appraisers, Realtors, and accountants are unable to establish an agreed upon value. They can provide assistance, but the final business value is an educated decision made by you.

I have developed a Net Profit approach when determining the value of a company based upon to your goals. The business has to meet or exceed the goals and expectations of the purchaser. The price may be undervalued and still not fall within the buyer's parameters. Just the opposite may be true. The business may be overpriced, and because the purchaser's objectives are accomplished, it qualifies for purchased. The bottom line is to buy a company that will meet your personal and business goals. Profit is not the entire answer, however without sufficient profit your dream can become a nightmare.

Phase I: Prepare Basic Information

Step 1: Prepare Home Budget.

Step 2: Compute Amount Available for Down Payment.

Step 3: Estimate Business Purchase Price

Step 4: Establish Amount of Loan Needed.

Step 5: Amortize Loan - Average Interest & Principal first Year.

Phase II: Compute Net Profit on Selected Business.

Step 1: Establish Monthly Gross Income

Step 2: Determine Cost of Goods Sold

Step 3: Establish Your Operating Expenses

Step 4: Determine Monthly Net Profit.

Step 5: Adjust the Net Profit Based on Your Projections.

Phase III: Adjusted Net Profit - Taxes

Step 1: Deduct Average Interest expense from Adjusted Net Profit to obtain Taxable Net Profit.

Step 2: Compute Social Security & Medicare (15.3%) on Taxable Net Profit. Phase III, Step 1.

Step 3: Estimate Federal and State Income Taxes (15%) on Taxable Net Profit. Phase III, Step 1.

Step 4: Subtract Payroll Taxes, Phase II, Step 2 and Income taxes, Phase III, Step 3 to determine the net profit available.

Phase IV: Compute Take Home Net Profit

Phase I – Prepare Basic Information:

Monthly Home Budget Amount, Phase I, Step 1	3,900.00
Amount available for Down payment, Phase I, Step 2	120,000.00
Estimate Business Purchase Price. Phase I, Step 3	480,000.00
Estimated Loan Needed. Phase I, Step 4	360,000.00
Interest Payable first year – Average –Phase I, Step 5	1,966.00
Principal Payable first year – Average –Phase I, Step 5	3,555.00

Phase II -: Compute Net Profit on Selected Business:

Monthly Gross Income, Phase II, Step 1	65,000.00
Cost of Goods Sold, Phase II, Step 2	14,300.00
Total Operating Expenses, Phase II, Step 3	38,200.00
Monthly Net Profit. Phase II, Step 4	<u>12,500.00</u>
Adjusted Net Profit, Phase II, Step 5	13,500.00

Phase III – Adjusted Net Profit - Taxes:

Adjusted Net Profit	13,500.00	
Average Interest paid	<u>1,966.00</u>	
Taxable Net Profit		11,534.00
Social Security and Medicare on Taxable Profit		1,683.00
Federal and State Income Tax on Taxable Income		1,730.00
Total Payroll Taxes and Income Taxes		<u>3,413.00</u>
Net Profit After Taxes - available for Investment Objectives		<u>8,121.00</u>

Phase V: Does the Adjusted Net Profit Meet Your Investment Goals:

Provide the reasonable wage for your work.
Service the business loan. (New Business Loan)
Provide a fair return on your investment.
Create a profit for growth and retirement.

Net Profit After Taxes - available for Investment Objectives	8,121.00
Monthly home Budget Amount	3,900.00
Month Principal Payment	<u>3,555.00</u>

Total amount Home and Loan payment   7,455.00

Balance available after living expenses and Loan Payment   666.00

In this example, we have established that the profit is sufficient to meet your investment goals. However, the balance of profit available is only $666.00 which may not be an adequate margin. I would recommend this business. There is one more phase to review before the final decision.

Phase VI: Significant Facts. You may discover other considerations. Be observant, it is impossible to detail every scenario. You will have to determine how each different anomaly will affect your offer and your decision to purchase. Many of the items below will not affect your purchase price, but you must consider each one and consider its effect upon your business. As an example many buyers, and for that matter new enterprises do not place the concern over the location it deserves. Many companies are for sale or facilities are for rent because of their poor location. However, many buyers are more concerned with price and therefore downplay the effect the location has on the success of the company. Consider other items:

✓ **Location:** Simply put, if customers can't find you, or it is too difficult to find you, the location sucks.

✓ **Easements**: Building easements or right-a-ways could impact your business plans.

✓ **Act of God Problems:** Has the business ever been a crime scene? Fires or even floods could affect the price.

✓ **Government Problems:** Does the seller have problems with the IRS, Sales Tax or other government agencies?

✓ **Zoning Concerns:** What is the business zoning? Check the zoning and don't assume the business is correctly zoned.

✓ **Hazardous Materials:** Will you have hazardous materials?

✓ **Why is the Seller Getting Out?** Besides retiring, health reasons or other opportunities, you need to make sure you find any hidden reasons which could influence you offer.

✓ **Seller Financing:** Will the seller carry back all or some of the purchase price? The seller participation in financing your purchase, may not have anything to do with his faith in the business. He may need the money for retirement, or he has personal debt he need to retire. If the company meets your investment goals it probably will meet the lender's criteria. Don't pass on an opportunity unless seller financing is your only alternative.

✓ **License and Permits:** Check all License and Permits before you finalize the purchase. What type of license is need depends on the kind of business and location. What state or local government issues licenses and permits?

✓ **Environmental Concerns:** If you are acquiring real property along with the business, it is important to check the environmental regulations in the area.

✓ **Can the Sales Income be increased?** You can make an educated projection depending on the current operation.

✓ **Can the Cost of Goods Sold be reduced?** Again a review of the purchases, the quality or other factors may allow you to decrease the Cost of Goods Sold

✓ **Can I cut the Operation Expenses?** It may be impossible to change fixed cost such as rent or utilities in the short term. However, concentrate on those costs you control.

✓ **Recorded and Hidden Liens:** In many states equipment claims are recorded in the County where the business is located. Check County and State records for hidden liens before the closing.

✓ **Sales Tax on Capital Assets Purchased:** Do not forget that you are required to pay sales tax on the purchase of hard assets such as equipment, fixtures, vehicles and machinery. Sales tax in some states and localities could be as high as 10 percent.

✓ **Leased Equipment:** Determine is any of the equipment is leased. Review the General Ledger, Lease Expense Account for payments on leases. Determine if the contract can be paid off or do you need to consider a price reduction.

✓ **Office, Store or Warehouse Rental:** What are the terms of leased facilities? Can the lease be assigned? What about rent deposits and guarantees? Obtain a copy of the lease contract and make sure you understand the terms and conditions. Are there any special provisions?

✓ **Business Loans:** Does the business have any loans on the books? Are the loans going to be paid off? At closing make sure the loan is paid with closing funds.

✓ **Accounts Receivable:** Is the seller collecting the Accounts Receivable? What about Bad Debts? I suggest you do not buy the Accounts Receivable.

✓ **Accounts Payable:** Do not assume the Accounts Payable unless you can verify outstanding debt. List those Accounts Payable to be paid at closing and make sure you either have the seller set aside funds to cover AP not disclosed or you take other precautions within the purchase contract. Your attorney needs to protect you against undisclosed debts.

✓ **Business Forced To Sale:** In Chapter 1, I covered the many reasons businesses fail. Many times it is impossible or extremely difficult to determine if the seller needs to sell his business or it is his choice. As a buyer identifying the motive for the sale can save you thousands of dollars. Whether you are buying to liquidate assets, reorganize or operate; your mission is to conclude the lowest acceptable purchase price.

✓ **Hire an Attorney:** This is where you need an attorney. You should negotiate with the seller on many details of the purchase as possible. Once the price has been determined, and you and the seller have agreed on the principal terms, get to know the seller. He can help you transfer the customer loyalties. I personally like cutting my deal and then letting the attorney write/check the contract to ensure the sale is reduced to the details I negotiated. I expect my lawyer to review with me the terms and conditions of the contract. Since any contract involves future problems, I expect my lawyer to point out any problems that may occur.

✓ **Reorganize, Buy and Sell:** Sometimes an opportunity is staring you in the face. Have you ever visited a fast food outlet managed by two 17-year olds playing loud music and waiting for closing? Not to be overly harsh on 17-year olds, but they do not have the experience, ability or the education to operate a business. Kids running a business without an adult can be an opportunity! Want to buy a business cheap then, check the operation ten times. Check for cleanliness, the bathroom, the tables and floor, the signs, food and of course check the service. If you want a turn-a-around business just look. They are all everywhere. Go directly to the owner – no realtor. This guy needs to sell he is losing his ass.

Phase VII: Complete the Purchase

Buy the Business Not the Company (Business Entity): If the company is a corporation or partnership/LLC do not buy the company stock or ownership shares. Buy the business assets including the registered name and the operation of the enterprise. Buying a stock means you are purchasing all the negative history of the business including any problems the company has with the IRS or maybe potential lawsuits. You will be responsible for unpaid taxes, unfiled tax returns and issues with the filed tax returns. There may be lawsuits and employee problems which follow the company ownership. This lesson is so important that it bears repeating: Buy the business operation and assets of the corporation, partnership or LLC. Do not buy the common stock or ownership shares from the owner.

My advice to the seller is to sell your business ownership position such as stock. If you can sell the company stock or an ownership position, you should do so. Selling stock is simple and fast, and 100% of your sale price is considered capital gain. Selling a business, and its assets by the company can result in a higher tax burden. Small Business are usually asset-based valuations.

Split-Out The Total Purchase Price: The final contract should split out the total purchase price for goodwill, fixtures, equipment, real estate, intangibles assets such as patents, and any other acquired right or guarantee. Remember that you will be required to pay sales tax on your purchase. However, the benefits of writing off the equipment cost on your income tax could be considerable. Also, you can setup hard assets as 179 Depreciation so the total investment can be written off in a few short years. See a CPA for details.

Non-Completive Provisions: If the business sales volume can be traced to the owner or maybe an essential employee, non-competitive language should be included in the contract. Restrictive trade clauses and restriction concerning the trade name, trademarks, and patents. Many non-competitive agreements are unenforceable so you will need an attorney.

Hire Attorney and CPA: Understand your future obligations and protect yourself. Form a business entity if necessary.

© Randy Glasbergen
www.glasbergen.com

"If you claim your fleas as dependents, you may qualify for the Earned Income Tax Credit."

Chapter 4
STEPS FOR STARTING YOUR BUSINESS
SMALL BUSINESS HANDBOOK
The best and most complete handbook for the Micro Business Entrepreneur.
Essential information for starting, buying, operating and succeeding.

The foundation of any business idea requires a two-phase process. Before tackling a comprehensive business plan, first create a preliminary plan. The initial business plan does not require the same level of research as your final comprehensive business plan, and it can save time and money. However, you need to research your product lines, customer base, competition, pricing, and profit margins. There are two primary goals. Your first goal is to test market your idea, and your second objective is to determine the level of interest by lenders and investors. Once your preliminary plan is completed, meet with trusted friends, relatives and peers for their reaction. Finally, meet with lenders or investors to obtain an opinion on your idea and suggestion on how to make your proposal stronger.

Prepare a more formal business plan once you have determined your idea has merit. You may not accept the opinions of your mentors and peers; however, feedback from lenders and investors should be of strictly evaluated. Tackling the comprehensive business plan may require hiring professionals or at a minimum, studying and educating yourself on the requirements of your enterprise. It has always been my contention that sales income is usually overstated without backup. Every step is completed to assure the reader that the financial projections are trustworthy. Your job is to convince lenders and investors that they can rely on your research. Backup your business plan with solid facts.

Phase 1: The Preliminary Business Plan

Reduce your Business Idea to writing: Hundreds of ideas surge through our brains daily. We usually have so many ideas we tend to discount most of them. Your dream will not suddenly materialize like a Genie in the bottle. You must take action. Your initial step is to create an outline summarizing your ideas. What is the idea about? What are the products or services, is there a market for you products and can I achieve my financial goals.

Opening a retail store selling high-end Scandinavian furniture may be difficult to accomplish, but the idea of a retail furniture store is relatively common. Off the wall ideas such as inventing a new internet App is not only difficult but would not be impossible for those of us without any understanding of computers. However, no idea should be scratched without completing an initial outline. Whether you want to start a restaurant, a home repair business or you have an invention that will transform the building industry, your story needs to be reduced to writing. The preliminary business plan should be an outline of where you intend to go and how you intend to get there.

Create a Summary Business Plan: The Preliminary business plan is a reduced version of the comprehensive plan. The goals are different. Much of the effort creating this initial plan can be use preparing a Master Business Plan required for SBA funding, investors or direct bank loans.

> **Introduction:** Short paragraph introducing yourself and any other principal owners who will participate in the management of the company.

> **What are my Products and Service?** Think through your new business idea carefully by creating a general product line or an outline of services you intend to offer. Your product lines will change as your market plan develops. You need to put considerable thought, and effort on your product line and services provided because most of your costs are directly related to your goods and services offered.

> **Requirements for your Business?** Besides the professional license such, as an engineer may need, you may also need information on zoning or a restriction on various products. Today everything is on the internet. States and cities have excellent websites and usually, the information you need is online. Complete a list of the legal requirements carefully noting the source and any fees necessary. This section may be lengthy because your business may require everything from a constructing a facility to creating a Website for internet marketing.

> **Is There a Market for Your Products or Services?** No simple answer. If your product or service is currently being offered, the solution can be obtained by reviewing trade magazines or government industry reports for your marketing area. If possible contact competitors in your local area or even in other cities. Define your marketing area or estimate the percent of potential customers who would benefit from your product or service.

When researching the possibilities for this handbook, I reviewed government statistics for the number of new business with ten of fewer employees which is my target market. I discovered that my market was over thirty-three million entrepreneurs, I then made an estimate of the number of people that need my handbook and would buy. There is no simple answer. I know my market, but I have no idea how many units I can sell even with an outstanding marketing plan.

Below is a list of variable to consider when forecasting sales volume for products and services. None of these variable will provide you with an acceptable formula or answer. Even experts are wrong. Ever heard of the Edsel? It was not even in my word dictionary.

✓ Who are my customers?
✓ Test market your product.

56

✓ Create a consumer panel.
✓ Knock on doors.
✓ Does my product fill a need?
✓ What is my total customer base?
✓ What percent of my customer base will buy?
✓ Why would customers buy your product or service?
✓ How would my business improve people's lives?
✓ Where are these customers?
✓ How do I tell potential clients about my business?
✓ Are my products or services a necessity or an impulse purchase?
✓ Is my market worldwide?
✓ What are the prices for 'Like' products and services?
✓ Is my market to a wholesaler or direct to the consumer?
✓ What is my competition?
✓ Is my product unique?
✓ Is my product meeting a trend?
✓ Is my product legal?
✓ What is the optimum price for my product?
✓ What price is the consumer willing to pay?
✓ Does my product equal or exceed my competitors?

The biggest variable is not price. An excellent marketing plan and control of Inside Competition will result is sales.

➢ **How do you intend to Market your Products or Services?** Every day you drive-by businesses that that have no idea how to get you to stop and enter their store. How are you going to get your message to customers? Creating customer excitement requires a marketing plan detailing your personal commitment, both in time and money. Why would customers buy from you? What unique and exceptional service or product are your offerings? Consider the price. However, price is not the most important ingredient. After all, someone was able to sale thousands of Pet rocks. Customer satisfaction is the key to success. We remember products and services in terms such as 'Good Buy' or 'Too Expensive,' but most often, we remember the quality and service we received. How does your business product or service stack up compared to your competition? How are you going to get your message out? Word of mouth to generate business is probably the best advertising, but you better have deep pockets waiting for the word to get around. Following are a few advertising ideas.

✓ Print Advertising – Newspapers, magazines, brochures and fliers.
✓ Radio and TV
✓ On Line
✓ Billboards and Kiosks
✓ Trade Shows and Events
✓ Movie Trailers

57

    ✓   Door to Door and Person to Person
    ✓   Business Cards and Mailings
    ✓   Employee participation promotion
    ✓   Telephone marketing
    ✓   Word of mouth incentives.

➤ **Can my Idea Make Money?** I had a client that opened a Franchise Golf Store. His product cost was 70%. $1,000 in sales resulted in a gross profit was $300. The store operating cost was $11,000 a month. With a product cost of 70% of sales, the company needed $36,666 a month in sales to survive. Overall the owner was an excellent operator but he completely overestimated his sales when preparing his business plan. He could not compete with major sporting goods stores, and he paid for his mistake by losing his 401K investment. Sales and cost of Goods sold are your number one priority.

The importance of accurate sales and cost of sales projections cannot be over emphasized. Your projected expenses will become a reality, but Sales and Gross Profit (Sales Income minus Cost of Goods Sold) usually are exaggerated. Strive for a 100% mark-up as an initial estimate. Many companies can create sales for an exorbitant price because their marketing plan has established a perceived value, real or not. First attempt is setting a selling price that will attract buyers. Secondly determine the cost of sales and those numbers will create your Gross profit. (Sales minus Cost of Sales equals Gross Profit.) Profit before operation expenses applied.

➤ **Financial Projections:** For the preliminary plan, you need to develop a simple income and expenditure forecast. Banks, investors, and the SBA will require two or more years of detailed projections but for this preliminary plan, estimate an average month of sales, cost of sales and expenses is necessary.

    Step 1: First tackle Sales Volume. Other than throwing a dart at a chart of numbers, you need to estimate potential sales volume using market information.

    Step 2: Cost of Goods Sold: Contact suppliers for dealer pricing. If you have a produce overseas or locally review your cost including freight and any other fees.

    Step 3: Estimate Expenses: Review the list of expenditure categories in Chapter 5, Chart of Expenses and use the expense categories as a guide in determining estimated cost required for your business operation.

Your financial projections need to cover three average months. The basic information needed is the estimated sales, Cost of Sales for determining

Gross Profit and of course an estimate of typical operating expenses. You are attempting to solve the four business goals:

Provide a fair return on your investment.
Service the business loan. (New Business Loan)
Provide a reasonable income for your labors.
Create a profit for growth and retirement.

Share Preliminary Business Plan: As stated above the goal of a preliminary plan is to test market your idea and determine the level of interest by lenders and investors. Form a group of friends, relatives, peers and other business people you trust. Present your preliminary plan and obtain their opinions concerning the success of your enterprise. You will receive negative input, and unless it is constructive, you should disregard such comments. However, most ideas will have merit. Before presenting your plan to lenders or investors, you need to consider all the ideas and suggestions and incorporate them into a revised preliminary business plan. You may discount any and all opinions and follow your dream no matter the obstacles. Congratulations, you are an entrepreneur.

Visit with a lender to get his ideas concerning your business plan. Although it is not necessary, you may want to prepare an estimate of the total investment required and your available cash and equity. Since lenders will need a personal financial statement, I would prepare one before visiting with the lender. In Chapter 2, there is a guide to determine the amount of investment necessary to determine the loan available. Bankers will be looking for a minimum investment of 25% of the total required investment, and the balance needs to be secured by equity in hard assets. As an example, if the total business investment is estimated at $150,000, lenders will require a $37,500 personal investment and hard asset equity for the balance.

You are not attempting to receive a loan approval. You are trying to determine the lender's interest in making an SBA or a direct loan. You want to make the bank your advocate and pick his brain for his ideas for financing your business. If any bank shows lack of interest move on. The bank's loan committee approves both direct loans and the banks participation in an SBA guaranteed loans. The SBA only guarantees a part of the loan and the bank is still liable for a large percent. Be prepared to cover the essential investment amount in the meeting with a lender. Do not forget, all lenders are interested in your ability to repay the loan and will you repay the loan.

Until you solve how to finance your business, spending money to create a corporation or an LLC entity and incurring legal fees to protect your name and even to meet with your insurance agent should wait.

Special Advice: Lenders will require Financial Statements on a quarterly or yearly basis. Many times investors, especially friends and relatives, do not realize their money is in jeopardy until the notification of bankruptcy is received. Make it an action item to inform them monthly of the financial status of your business by forwarding them your financials. Make it a practice to send monthly Financial Statements to investors or lenders. Many times a friend or a relative is blindsided with the news of a business failure. Sharing monthly financial Statements will assure investors and lenders that their loan funds were used by the business and not personally.

Legal Entity – Protection & Tax Benefits

Before reviewing the steps necessary for a comprehensive business plan; this section deals with your business entity. I recommend you consult with an attorney and a CPA when selecting a business entity. Each discipline is necessary. This manual covers five business *entities:*

  ➢ Proprietorship,
  ➢ Partnerships,
  ➢ C-Corporations
  ➢ S-Corporation
  ➢ Limited Liability Company.

For a small start-up business, I recommend that you choose a proprietorship, with some reservations. The reservations I have concerning a proprietorship is the unlimited personal liability of a proprietorship. However do not be fooled into believing an LLC or a corporation will provide unlimited protection. Forming a separate entity will not protect you from all liabilities. Personal responsibilities such as a vehicle accident, where you were the driver and actions by a lender for personal loan guarantees could not be avoided.

The next best business entity is a Limited Liability Company, again with reservations. Similar to any business entity, an LLC will not protect your personal assets from individual events caused by you and loan guarantees you made. However, those liabilities that are incurred by the LLC or corporation in its normal day to day business operations do not flow through to you individually. Unless you guarantee a loan or even company accounts payable, the lender cannot hold you personally responsible. An individually owned LLC reports income and expense the same as a proprietorship, and your personal assets can be protected.

Many entrepreneurs falsely believed a separate business entity such as an LLC or a corporation will protect all your personal assets. A business entity will not protect you from personal liabilities such as drive drunk or causing an accident driving a company vehicle. Most risk can be protected with a combination of business liability insurance and a business entity.

It is not simple to pick a business entity. You must consider lenders, investors, many types of risks such as financial liabilities and your income tax burden. Most new businesses automatically assume that they should form a Limited Liability Company. I believe the advantages of this business entity are considerable; however I do not think it is the best entity for limiting your total income tax liability. An LLC taxed as an S-Corporation is recommendation.

Contact your CPA and your attorney for your situation. It cost extra money to operate as an LLC or corporation.

When considering a business entity the state franchise fees, legal and accounting cost may be prohibited. If you are a very small business, these costs may many entrepreneurs to form the simple business entity of a Sole Proprietorship. LLC's, corporation and partnerships require additional expense. As a sole-proprietor, the accounting, tax preparation, and legal requirements may create a significant financial burden. As a proprietor, you report your income and expenses on your personal return with little cost for an attorney or a CPA.

Cost of Registration: You can register your company without an attorney or a company on th einternet. Study your state on-line website for help. When you are ready to obtain a Federal Identification Number go to the IRS web site. I was obtaining an ID for a client and used a commerical ID web-site. The company wanted $246.00 for something that is free from the IRS. Study and read about state and fedeal requirements before you plunk down money.

DISCLAIMER

Picking a business entity can be difficult. The information below is only an outline to guide you through several aspects of each entity. It will assist you in asking the experts meaningful questions. I recommend that you hire both an Attorney and a Certified Public Accountant as a team. An attorney will guide you through your legal concerns, and the accountant will guide you through accounting and tax problems. It is important that you hire both disciplines.

Although this manual touches on legal aspects concerning your business operations and determining a business entity, you need to consult with an attorney. This writer is not an attorney and the general legal information included in this manual may or may not be applicable to your business.

© Randy Glasbergen.
www.glasbergen.com

GLASBERGEN

"Our Legal Department has seen substantial growth
over the last quarter, producing 21% more
mumbo and 17% more jumbo."

SOLE-PROPRIETORSHIP

A sole proprietor is someone who owns an unincorporated business by himself or herself. It is a business entity which an individual is considered a single entity for tax and liability purpose. Other than a licensing requirements in some municipal or state governments, a Sole Proprietorship is not registered. The Sole Proprietor's legal entity is his name unless a Doing Business as (DBA) is registered. The owner is inseparable from the business they are personally liable for any business debts.

Advantages and Disadvantages of a Sole-Proprietorship: The most significant disadvantage of using a proprietorship is lack of financial protections.

Single Owner: An individual owner makes all the decisions without consulting anyone.

Easy to start: Unless you need a local license there are no formalities, begin your business without any notifications or license. (You may be required to obtain a local or state license, such as a bar or a restaurant)

Federal ID not Necessary: Unless you have employees you do not need to get an Employers Identification Number, and you can use your social security number.

OK to Co-mingle funds: As opposed to a corporation or an LLC, the owner can transfer funds in and out of the business for any reason. You can use the money from your company for persona expenses. Of course, personal expenses are not a deductible expense, but if you want you can have one checking account. A word of caution; co-mingling personal and business funds can create confusion, and non-business depsoits could be reclassified as taxable income in an IRS audit. I strongly suggest you do not co- mingling personal and business money.

Easy to dissolve: Sole proprietorships are easy to end. Although all the debts must be paid, and you are personally liable for such business debts, ending the company is as simple as walking away. You will also have no lawsuits from angry investors as you would have with a corporation or an LLC provide you have no loans.

Half of Your SE Tax is Deductible: The IRS allows you to deduct ½ of the total social security tax as a direct deduction against any income listed on Page 1 of the Individual Tax Return.

Easy Tax Return and Bookkeeping: A sole proprietor reports revenues and expenses directly on an IRS Schedule C that is a part of the individual tax return. No Balance Sheet is required. Bookkeeping is as simple as reporting income and business expenses.

Tax Advantages for your Children: Children under the age of 18 are exempt from Social Security Tax and Federal Unemployment Tax. If you pay your child an amount equal to or less than your child's Standard Deduction on the Tax Return, no income tax will be due. However, child's tax bracket could be lower that the parents, so review the amount to be paid by your accountant.

Child Retirement Fund or College Fund: Children can fund an IRA or a Roth IRA. Your child's wages are deductible on your tax return as a business expense. The child's wages are not taxable under the standard deduction so if you plan this correctly your child can save for college using non-taxable income. See your Tax Accountant for details to ensure the procedures meets IRS code.

Health Insurance & Medical reimbursement: Set up health insurance for the owner, spouse, employees and dependent children. The cost of group health insurance for your spouse is deductible if she is receiving a salary. Also consider a medical reimbursement plan. Business can deduct up to $2,500.00 for out of pocket medical expenses for employees and their spouse.

Health insurance premiums are deductible on Form 1040, however, since the health insurance is not deducted as a business expense the amount of the health insurance is subject to social security taxes. If your health insurance cost $10,000.00 a year the payroll tax would be $1,530.00.

GENERAL PARTNERSHIP

A partnership is the relationship existing between two or more persons who join to carry on a trade or business. Each person contributes money, property, labor or skill, and expects to share in the profits and losses of the enterprise.

Profits and losses are passed through to the partners on Form 1065, Schedule K-1. A partnership must file an annual information return. Each partner includes his or her share of the partnership's income or loss on their individual tax return.

Partners are not employees and should not take a salary nor should a Form W-2 be issued. Partners receive Guaranteed Payments that are subject to payroll taxes on the partner's individual tax return. The guarantee payments are considered an expense of the Partnership. The partnership must furnish copies of Schedule K-1 (Form 1065) to the partners by the date Form 1065 is required to be filed, including extensions.

As a general partner, you can be held responsible for the debts of the partnership, and you may be held liable for the liabilities of the other partners. If a partner incurs a partnership liability, other partners may be liable for such a liability. The Partnership entity is not recommended for small businesses. A Limited Liability Company or the corporation entity will provide liability protection without the negativities of a General Partnership. Very few general partnerships survive because partners can't get along.

Advantages and Disadvantages of a Partnership: Below are advantages and benefits of a general partnership.

> **Easy To Establish:** Many partnerships can be organized without the benefit of a written formal agreement.

> **Profits Flow to Partners Tax Return:** Profits from the business flow directly through to the partners' personal tax returns. No

> **Shared Investment:** With several owners there may be more money available for investment.

> **Shared Responsibilities and Work:** Different individuals bring different abilities to the table. Center

> **Shared Business Risks and Expenses:** Can be a positive however some partners have no credit rating or very little available front-end investment.

> **Complementary Skills:** Each partner can lead to the achievement of greater financial results together than would be possible apart.

> **Mutual Support and Motivation:** Big deal if you are fighting about everything.

> **Partnership Require Sharing Decisions:** Shared decisions require the ability of solving problems jointly. Disagreements will occur and sometimes tear the company apart.

Some Benefits not Deductible: Some employee benefits are not deductible from business income on the partnership tax return.

Joint Liability: Partners are liable for the financial actions of other partners within the partnership organization. Joint liability is the major flaw of a Partnership entity. The partnership liabilities flow through to all partners regardless of ownership. For this reason, a different entity is recommended. (See Limited Liability)

Shared Profits: Becomes a problem when and if any partner determines they are caring more of his share of time and ability.

Business Decisions: Disagreements will occur concerning small and large business details. These differences may become unsolvable making working conditions unbearable.

Limited Life: The partnership may end upon the withdrawal or death of a partner.

LIMITED PARTNERSHIP

A limited partnership is a special type of partnership which is very common when people need funding for a business, or when they are putting together an investment in a real estate development. A limited partnership requires a written agreement between the general partner and the limited partners. Each limited partner makes an investment of funds into the partnership for a percent of the profit. The pre-stated share of the profit is ordinarily greater than that of each of the general partners.

The profit and losses flow through to partners individual tax returns. State law sets the maximum number of limited partners.

Although this entity can be used to operate your Micro Business, usually this entity is advantageous for General Partners to secure funding from Limited Partners for Real Estate investments.

LIMITED LIABILITY COMPANY

An LLC is an entity created by state statute. Depending on elections made by the LLC and the number of members, the IRS will treat an LLC either as a corporation, partnership or as a proprietorship. The profit or loss is reported by the LLC owner on Schedule C and is treated the same as a proprietorship. Specifically, a domestic LLC with at least two members is classified as a partnership for federal income tax purposes unless it files Form 8832 and affirmatively elects to be treated as a corporation.

A Limited Liability Company is a non-corporate business entity. The owners can participate in the organization's management and are protected against personal liability for the organization's debts and obligations. A Limited

Copyright ©

Liability Company entity was created to include the characteristics of a corporation and a partnership. The owners are called Members and have corporate-like protection against personal liability.

Advantages and Disadvantages of a Limited Liability Company: Below are advantages and benefits of a Limited Liability Company.

Tax Benefits: LLC offers pass-through tax status similar to that of a partnership however a single member LLC is taxed as a sole proprietorship. Unless the LLC elects to be treated as a C-Corporation, the LLC itself does not pay taxes.

Less Paperwork: Corporations are required to hold meetings and record minutes of those meetings each year. The LLC is not required to maintain meetings. The amount of paperwork needed to purchase assets, open bank accounts or make significant changes within the company is also reduced.

Liability Protection: A LLC will provide the owner(s) with a degree of responsibility protection, such as a C & S Corporation. Owners of corporations and LLC are typically not personally responsible for the debts and liabilities of the business. The degree of legal protection offered by an LLC has been challenged in some states. If liability protection is your primary concern, you need to seek advice on the legal precedents in your state before choosing an LLC.

Hard to Change Entity: While it's relatively easy to change from an S to a C-Corporation or vice versa. Changing from an LLC to a C or S corporation requires a new corporate entity, with all the paperwork involved.

Single-Member LLC: Some states don't allow single-member LLC, so one-person companies need to check the rules in their state.

C-CORPORATION

A C-Corporation is a business entity created and organized within your state. The organizer submits the required forms to the office of Secretary of Corporations. An organizer may be a shareholder, however, usually an attorney organizes the corporation. Stock certificates or stock shares reflect ownership in the C-Corporation and are issued to shareholders in trade for cash or assets. The corporation must be registered in each state that it conducts business. If you do business in Colorado and you are a Nevada or Delaware corporation, you must file as a 'foreign corporation' in Colorado, and you will be required to file a Colorado business tax return.

A corporation is considered an independent entity which conducts business under the corporate name. For federal income tax purposes, the C-Corporation is a separate taxpaying entity. A C-Corporation conducts business, realizes net income or loss, pays taxes and distributes profits to the shareholders. It can be sued or sue. I have had clients who have been sued at the same time their corporation is being sued. Remember, operating as a corporation may be a defense, but it will not stop lawsuits. When attorneys file lawsuits usually the company, and the owner are sued.

The profit of a C-Corporation is taxed and paid by the C-Corporation when earned. The profits of the corporation are posted to an <u>Account</u> named *Retained Earnings*. Retained Earnings are distributed to shareholders as dividends. The dividends are taxable on the shareholder's individual tax return. This procedure creates a double tax. The corporation does not get a tax deduction when it distributes dividends to shareholders. Shareholders cannot deduct any loss of the corporation.

Summary of the Corporation Structure and Organization

Organizer creates corporation
By filing with Secretary of State
(The Registered Agent named)
The number of shares of stock is determined
The stock is assigned a value. No-par
Stock is not assigned a value.

Individuals purchase the
Common stock and become
Shareholders (owners)

Shareholders elect
Board of Directors

Directors manage the business.
The Directors determine long-range goals and establish
Company policy. The directors hire the Chief Operating Officer.

Directors hire the Officers (Chief Operating Officer)
(Officers manage day-to-day business)

Every state allows the creation of a General Corporation or called a "C" Corporation.

Advantages and Disadvantages of a C-Corporation: Below are advantages, benefits and disadvantageous of a C-Corporation.

Two ways to take money from the corporation: As an employee you receive wages, bonus, commissions or even stock options. All of which are subject to employment and income taxes. Wages are a deductible expense for the corporation. As a shareholder, you invested money into your business and expect a return on such investment. A corporation distributes profit to its shareholders usually once or twice a year, and such a distribution is called dividends. Although your company may not be as large as General Motors, it still has the option to pay dividends from profits to its shareholders. (See Taxes below)

Limited liability: The C-Corporation is legally a separate entity. The owners and shareholders cannot be held responsible for any debts of the C-Corporation or any lawsuits brought against it. (Officers and Directors have been charged with illegal acts) In other words, your personal assets will not be affected by the actions of the corporation. However, payroll taxes withheld from wages can be can collect from a corporate officer responsible for the corporations payables. Withheld Payroll taxes are considered 'held in trust' and the corporate officer responsible, may be required to pay.

Investors: A C-Corporation can sell stock or shares, either common or preferred, and there's no limit to the number of shareholders. When planning to raise capital or to take your business public, a C-Corporation is necessary.

Taxes: Because the C-Corporation is a separate entity, the profits, and losses are earned by the company and retained by the company. Profits kept by the corporation are called retained earnings. Dividends paid to the shareholders come from retained earnings. Unless you or your shareholders receive dividends, the shareholders are not be taxed on the corporation's income. C-Corporations enjoy a lower tax rate but once the taxed profits are distributed as dividends, they are tax again on the shareholder's tax return.

Perpetual existence: A C-Corporation will exist indefinitely, even if a shareholder or owner leaves, becomes disabled, dies, or sells off their shares.

Higher costs: A corporations must register in each state they conduct business. Registration fees in many states are very high. California's yearly fees start at $800.00 whereas Texas has a franchise fee which could be considerable. However, Texas does not have a state income tax. Check with your state concerning fees and registration cost.

Increased paperwork: Corporations required additional bookkeeping. A proprietorship and a single owner LLC allow the simplest record keeping. Because of IRS regulations and tax codes, the accounting and income tax preparation can be a significant expense. Increased regulations may require additional documents such as Articles of Incorporation, corporate bylaws, corporate minutes and certificates of good standing.

Double taxation: The C-Corporation pays income tax on profits generated from operations. The after-taxed profits are retained in an Account, called *Retained Earnings*. Many C-corporations distribute their retained earnings to the shareholders (Owners) as dividends either on a quarterly, semi-yearly or yearly basis. Dividends are simply C-Corporation profits that have already been taxed and are taxed again on the shareholder's individual tax return. As a small C-Corporation, you can limit direct corporate taxes by increasing shareholder/officer salary. By increasing your salary, you decrease corporate profits subject to corporate-level income tax.

One of the biggest problems I have with a small Business using the C-Corporation structure is the problems created when you sell your business. Remember that the C-Corporation owns the business. You own the C-Corporation, but the C-Corporation owns the business assets and business operation. When the C-Corporation sells the business, the profit from the sale is taxable at the corporate level and again at the individual shareholder level when the profit is distributed as dividends to the shareholder.

S-CORPORATION

First set up a traditional corporation. You file the necessary documents called Articles of Incorporation with your state. Once you have complete organizing the C-Corporation you need to complete IRS Form 2553 to have your business treated as an S corporation. Form 2553 request that the IRS allow your company to pass-through income and losses to the individual shareholders. The profits and losses are claimed on the shareholder's tax return. The corporation structure and organization is the same for an S-Corporation as it is for a C-Corporation.

Shareholders must be individuals, a resident or a U.S. Citizen, and currently an S-Corporation cannot have more than 100 shareholders owning one class of stock. The S-Corporation must use a December 31 year-end. Such income as net profit, interest, dividends and capital gains are passed-through to the shareholders and claimed as income or loss.

The major downside to a C-Corporation is double taxation. Profits are taxed at the corporate level, and when distributed to the shareholders, they are taxed once again. S-Corporation profits are only tax one time. When an S-Corporation has profits, the company's directors have the option to distribute those profits or retained them within the corporation as retained earnings. S-Corporation retained earnings have been taxed are not taxed again when distributed.

Advantages and Disadvantages of an S-Corporation: Below are advantages, benefits and disadvantageous of an S-Corporation. An S-Corporation is a C-Corporation that the profits are taxed on the owner's individual tax return. Many of the attributes of a C-Corporation apply to an S-Corporation.

Two ways to take money from the S-Corporation: As an employee, you receive wages, bonus, commissions or even stock options, and all are subject to payroll and income tax. Of course, wages are a deductible expense to the corporation. As a shareholder, you invested money into your business and expect a return on such investment. A company distributes profit to its shareholders usually once or twice a year, and such a distribution is called dividends. Profit from the S-Corporation is taxed on the shareholder's tax return. When and if the profit is distributed to the shareholders it is not taxed again.

Limited liability: The S-Corporation enjoys the same legal protections as a C-Corporation. See Limited Liability above.

Investors: An S-Corporation can sell only one class of stock. If you ever plan to go public, you'll also need to be structured as a C corporation.

Taxes: Profits and losses flow through to the individual shareholder.

Perpetual existence: An S-Corporation will exist indefinitely, even if a shareholder or owner leaves, becomes disabled, dies, or sells off their shares.
Higher costs: Corporations must register in states where they operate. Registration fees in many states are very excessive. California yearly fees start at $800.00. Check with your state concerning fees and registration.

Increased paperwork: Corporations required additional bookkeeping. A proprietorship and a single owner LLC allow the simplest record keeping. Because of IRS regulations and tax codes, the accounting and income tax preparation can be a significant expense. Increased regulations may require additional documents such as Articles of Incorporation, corporate bylaws, corporate minutes and certificates of good standing.

Double taxation: Profits are only taxes once. One of the biggest tax benefits of an S-Corporation is the income tax liability when selling your business. Of course, it is beneficial to sell your stock to the new owner but usually the buyer buys the business from the S-Corporation. The S-Corporation owns the business operation and the assets. The sale proceeds (profits) flow through to the shareholder's individual tax return.

Most of the profits generated by the sale of the business are capital gain income and subject to a much lower tax than ordinary income. Check with your tax accountant.

Copyright 2007 by Randy Glasbergen.
www.glasbergen.com

GLASBERGEN

"If I walk past your desk without stopping to criticize your work, that counts as a compliment."

Notes

_____

_____

_____

_____

_____

_____

_____

_____

_____

_____

Summary of Business Entities

Sole Proprietorship:

A Sole Proprietorship is a business entity that is owned and operated by a single person. The Sole Proprietorship is the simplest business entity available. The company is formed with little effort and can be conducted using owner's Social Security Number unless employees, and then a Federal and State EIN – Employers Identification Number is required. Unless there are state or city license requirements, no other filing are necessary.

1. **Ownership** - One Owner
2. **Liability** - Unlimited Personal Liability for company debts and liabilities.
3. **Taxation** - Profit and Loss reported on Owner's Tax Return and taxed at owner's rates. Schedule C prepared reflecting Profit and Loss amounts.
4. **Documents & Filings** - No Federal or State Filings Required.
5. **Business Management** - Owner in complete management control
6. **Capital & Investment** - All capital from Owner – loans

C- Corporation

Allow to form a C-Corporation in every state and created by filing corporation documents. C-Corporation is established in the state but files Federal Tax Return. Starting a C corporation is similar to creating another person. Corporation can sue, be sued, borrow money, buy assets and in general act as a separate entity.

1. **Ownership** - Unlimited number of shareholders (Owners)
2. **Liability** - Limited or no personal liability for Corporation debts.
3. **Taxation** – Corporation files a tax return has its tax rates and the liability is not personal. After tax profits are distributed to shareholders as dividends and are taxable on shareholder's tax return. Double taxation, corporation, and owners.
4. **Documents** – Required to file Articles of Incorporation, maintain minutes of meetings and issue stock certificates to shareholders
5. **Business Management** – Shareholders elect Directors; Directors hire management and management run the company.
6. **Capital & Investment** – Shareholders purchase stock, Corporation can borrow money without owner's being obligated.

S- Corporation

An S-Corporation is created from a C-Corporation. It is a closely held corporation that files with the IRS requesting to be taxed under Subchapter S of Chapter 1 of the Internal Revenue Code. An S corporation does not pay federal income taxes, and the profits and losses are divided among and passed through to its shareholders.

1. **Ownership** - Unlimited number of shareholders (Owners)
2. **Liability** - Limited or no personal liability for Corporation debts.
3. **Taxation** – Corporation files a tax return. Profit and Loss flow through to the shareholder and are taxed on shareholders individual tax return.
4. **Documents** – Required to file Articles of Incorporation, maintain minutes of meetings and issue stock certificates to shareholders. Request Sub Chapter status from the IRS.
5. **Business Management** – Shareholders elect Directors; Directors hire management and management run the company.
6. **Capital & Investment** – Shareholders purchase stock, Corporation can borrow money without owner's being obligated. Shareholders may be liable if personally signed on debt.

General Partnership

A General Partnership is an agreement between parties to share management, profits & losses and operate as a business. There can be General Partners and Limited Partners.

1. **Ownership** - Unlimited number of partners or limited partners.
2. **Liability** – General partners have unlimited liability for company debts and maybe actions of other general partners. Limited partners are usually limited to their investment.
3. **Taxation** – Corporation files a tax return. Profit and Loss flow through to the General Partners and Limited Partners and taxed on their individual tax return. Profit may be subject to Social Security Taxes.
4. **Documents** – Limited Required to file Articles of Incorporation, maintain minutes of meetings and issue stock certificates to shareholders
5. **Business Management** – Shareholders elect Directors; Directors hire management and management run the company.
6. **Capital & Investment** – Shareholders purchase stock, Corporation can borrow money without owner's being obligated. Shareholders may be liable if personally signed on debt.

Limited Liability Company

A Limited Liability Company (LLC) is a private business structure. Profit and losses are passed to the members similar to a partnership. An LLC has the additional benefit of limited liability for the owner's called members. It is not a corporation. In many states, individuals who provide professional services are not allowed to form an LLC.

A Limited Liability Company (LLC) is a company whose owners and managers enjoy limited liability and some tax benefits, but avoid some restrictions associated with S corporations. The LLC is organized and created by filing documents with the state. All state recognize and allow LLCs.

1. **Ownership** - Unlimited number of members or owners.
2. **Liability** – Members have limited liability for company debts and maybe actions of the LLC.
3. **Taxation** – LLC files a tax return. Profit and Loss flow through to the Members and are taxed on their individual tax returns. Profit may be subject to Social Security Taxes.
4. **Documents** – Required to file Articles of Organization with the state.
5. **Business Management** – Member management.
6. **Capital & Investment** – Usually investment by member-owner.

Phase 2: Comprehensive Business Plan

There are hundreds of websites devoted to writing a business plan, including the SBA website. Not only is the detailed business plan necessary for banks and lenders, it is a guide for operating your business. The business plan tells a story. The story needs to be as short as possible, clear and focused. Your plan needs to cover basic information such as your business background, description of your new business, startup cost, real estate cost (renting or buying), and your marketing plan. You will need personal financial statements, tax returns and projections of income and expenses. Banks and investors appreciate and demand full disclosure.

Business Plan Steps

Step 1: Business Summary
Step 2: Management Information
Step 3: Review Personal Finances & Household Budget.
Step 4: Pick Your Name and Protect It
Step 5: Start-Up Cost
Step 6: Protect Your Butt – Insurance and Bonds
Step 7: Management & Legal Entity
Step 8: Product and Services Offered.
Step 9: Market Analysis.
Step 10: Marketing and Sales.
Step 11: Financial Projections
  ➢ **Profit and Loss Projections**
  ➢ **Balance Sheet Projections**
  ➢ **Cash Flow Projections**
Step 12: Funding Request and Financing Your Dream
Step 13: Federal ID.

The purpose of the business plan is to 1. Obtain a loan, 2. Entice an Investor or 3. Create a Plan for your company development. Your plan must project that you have the knowledge and the ability to organize a new business, operate that business and that you are committed financially. Lenders and investors require that you have researched your business concept that you understand your competitive market.

Step 1: Business Summary: The summary needs to grab the reader attention. Include the following information.

> ➢ Start by covering a description of your business.
> ➢ Detail description of the organization and management
> ➢ When was your company formed?
> ➢ Who organized your company?
> ➢ Short description of your Products and services.
> ➢ Who are your customers? Why is your company different?
> ➢ Concise information on your market analysis. Who is your target market?
> ➢ Why can your company compete?
> ➢ How you intend to market your products and services? Retail, wholesale of even internet.
> ➢ Finish with why you will succeed.

Step 2: Management Information: This manual is for a Small Business as a single owner to ten employees. Keep it simple.

Just introduce yourself. Include personal information, experience and any professional licenses you currently hold. A one-page resume format is acceptable. The reader needs a glimpse of who you are by creating a positive respect for your business idea through the personal summary. Discuss your experience and why your background has prepared you for success. In a few simple words, convey to lending institutions, investors and even friends and family why they can trust you with their money. This page is developed to establish the reader's confidence in you without boasting.

If your business is going to require a small staff and you have already picked that individual, you need to cover their background. Lenders and investors may want information on anyone who will be instrumental in the success of the business.

Step 3: Review Personal Finances & Prepare a Household Budget. Review your household finances. Lenders and investors will require personal financial information on the amount of money required each month to support you family. You will need to provide a Personal Finance Statement, two years of individual tax returns and many times a Personal Budget Plan.

> **Personal Financial Statement:** A financial statement or personal financial balance sheet is a complete and detailed recording of all your assets less your liabilities resulting in your Net Worth. You can obtain a blank financial statement from a lender or use the outline attached.

> Assets such as cash in the bank and even stock holding can be easily valued however real estate and vehicles take some research. Bankers will discount

your estimates, and it is a good idea to include information that supports your estimates of Fair Market Value. Car values are available on-line, and you should be able to obtain home market value from a local realtor.

Cost of Living Budget or Household Budget: If you are currently living on a fixed amount and you believe, your home expenses will remain the same, use the current fixed amount as your budget. As an example, if your net take home is $4,800.00 per month and this is a reasonable amount for your household, use that amount as your budgeted amount. Lenders may require details that you can easily furnish by reviewing your checking accounts.

1. Start with the cost of maintaining your home. If you are renting or own use the rent amount or the payment as your first cost.

2. Next include all the monthly re-occurring cost such as electric, gas, water and sewer. Use the last twelve payments and average your cost per money.

3. Next tackle the cost of food and supplies. Again you will need to average these amounts. Include the cost of clothing in your household budget.

4. Include individual cost such as school tuition, books and supplies and special travel or lunch cost.

5. Cover Vehicle payments and a monthly average cost of operating such as gas, oil, repairs and general maintenance.

6. Include a provision for entertainment and eating out.

7. Always add a fudge factor.

   Step 4: Pick Your Name and Protect It: There are two separate issues concerning your business name. The first is picking the right name, and the second is protecting your business name.

Pick the right Name

The first mistake we all seem to make is selecting a business name after ourselves. However, there can be two reason to choose your name. The first is a professional requirement. Doctors, attorneys or CPAs may be required by state law to use their given name. Secondly, your name may be well known and have a local or even national recognition. In Denver, Colorado, John Elway allowed the use of his name for car dealerships. I suspect he owned the dealerships or at least he had partial ownership, and his name was and still is locally and nationally recognized. If your name is established in your community by all means use it for your company name. If your name is tied to the business, it may be difficult to sell or transfer.

Although there are many successful businesses using the name of the founder, it has taken years and many dollars to establish name recognition. One of the first rules of selecting a name is picking a name that the customer recognizes immediately when seen. If using your name is desired, combine it with the business occupation. Jones Plumbing or Smith Hardware accomplishes your wish to use your name while identifying your business. Your name alone does not have value.

Using a generic name is also possible but picking a name that is short, and that quickly identifies your business is the goal. A trade name or a DBA, Doing Business As, is a fictitious name under which the business operates. Most names that are less than six letters have been taken as Internet Domain names, so discovering a short, catchy name probably is impossible. I recommend a name that clearly identifies the product or service being offered. Many times I have driven down the street and wondered what business is that? The business has a huge sign which cost thousands, but is a deterrent to the business. Potential customers may not enter a store unless they know what products and services are being offered. Think about it; you are driving down the street, you must find a parking spot or navigate a busy sidewalk just to discover what this store has to offer. Make your name count.
Pick a name that is simple, easy to spell and pronounce. Is the name meaningful to potential customers? Does your name explain what you are offering? Sometimes catchy names are a hit and not because the name describes your business, but because the name is distinctive and fun. Give a lot of thought to your name.

A short name is best for an internet search. However, using a name that is intentionally misspelled is a problem for internet searches.

Protecting Your Name or a Trademark

A trademark protects symbols or words that a business uses to distinguish themselves from other companies. There are many trademarks that are not accepted. Before picking a name or a symbol, you need to research to see if someone else has your name or logo. Even similar sounding names or appearance may disqualify your trademark. Check with the County, State and the US Trademark office before finalizing a business name you created.

Every state has a department assigned to regulate the registration of corporations and Limited Liability Companies. Unusually this office is under the Secretary of State department. A few states require days to check on a name, but most states allow access to their database. Next check with a company named 'KnowEm' for a free search nationwide. One of the quickest ways to determine if your name is taken is a Go Daddy search. Type in your name and Go Daddy will conduct a search of their database. Within a few seconds, you will know if the name is available. You can change the name maybe end up with a name you like. I was able to obtain the name smallbusinesshandbook.biz after a couple of tries.

Registering you name or trademark is an option and not required by any law. Using a name that is not currently being used, grants you the legal right to use the name legally, first come, and first serve. Creating a Corporation or an LLC in your state protects your name within that state from someone else using the name.

As with all legal actions, I suggest the help of an attorney for any filing. The problem of a trade name, corporation or LLC name can be confusing. Attempt to solve this issue early on in your businesses, as the problem will be magnified when your company wishes to go national. If you have any inkling that your company could become widespread, register for a Federal Trademark as early as possible.

Step 5: Start-Up Cost: Your first budget was your household budget to determine the amount of money you need monthly to support your current or adjusted lifestyle. The Start-up budget may be more difficult because the cost of equipment, fixtures, remolding and building construction are difficult to research. However, this is an important step, and you must attempt to create a budget that is within 10% of the actual cost.

New equipment and fixture cost is available on-line however establishing the cost for used equipment is difficult unless you do a hands-on inspection. Whatever it takes you need to determine an acceptable cost. Equipment is one problem; however, remodeling or construction can present a whole new set of problems.
Years ago we would use the figure of $20.00 per square foot cost for a strip-mall or building remodel. However, that cost has increased substantially. Depending on the job, remodeling cost could be as high as new construction. Building a warehouse or a fast food facility requires detailed architectural blueprints and competitive bidding. Experience has taught me never to pay any contractor an up-front payment. You may need to pay for an estimate, but pre-paying contractor is a gamble. The key to establishing an accurate construction bid is precise and detailed blueprints. When contractors or sub-contractors are using the identical plans, you can compare apples to apples.

Began your start-up budget by making a list of all the equipment, fixtures and tools you will need for your business. As a plumber, you may need thousands of dollars in small hand tools so your list could be extensive. A retail store will have thousands of dollars in display racks, and shelving and a restaurant will have a complete kitchen including everything from stoves to prep tables. Visit used equipment outlets and attended auctions if possible. Of course, everything is on the internet and pricing equipment and fixtures has become easier than visiting outlet stores and comparing prices.

If your small business requires, a van or truck, prices can be obtained from the internet. It has been my experience new vehicles may be cheaper in the long-run. Dealing with used equipment can be costly in repairs and downtime. If you are a one-man shop having a reliable vehicle is a requirement. Check on the internet for the average repair cost of used vehicles or equipment you intend to purchase. Remember the cost of lost business could be higher than the expense of the repair. I convinced a small foundation contractor to use new vehicles and because of the reliability his downtime became negligible and his profit increased. The major cost items of start-up cost are:

Professional Fees: The cost of hiring attorneys, business consultants, accountants and other professionals can be expensive and challenging. Obtain a firm estimate from professional if possible.

Real Estate Cost: Purchasing, constructing (new facility or remodel a purchased property), leasing or completing leasehold improvements to a leased property.

Operational Equipment and Fixtures: This includes everything from machinery for a manufacturing business, equipment for a construction business, retail business

Soft Cost: such as purchasing blue sky, franchise fees, computer software programs or technical reports.

Working Capital: You will need operating capital for the day to day operations. I suggest an operating fund of 20% to 30% of your projected monthly revenue. If you anticipate sales of $30,000 a month, the operating fund of $9.000 is not unreasonable.

Inventory and Supplies: You will need to fund your initial investment in inventory and supplies. Establish your product list and proceed to contact wholesalers or manufacturers. One of my clients' ordered her initial stock from a commission broker who had connections in Asia. The first order worked out great, but restocking became a problem and she had to turn to domestic suppliers.

Step 6: Protect Your Butt – Insurance and Bonds: Your business entity will not protect you and your business from losses such as fire, accident, floods and property damage. Review you insurance requirements with an insurance agent.

Vehicle Insurance: You need to update your vehicle insurance by contacting your agent. Your insurance agent understands the problem of using your personal vehicle for business and probably will suggest increasing your coverage. Your insurance company may want an additional premium however many insurance companies may not cover damages if your insurance is based only upon personal use, and the insurance company discovers business use after an accident.

Health Insurance: Contact your agent about health insurance. Once you leave your employment you will need your company to purchase insurance. The rate will be the same, but due to IRS deductions for health insurance you need to register your health insurance in the business name. With the new

Worker's Compensation (WC): Workers' compensation is insurance intended to make sure employees who are injured, disabled or even killed while working have insurance coverage for medical bills and are provided with compensation sufficient to cover loss of wages. Also employees are compensated for permanent physical injuries. Worker' compensation is intended to provide benefits without the need to prove the employer was at legal fault.

Include are benefits for dependents of workers who are killed because of work-related accidents or illnesses. These are state laws and each state has their own set of parameters. States statutes protect employers by limiting the amount of money that can be recovered. There is considerable controversy over workers compensation laws. Many employers refuse to purchase this insurance because of the cost and sort of throw the dice in order to gain a competitive edge. Some states do not require worker's comp. insurance and many employees must sue to receive benefits. Requirements are all over the board and you need to check your state statues.

Many small business elect to become a LLC of a corporation to protect them. If the company does not have sufficient capital to pay the premiums or to pay medical or other benefits to injured employees, they simply go out of business. If your corporation does not have a great deal of assets this could be an option. Contact your attorney, state or your insurance agent for information applicable to your business.

Errors and Omission Insurance: Errors and omissions insurance will protect businesses and individuals from claims and lawsuits arising from failure to perform contracted work. It can also cover mistakes made in the course of doing business. Professionals purchase insurance because some errors can be very expensive. Forgetting or omitting a clause in a legal document or an error in an income tax return can cause considerable damage. Professionals purchase this insurance to limit their exposure to these types of mistakes. Of course, doctors and nurses all purchase malpractice insurance that is similar to Errors and Omissions Insurance.

Liability Insurance: Liability insurance will protect you financially from Acts of God, Fire, tornados, wind and flood. Liability insurance pay damages where a person or organization is found responsible for injury or harm in the case of negligence

Performance Bonds: Many companies purchase performance bonds to protect their clients by insuring their performance. A performance guarantee assures contract completion and is typically issued by a specialized insurance company.

To protect your personal assets against failure is possible by organizing a corporation or an LLC. A few liabilities incurred by your LLC or a corporation can also become personal. If your company handles and collects funds belonging to others, such as sales tax, trust accounts and payroll withholding funds, the individual responsible for remitting such funds when due can be held financial responsible if such funds are not forwarded.

Step 7: Management & Legal Entity: The business summary should include the details of the operation. If you have formed a corporation or LLC, you need to detail that information. Include the companies organization structure; officers, directors, CEO, and managers. Key personal are of particular interest so Include their background.

- Names of Partners and Owners
- Education and Experience.
- Prior Employment
- Special Skills
- Who Owns the Company - Percentages?
- Corporation – Shareholders, Directors, Officers and Managers
- Authorized Corporation Stock And Classification
  - Issued Stock
  - Par Or No-Par-Value
  - Minutes Of The Corporations Meetings
- Partnership – Name Of Partners And Percentage Of Ownership
- Prior Owner And Management Experience Of Startup Companies

Step 8: Product and Services Offered: Services or Produces Lines: Detail e information regarding your goods or services in detail. Make sure to mention patents, exclusive process, copyrights or anything unique. If your goals include conducting research and development, you need to detail the end product information.

Include information concerning inventory and any factors affecting the turn-over. Inventory management can be involved and how often your stock needs to be replaced is important. Shrinkage, obsolescence, and spoilage are other factors when determining the investment in your inventory. Incorporate Information about patents, copyrights and even trade secrets and agreements with suppliers or specialty manufacturers.

Step 9: Market Analysis. This section of your business plan should explain who and where is your market. Include information on how you conducted your research. Describe your industry, customer base, projected growth, and target market. As an example, your research may be as simple as obtaining traffic counts or conducting consumer interviews.

Include information on your target market such as the size and average income. You may want to include local data on the number of users in your area within a mile or two. Define your pricing structure including special offers or discounts you intend to provide. A more complicated analysis is determining your market share. As an example, one of my clients opened a Gym, they counted the number of customers entering competitive health clubs for over ten days. They then conducted a survey of health club members to determine the amenities that attracted them to a particular facility. From this information, they were able to determine the potential market share.

Review your competitor's goods and services and pricing. Evaluate your competition by studying the following.

Strength and weakness of each competitor.
Can you offer consumers an alternative?
Is the market already saturated?
Can you be competitively priced and still realize a profit?
How do you intend to entice customers?
Are you able to provide state of the art technology?

Finnish this section by including any government regulatory requirements and their effect on your propose business.

Step 10: Marketing and Sales: Many business plans do not address how they intend to market their products and services. Include information concerning your competition and why your operation can compete because of location, unique goods or services, price or even your personal ability to create sales. Who are your Customers? How do you Plan to Market Products & Services? What type of adverting are you planning such as Yellow Pages, Print Media, and Coupon Specials? Do you need a Website and finally what is Your Marketing Budget? Before you prepare financial projections cover in detail how you expect customers to find out about your business and what is your marketing budget. Marketing is as simple as who are my clients and how do I get them to spend money with my company.

Your location is also a segment of your marketing plan. As discussed, you need to get potential customers off the road and into your business. Think of the thousands of companies you drive by each day and why you never became a customer. Does the company name clearly reflect the products and services your business offers? Do you have adequate parking and is your location easy to find? Many small business offices at home so that is not a concern, however, if your business plans include rental space, lease payments must be a part of your budget forecast.

Step 11: Financial Projections: Detailed financial projections are necessary when seeking a commercial loan or investors. SBA lenders and most other creditors require Income and Expense Projections, Balance Sheet Forecast and Cash Flow Projections for a five-year period.

I disagree with preparing five years of financial projections. Usually, the first year is only an educated guess and anything after that is simply a government make-work project. Our government can't prepare a budget for one year, however the SBA requires financial projections for five years. You have to play

Copyright ©

the game, and although the last three-years of forecast are ridicules, you must respond if you want an SBA loan.

Financial projections can take hours of work and require an accounting professional. Your projections could easily cost you over a thousand dollars. The numbers are yours, and your accountant will record them for a professional presentation.

There are five financial projections required by lenders, the SBA, and investors.

> ➢ Personal home budget.
> ➢ Capital equipment projections.
> ➢ Profit and Loss Projections for five years.
> ➢ Balance Sheet projections for five years.
> ➢ Cash Flow projections for two years.

Included at the end of this chapter is a one-year example of Profit and Loss Projections, Cash Flow Projections, a projected Balance Sheet and Capital Expenditures forecast for a small company. Along with the projections you are required to submit an explanation of significant line items. Lenders and investors are more interested in how you determined your income and expense projections than the numbers themselves. There are many financial projection software programs available. Search for Software for financial projections in Google or Bing. Create revenue and expense categories that fit your business

Profit and Loss Projections: In Chapters 5 information concerning financial statements is cover in detail. At the end of this chapter is an example of a Profit and Loss Projection for a small plumbing company. You can use the outline in Excel for your companies forecast.

The income reflected on a profit and loss statement may reflect sales made on credit. The P & L projections following this chapter indicate that the plumber has decided to extend credit to a large apartment house. Service sales are on a cash basis, no Accounts Receivable. The P & L Statement correctly reflect the credit sale as income, but the cash flow statement reflects actual money collect. Income is hard to predict. Use the information from the market analysis and make

Cash Flow Projections: A profit and loss statement does not reflect principal loan payments, Equipment principal loan payments and owner's draws. The monthly business mortgage payment is for principal reduction and interest expense. Interest is deductible and will be reflected in the profit and loss projections as an expense. Principal payments are expenditures are not recorded on the P $ L statement but are disbursements on the cash flow statement. Also, the purpose of the household budget is to determine the amount needed for a draw or salary.

The number needs to be a fixed amount and is imperative when preparing Cash Flow Projections.

An analogy of a cash flow statements is similar to a cash flow statement of your personal finances. First review your current bank balance plus known amounts you will receive for the month:

Cash in the Bank	5,985
Net Wages expected for the month	6,458
Loan for the bank (for whatever)	3,000

Total cash available of the month
15,443

Next you review your past personal disbursements:

Rent for home	3,500
Utilities	900
Food	800
Auto Payment	650
Miscellaneous Disbursements	855

Total projected disbursements for the month
6,705

Cash remaining at the end of the month
8,738

The $8,738 is the amount you have as current bank balance beginning the next month. Each month's ending cash balance is the starting cash balance for the next month. Cash flow projections can reflect two significant problems. When granting credit a business needs capital to replace insufficient cash receipts. Expenses continue but income may be lagging and, therefore, current operating expenses and too many credit sales requiring considerable investment.
 Lenders request cash flow projections before funding the loan. Lenders are only interested in two things; is the money avaiable to make the payment and will you make the payment. Extending credit can easily but a strain on your business finances. Your expenses and disbursement requirements for wages, rent, and other operating cost do not stop. You may have a profit however, you are cash strapped.

It is important to consider 'Working Capital' when preparing your cash flow projections. Business require capital to operate day to day and until cash flow from profits is relaized, the company survices on working capital. Extending credit or increase in inventory can create a cash flow problem. The company has a profit but the money is not avaiable for day to day operations. Working capital is the amount of money a company has available to operate a business.

Prepare a Break-Even Point: Preparing a break-even chart is one of the essentials of any business plan. At a point in time when revenue equals cost, losses end and profit begins. At this point, the business becomes financially stable. One problem with calculating a Break-even point: it keeps changing. We can conclude that the cost of materials and products will remain a constant percent of sales income. Other expenses such as labor cost, employee benefits, operating supplies and even company vehicle cost may vary as sales volume increases. As an example: a restaurant reaches sales income of $1,200.00 per day with three servers and one cook. Any increase in sales volume could increase the need for an additional server and a second cook. The restaurant broke even as $1,200.00 a day in sales but with sales of $1,400.00 a day the restaurant could be losing money.

In a retail outlet or even in a restaurant the effect of an increase in sales in relationship to the labor cost is complicated to measure. Many companies manage this problem with part-time workers or overtime. It takes considerable skill to maximize sales with no increase in labor cost. In a business providing services, the effect of a sales increase could be devastating. As a Small Business providing professional services the cost of hiring another CPA, Doctor or Attorney will have an adverse effect upon your Break-even point.

When forecasting financial statements and break-even points, I prefer using a program like Excel because of the math formulas I can apply. I can assign a percent of sales for labor expense or record and additional employee amount in my projections and easily understand the effect this increase has on my profit. The break-even point is calculated at the same time financial projections are prepared.

Notes

_____

_____

_____

_____

_____

_____

_____

Cash Flow Projections without Loan

Item	January	February	March
Starting Cash 1st Month		1900	-14756
Deposit by Owner	48,000		
Bank Loan			
Income - Sales		2,000	12,500
Total Cash Available	48,000	3,900	(2,256)
Disbursements			
Start-up Cost	46100		
Inventory			
Monthly Operating cost		15400	19500
Owners Draw		3256	3256
Loan Payments			
Total Disbursements	46100	18656	22756
End of Month Cash	1,900	(14,756)	(25,012)

	April	May	June
Starting Cash 1st Month	-25012	-34308	(32,601)
Deposit by Owner			
Bank Loan			
Income - Sales	16,500	29,000	29,700
Total Cash Available	(8,512)	(5,308)	(2,901)
Disbursements			
Start-up Cost			
Inventory			
Monthly Operating cost	22540	24037	25,985
Owners Draw	3256	3256	3,256
Loan Payments			
Total Disbursements	25796	27293	29,241
End of Month Cash	(34,308)	(32,601)	(32,142)

Cash Flow Projections without Loan

Item	July	August	Sept.
Starting Cash 1st Month	(32,142)	(31,045)	(27,631)
Deposit by Owner			
Bank Loan			
Income - Sales	30,458	32,140	33,056
Total Cash Available	(1,684)	1,095	5,425
Disbursements			
Start-up Cost			
Inventory			
Monthly Operating cost	26,105	25,470	26,750
Owners Draw	3,256	3,256	3,256
Loan Payments			
Total Disbursements	29,361	28,726	30,006
End of Month Cash	(31,045)	(27,631)	(24,581)

Item	Oct	Nov	Dec	Total
Starting Cash 1st Month	(24,581)	(21,607)	(17,013)	
Deposit by Owner				48,000
Bank Loan				
Income - Sales	34,120	36,250	36,520	292,244
Total Cash Available	9,539	14,643	19,507	340,244
Disbursements				
Start-up Cost				46,100
Inventory				
Monthly Operating cost	27,890	28,400	26,380	268,457
Owners Draw	3,256	3,256	3,256	35,816
Loan Payments				
Total Disbursements	31,146	31,656	29,636	350,373
End of Month Cash	(21,607)	(17,013)	(10,129)	(10,129)

Cash flow Projections with Loan

Item	January	February	March
Starting Cash 1st Month		44,900	27,159
Deposit by Owner	48,000		
Bank Loan	43,000		
Income - Sales		2,000	12,500
Total Cash Available	91,000	46,900	39,659
Disbursements			
Start-up Cost	46,100		
Inventory			
Monthly Operating cost		15,400	19,500
Owners Draw		3,256	3,256
Loan Payments		1,085	1,085
Total Disbursements	46,100	19,741	23,841
End of Month Cash	44,900	27,159	15,818

	April	May	June
Starting Cash 1st Month	15,818	5,437	6,059
Deposit by Owner			
Bank Loan			
Income - Sales	16,500	29,000	29,700
Total Cash Available	32,318	34,437	35,759
Disbursements			
Start-up Cost			
Inventory			
Monthly Operating cost	22,540	24,037	25,985
Owners Draw	3,256	3,256	3,256
Loan Payments	1,085	1,085	1,085
Total Disbursements	26,881	28,378	30,326
End of Month Cash	5,437	6,059	5,433

Cash Flow Projections with Loan

Item	July	August	Sept.
Starting Cash 1st Month	5,433	5,445	7,774
Deposit by Owner			
Bank Loan			
Income - Sales	30,458	32,140	33,056
Total Cash Available	35,891	37,585	40,830
Disbursements			
Start-up Cost			
Inventory			
Monthly Operating cost	26,105	25,470	26,750
Owners Draw	3,256	3,256	3,256
Loan Payments	1,085	1,085	1,085
Total Disbursements	30,446	29,811	31,091
End of Month Cash	5,445	7,774	9,739

Item	Oct	Nov	Dec	Total
Starting Cash 1st Month	9,739	11,628	15,137	
Deposit by Owner				48,000
Bank Loan				43,000
Income - Sales	34,120	36,250	36,520	292,244
Total Cash Available	43,859	47,878	51,657	383,244
Disbursements				
Start-up Cost				46,100
Inventory				
Monthly Operating cost	27,890	28,400	26,380	268,457
Owners Draw	3,256	3,256	3,256	35,816
Loan Payments	1,085	1,085	1,085	11,935
Total Disbursements	32,231	32,741	30,721	362,308
End of Month Cash	11,628	15,137	20,936	20,936

89

Profit and Loss Projections

Item	January	February	March
Income - Sales		2,000	12,500
Total Cash Available	-	2,000	12,500
Disbursements			
Depreciation on Equip.		768	768
Monthly Operating cost		15400	19500
Owners Draw		3256	3256
Interest Payment		251	247
Total Disbursements	0	19675	23771
End of Month Cash	-	(17,675)	(11,271)

Item	April	May	June
Income - Sales	16,500	29,000	29,700
Total Cash Available	16,500	29,000	29,700
Disbursements			
Depreciation on Equip.	768	768	768
Monthly Operating cost	22540	24037	25,985
Owners Draw	3256	3256	3,256
Interest Payment	244	240	237
Total Disbursements	26808	28301	30,246
End of Month Cash	(10,308)	699	(546)

Profit and Loss Projections

Item	July	August	Sept.
Income - Sales	30,458	32,140	33,056
Total Cash Available	30,458	32,140	33,056
Disbursements			
Depreciation on Equip.	768	768	768
Monthly Operating cost	26,105	25,470	26,750
Owners Draw	3,256	3,256	3,256
Interest Payment	233	230	226
Total Disbursements	30,362	29,724	31,000
End of Month Cash	96	2,416	2,056

Item	Oct	Nov	Dec	Total
Income - Sales	34,120	36,250	36,520	292,244
Total Cash Available	34,120	36,250	36,520	292,244
Disbursements				
Depreciation on Equip.	768	768	768	8,448
Monthly Operating cost	27,890	28,400	26,380	268,457
Owners Draw	3,256	3,256	3,256	35,816
Interest Payment	222	219	215	2,564
Total Disbursements	32,136	32,643	30,619	315,285
End of Month Cash	1,984	3,607	5,901	(23,041)

Cash Flow Projections

The first set of charts demonstrate the company cash flow for the first year without a bank loan. As you can see the maximum negative cash flow is $32,142. This amount determines the bank loan needed. When we insert a bank loan of $43,000 we easily see that our cash flow remained positive. In fact, we probably did not need a loan as high as $43,000 but it is important to consider contingencies.

Profit and Loss Projections

Since can flow is different than the profit and loss we can now see the company is operating at a loss for the first year of operation which is expected. We borrowed $43,000 to level out our cash flow and the loan also provided us with staying power until the company produces a profit.

Step 12: Funding Request and Financing Your Dream: Securing a business loan is the most difficult step of Starting a Business. Even when our economy was roaring, business loans were difficult to obtain. On line, there are hundreds of lenders requesting your business. The first general rule is never pay a front-end fee for any loan unless a lender is a bank or commercial lender directly known by you. There are thousands of fake lenders operating on the internet who cannot be trusted.

Commercial lenders usually require 30% or more as a down payment for the purchase of a business provided that business assets and earning are acceptable to the banks' lending policies. Starting from scratch has the same requirements. Each asset has a loan-to-value amount. Raw Land loans typically require a 50% down payment and at the other end of the scale many home loans are for 100% of the Fair Market Value (Appraised Value). Business loans of any type can be risky, and many lenders turn to the SBA to reduce their risk. The SBA guarantees 85% of a business loan up to $150,000.00, and it is a common belief that an SBA loan can be obtained with a small or not down payment.

The SBA's primary lending program the 7(a) Loan Program guarantees as much as 85 percent of loans up to $150,000 and 75 percent of loans of more than $150,000. The maximum loan amount is $5 million. Loans for as long as 25 years are avaiabl efor Real estate, 10 years for equipment (as long as the equipment is likely to stay useful during that time) and usually up to seven years for working capital. Interest rates are also competitive because the SBA limits the interest rate spread that banks can offer.

SBA Advantage: The SBA guarantee gives banks some comfort room to approve loans or allow borrowers to repay loans over a longer period. You might want to consider an SBA loan if you are looking for a long team loan. Many banks will not make business loans unless the collateral fully covers the loan amount. Therefore, an SBA loan could be the answer if your collateral is inadequate or you have a limited operating history. Take to your banker.

The Disadvantageous of an SBA Loan: Even though the SBA has tried to make the application easier, and less time-consuming, the paperwork and red tape surrounding SBA loans is well-known. Using a professional to prepare your SBA documents can cost several thousand dollars and then there is no guarantee that you will be able to secure a loan. One potential solution might be to find a bank participating in the SBA Express program, which promises a 36-hour turnaround in return for only guaranteeing half of the loan's value. The maximum loan amount of $350,000 is also a fraction of the 7(a) loan program.

Where to go: Banks such as Wells Fargo and U.S. Bank are the most active SBA lenders. However check out local community banks which focus on business lending. Many of these smaller banks are easier to deal with because they have more flexibility when it comes to approving loans. I have also discovered many of these local community banks have a wealth of lending knowledge and business information. Historically my interface with smaller community banks starts with a pre-loan meeting and develops into the bank becoming a mentor for your company.

Is Your Bank an SBA Preferred Lender? Many banks are SBA Preferred Lenders and as such the SBA delegates much of the decision making and loan servicing to the bank. Such banks will have more SBA loan expertise and should be able to mentor and service your lending needs. Using a small community bank who designated as a Preferred SBA lender will increase your chances of obtaining a loan.

We see an upsurge in small Business financing. A growing group of entrepreneurs are turning to financing their business through smaller easier to obtain loans secured by personal assets, business assets and loan guarantees by a friend or relative. The SBA also has loan guarantees for non-profit organizations that provide small loans to minority entrepreneurs. Banks have become increasingly harder to deal with, so many entrepreneurs have turned to these sources to secure small loans.

First off we have to remember what the banker is attempting to accomplish. Banks sell the use of money. The simplest explanation is that banks accept deposits and make loans and derive a profit from the difference in the interest rates paid and charged. They may pay 1% on deposits and collect 5% and up on loans. The difference is gross profit. It is interesting to note that the banks inventory is money. Although a banks inventory is never consumed, banks do lose inventory from time to time. Not everyone repays their loans. Loaning money is risky. The more risk the higher the interest rate. Of course, if the bank loses money their profit (interest) is also lost. Banks are looking for low-risk loans that will be repaid with the interest charged. Below are some the factors banks consider when making business or commercial loan.

No Commercial Loans or Time in Business Requirements: Many banks do not make commercial loans, and some lenders will not consider a business loan unless you have a proven business track record. A large number of businesses fail in the first five years. Many banks require two or more years of successful operation before the bank will qualify a borrower for a loan. Business realtors should be able to direct you to a bank that not only makes commercial loans, but will entertain first-time buyers.

Solid Financial Statement: Banks are looking for individuals who have a substantial financial statement, both personal and business. Banks prefer liquid assets such as savings accounts, stocks, and bonds and of course they prefer that you have a large balance in your checking account and savings account.

Your Ability to Generate Income: The next element the bank reviews is your ability to generate income in your current business or your new start-up. The first-line item on your Profit and Loss Projections is sales income. The bank realizes you must achieve your income goals in order for the loan to be collected. It is essential that you convince the bank that your sales revenue projections are realistic. You may have a desire to pay, but your ability to pay may be lacking.

Ron White, the comedian, explains in one of his routines that he was arrested for public intoxication and although he had the right to remain silent he did not have the ability. You may intend to repay, but that is impossible if you don't have the ability. Banks and their attorneys always believe you have the money, but you just don't intend to pay.

You Choose to Pay: Credit ratings provide the bank information on your intent to pay. A good credit history demonstrates that you had the ability to pay your debts, and you elected to pay your debts on time and in full.

Net worth Ratio: By any other name your "Net Worth Ratio" is simply a comparison between the fair market value of your assets and your existing liabilities. Banks compare your assets against your liabilities. They then review this ratio by including your new proposed debt. Another ratio that banks consider is debt to income. Again the bank is attempting to determine if you have sufficient income to service all of your debts.

Asset Value V's Total Debt: This is what I call the 'Fire Sale Ratio.' If your business fails what is the fair market value of the remaining assets compared to the bank's exposure. Can the bank sell all the assets resulting in full payment? Inventory and specialize equipment values are not only difficult to compute but because the market for both types of property fluctuates. Banks many times refuse stock and specialize equipment loans because they have no assurance of getting paid in case of a business failure.

Special use buildings and leasehold improvements are also especially difficult to finance. We all have seen buildings sit empty for months and even years because a buyer cannot be found. Even the value of the land is questionable because of the cost of removing an albatross structure is prohibitive. Specially designed building such as a Mexican or Italian restaurant may be impossible to finance.

As you can see from above information lenders will consider business loans based upon a percent of the fair market value of the hard assets. It is simple: banks not only review your ability to repay the loan but place considerable emphasis on the lender's ability to sell assets if the business fails. Lenders, including the SBA are not in the business of risk loans. Usually, an SBA loan will require hard assets in the amount of 70% of the loan to value. Remember an SBA loan only covers 80% of the needed cash and an SBA lender loans the additional 20%. Therefore, if you were borrowing $70,000.00 you would need hard assets with a fair market value of $100,000.00. The common perception is that SBA will loan 100% of the needed funding. The SBA requires collateral.

Always check other sources of money such as a seller carry or a loan from a relative. Do not make the mistake of borrowing money from a relative without loan documents. Money will change most relationships, reduce everything to writing. Parents are an easy mark until the loan payment is missed. Usually, loans from a parent come from equity in their home or a retirement fund. A loan default can make Thanksgiving Dinner very tense. Brothers and sisters should be consulted unless these relationships are expendable. I do recommend that all loans should be reviewed by a CPA or business consultant for risk assessment. Relatives should know the downside and not just the rosy picture painted by the borrower.

Procedure for Pre- Loan Approval

Last week I called a commercial lender to discuss a new loan for one of my clients. The loan officer's attitude was appalling. He did not know my client, and I could tell from his questions he not only did not give a damn. His comments bordered on slander. When he realized who my client was, I received a call that dripped with sugar and honey. He had pre-judged my request and my client before realizing my client's status in the community and of course his net worth. I include this story to prepare you for the current lender attitudes. It is beyond me why some loan officers disqualify you before you presented any loan documents.

I want the bank to become part of the solution and not part of the problem. I expect commercial bankers to share their experience, provide guidance and assist in the loan process.

Step 1: Review the equity you have in the assets you currently own. Are you willing to borrow money against those assets? Most lenders will require a mortgage on your home as additional collateral, and if you have a first mortgage, they will want a second mortgage. It can be difficult borrowing against your home for a down payment on a business because of the loan payment. Lenders are very hesitant when you create additional debt that requires a substantial payment and most lenders will not even consider a business loan with money borrowed for a down payment.

Most lenders require a 20% to 25% down payment of the business purchase price. There are other considerations such as the type of assets included in the acquisition price but your first consideration is to determine the purchase price compared to your available cash. This is a general rule. There are many ways to creatively finance a business but use the percent calculation to start your search. As an example if you have $75,000.00 available, you can look at businesses selling for as much as $375,000.00.

Step 2: You and your Realtor had found a business and have dissected the purchase price. This business is one that you would like to buy however at this time you only know the type of business, purchase price and an estimation of the value of all the business assets including Goodwill.

Step 3: Prepare the following documents. Spend some time, so you understand all aspects of your loan proposal. Organize your documents and be ready to answer any all questions concerning your credit.

> - Prepare a short resume. Include personal information such as education and the most important business/employment information. Why are you qualified to operate your new business?
> - Prepare a one-page outline of the business we wish to purchase.
> - Provide copies of your last two years of tax returns. Copies of the business tax returns or at the minimum current financial statements.
> - Prepare a "Statement of Net Worth". (Personal Statement).
> - Prepare a one-page estimate of the purchase price broken-down between the different assets included in the price.
> - Reflect the amount of down payment and the source of your equity.
> - Provide the banker with a copy of the listing information including a detail asset list with suggested Fair Market Value numbers.

Step 4: The bank and the applicant then review the pre-loan submission together. You are not expecting a commitment, but you are attempting to gain information concerning your ability to secure a loan including information on how you can make your application stronger. You may want to download a credit report for his consideration since your credit rating, and personal finances are paramount to his approval. I have always taken the position with people in authority that you are very confident of your proposal but since you lack lending expertise you need his input as a mentor. You only are blowing smoke up his butt, but most people in authority will respond with a helpful attitude.

Chapter 5
UNDERSTANDING FINANCIAL STATEMENTS
THE ESSENTIAL SMALL BUSINESS HANDBOOK
The best and most complete handbook for the Micro Business Entrepreneur.
Essential information for starting, buying, operating and succeeding.

Three Financial Statements

> ➤ **Balance Sheet**
> ➤ **The Statement of Income (Profit and Loss Statement)**
> ➤ **Statement of Cash Flows**.

In Chapter 4, Legal Entity – Protection & Tax Benefits, this handbook covers business entities and the entity I recommend. Whether you operate as a Sole Proprietorship, Partnership, a Sub-S Corporation, and a C Corporation or as a Limited Liability Company, you will need timely and accurate Financial Statements designed for making sound financial decisions. Precise Financial Statements are necessary for enticing investors, securing loans and preparing the company tax returns.

The information in this Chapter will provide you with the ability to understand your financial statements. In Chapter 6, I suggest a three-step approach when preparing your accounting by focusing on your participation. If you participate in the Bookkeeping function or rely on an outside service, it is important that you review and understand your Financial Statements monthly. Ask questions of any line items that seem confusing and gain an overall understanding of your company's financial condition. Using the knowledge in this Chapter, a monthly review and understanding of financial statements will enable you to make difficult business decisions based upon reliable information and not gut instinct.

The Balance Sheet and the Profit and Loss Statement are two Financial Statements that will provide you with the main indicators for managing your business. The Statement of Cash Flows displays historical cash flow information. The Cash Flow Statement is money-in and money-out, however, the report does provide detail disbursement information. Most entrepreneurs have their finger on the money available. However, the information on future cash requirements is more important. The solution for cash shortages is solved with a loan or additional investment and both solutions require an accurate and current financial statement.

Complicated Financial Statements

Over the years, Financial Statements have become increasingly more complex and challenging to understand. It is a good bet that most mortgage bankers, investors, managers, and company CEOs do not comprehend the information presented in a financial statement. I find it interesting that many underwriters do not understand the information given even with training and certification. The professional charged with the task of approving or denying your loan

Copyright ©

cannot understand your financial statement. It is a wonder self-employed individuals can obtain a loan.

I sometimes wonder how CPA's came up with such Account terms as *Marginal Revenue*, *Spending Variance* or an Account called Accumulated Deficits. I have been active in the accounting industry as a Public Accountant and a CPA for 30 years, and I can make an educated guess as to the meaning of these accounting terms. However, using complicated Account names for a small business is not acceptable. We may have dumb-down our educational system, but many CPA firms believe in the Mushroom Theory: keep the client in the dark and covered with manure. I know; I have used the same statement several times. However, attorneys and accountants refuse to discuss legal or financial information with their clients. Demand an explanation of any confusing line-items on your Financial Statements.

Keep it simple stupid. Every line item on a Financial Statement tells a story yielding information concerning the financial condition of your business. Learn how to use this information to manage your operation, secure loans, and investors. Accurate Financial Statements minimizes your tax liabilities and provides information for tax planning. Simple and precise statements are indispensable, and your understanding of these statements is a requirement for success. Things have gotten, complicated, keep your financial statements simple; the benefits are worth the effort.

Standard Financial Statements

Balance Sheet: Balance Sheets are a financial presentation of your Assets minus your Liabilities equaling your Net Worth (equity) at a point in time. Accountants and Bookkeepers use the term Accounts to describe the different categories within the Financial Statements.

Assets – Liabilities = Net Worth

Statement of Profit and Loss: A Statement of Profit and Loss is a financial presentation of your Sales Income minus your Business Operating Expenses resulting in Net Profit or Net Loss.

Income – Operating Expenses = Net Profit (Loss)

Statement of Cash Flows: A third financial statement is the Statement of Cash Flows. The Cash Flow statement is Money in and Money Out. On the first of each month, the statement reflects starting cash-on-hand, shows deposits and disbursements that occurred during the month, and indicates the cash-on-hand at the end of the month. Money is considered 'King' by investors and lenders.

Starting Cash (+) Plus Cash Increases (-) Minus Cash Disbursements (=) Equals Ending Cash balance.

Monthly Budgets: A more important document for a Small Business is the preparation of budgets. Monthly prepare a budget for the next three months. The budget for the next month is the most important. You can prepare a cash flow budget or income and expense budget. Both the cash flow and the revenue and expenditure budgets are projections used to guide managers when making financial decisions that affect the company's future.

Most Bookkeeping Software programs allow for the input of budgets, and the monthly reports compare budgeted amounts against actuals, creating positive and negative differences. Reviewing and understanding budget variances is an indispensable tool for guiding your company on its financial road map.

Financial Statement Categories – Name of Number: Accountants have assigned different Account numbers to each category within the Assets, Liabilities, Net Worth, Income, Cost of Goods Sold and Expenses groups. These Account numbers are a technique for posting our financial transactions. The largest bookkeeping software company does not use numbers for the various Accounts but relies upon name recognition. I dislike using only name designations because an important aspect of accounting is combining like expenses for analysis and review. It is hard remembering basic headings without remembering 100 different word titles. I also like operating expenses recorded in alphabetic order. I have seen Account titles such as *Office Supplies*, *Office Supply Cost* and *Office Supply Expense* all on a single financial statement. Of course, these are all the same category of expenses and the information is recorded in three locations. Below are examples of Account Numbers, the section in the financial statements and the Account name.

Account Number		Section within Financial Statement
10000 to 14999	Debit	Current Assets
15000 to 19999	Debit	Non-current Assets
20000 to 24999	Credit	Current Liabilities
25000 to 29999	Credit	Non-Current Liabilities
30000 to 39999	Credit	Equity or Net-Worth
40000 to 49999	Credit	Income
50000 to 59999	Debit	Cost of Goods
62000 to 89999	Debit	Expenses

The term Debit and Credit denote the fallback or automatic posting of the amounts within a section. Accounting software programs automatically displayed Assets as a Debit or a positive value. Liabilities are automatically posted as a Credit or a negative quantity. The signs (+) and (-) do not appear, however, unless an amount appears in (Brackets); the fallback is a built-in Debit or Credit. If an Account within a Section appears in (Brackets) the Account is considered a Contra Account amount.

CONTRA ACCOUNTS: A Contra Account offsets another Account. Under Current Assets, we could have an Account called *Accounts Receivable* that reflects the amounts due from customers. Asset Accounts such as *Accounts Receivable* are shown as a positive number. Sadly not all the receivables are collected. Businesses extend credit, and a few customers fail to make payment; the receivable will not be collected. Accountants attempt to project this loss by creating an Account called *Doubtful Accounts*. The amount recorded is an estimate of the accounts receivable uncollectible and is posted and displayed as a negative under the Account *Accounts Receivable.*

The Account term is named *Allowance for Doubtful Accounts*. This entry demonstrates to the reader that the business understands that a percent of the credit sales will not be received and by using the Contra Account we tell the world this information.

Accounts Receivable - Trade	10,000
Allowance for Doubtful Accounts 1.5%	(150)

The two Accounts demonstrate the Accounts Receivable have an estimated value of $9,850

A more common Contra Account is called *Accumulated Depreciation*. Company vehicles are Assets and are recorded at cost. Over a period, the vehicle's value decreases. As an example, a $20,000 car may drop in value to zero in five years. Each year we would record $4,000.00 as a negative in a Contra Account called *Accumulated Depreciation*. The asset Account called *Vehicles* displays the cost and the Contra Account reflects the decline in value. The difference between the two Accounts indicates Book Value. Cost minus depreciation. Depreciation is only an educated estimate of the decrease in value and does not reflect the actual fair market value; however, depreciation is a procedure to reflect an estimate FMV.

Vehicles	20,000
Accumulated Depreciation (After 1st year)	(4,000)

Book Value estimate - $16,000

Financial Accounting: Understanding Financial Statements can be confusing. The Financial Accounting Standards Board (FASB) was established by the Security and Exchange Commission to ensure uniform financial reporting that reflects the company's financial condition by establishing 'Generally Accepted Accounting Principles,' GAAP.

Tax Accounting: At the end of the year the Financial Statements are used to prepare a Business Tax Return. One would think that the IRS would use the same Financial Statements required by GAAP, when such usage clearly represents the most accurate reflection of actual Income or Loss. However, the income amounts and expense deductions are controlled by Congress, who have a different agenda than just taxing profits. The Tax Code has come to pass because of lobbying efforts by special interest groups, an economic purpose and many times an attempt to solve a social problem Congress perceives. Whatever the reason, income recorded on a tax return and the allowable expenses may or may not agree with the Financial Statements prepared using GAAP.

As an example, Financial Accounting allows you to deduct (expense) the cost of business equipment over the life of the equipment that matches income called the 'Matching Principle.' Tax Accounting allows, under certain conditions, the deduction (expense) of the total cost of the equipment in the year of purchase. Apparently the inducement works. Businesses can save thousands in the short term on the acquisition of business capital assets, and such an inducement does stimulate the economy.

CASH, ACCRUAL AND HYBRID ACCOUNTING METHODS

The Cash Basis Method and the Accrual Basis Method of accounting are the two primary approaches for tracking income and expenses and preparing the financial records for all businesses. A third method uses a combination of the Cash and Accrual Method and is called the Hybrid Method.

Company financial statements and tax returns are prepared using any of the three methods of accounting. The term Bookkeeping and Accounting are used herein to describe the process of preparing a report that records business's financial information and transactions.

Cash Accounting: The Cash Method of Bookkeeping is Money in – Money Out. When money is received the amount is posted to the books as income and when a disbursement is made, the amount is considered an expense or a deduction.

Accrual Accounting: Record income when a sale occurs and not when the company receives the money. As an example; I sell a Widget for $10.00 and the customer agrees to pay for that Widget next month. I post the sale in my books at the time of the sale, not at the time I receive payment. I post to the *Income - Widgets* Account and *Accounts Receivable – Trade* Account.

Record expenses when items are purchased not when paid. I buy office supplies from a local office supply store on credit. I pick up the supplies and agree to pay the Office Supply owner next month. Record the cost on the books as an expense at the time of purchase, not when paid.

Hybrid Accounting: Combination of Cash Method and Accrual Method of bookkeeping. Accrual Method is used for Inventory accounting. When a company purchases inventory, the cost of the inventory is recorded as an asset. As the stock is sold or consumed, the cost of the product sold or consumed is recorded as a Cost of goods sold. Use the Cash Method for non-inventory income and operating expense.

Example: The Company sells apples. Ten apples purchased for $1.00 each. The inventory <u>Account</u> reflects $10.00. The company sells one apple for $1.50. The cost of the Apple sold is $1.00. A $1.00 is transferred to *Cost of Goods Sold - Apples*. The result of the two transactions is:
  ➢ Inventory started at $10.00,
  ➢ Sales - Apples of $1.50,
  ➢ Inventory is now nine apples or $9.00 and
  ➢ Cost Is Goods Sold is $1.00.

Accounting Method – In-House Financial Statements: You can prepare your in-house financial statements using any Accounting Method which will clearly reflect your financial condition. For a Small Businesses, I recommend the Cash Method of Accounting unless your company is based upon the sale of merchandise. The Hybrid Method, as explained below, is used for the calculation of Cost or goods Sold and is considered a combination of the Cash Method and Accrual Method of Accounting.

Accounting Method - Business Tax Return: The Accrual Method of preparing your tax return is allowed for all business taxpayers. The IRS has regulations when you are allowed to use the Cash Method.

  ➢ Self-employed or Proprietorships: You can use Cash, Accrual or Hybrid Method when preparing your business tax return. Once gross revenues exceed five million dollars you are required to use the Accrual Method.

  ➢ "C" Corporation: C corporations can use cash accounting preparing r a federal tax return if the average annual gross receipts of the business over the past three years is $5 million or less.

  ➢ "S" Corporation: A S Corporation specializing in professional services can use either cash or accrual methods. If the business maintains an inventory, it will normally have to use the accrual method unless it can meet one of the following two tests, in which case the cash method is allowed.

    ✓ Three-Year Rule: The businesses average gross yearly income for the last three years does not exceed $1 million.

    ✓ Services Based Rule: The second test also requires that, while the business does have some activity requiring an inventory, its primary business activity is service-based.

TAX TIP

Companies often use the Accrual Method preparing internal Financial Statements and convert to using the Cash or Hybrid Method when preparing their tax return.

Accrual accounting procedures requires claiming sales when made not when the money is received. Uncollected sales or Accounts Receivable are included as Income on your tax return. Therefore, this income is subject to income tax. Companies with large accounts receivable may have a difficult time with cash flow and paying taxes on uncollected Sales Income.

Using Accrual accounting allows the deduction of expenses before paid but after incurred. Deducting expense when incurred and not paid is a benefit when preparing your business tax return.

Understanding the Balance Sheet

The Balance Sheet is a statement listing in detail all the assets owned by a business and a detailed listing of all the liabilities of the company currently owes (debt). The result of subtracting the liabilities (debt) from the assets equals the net worth or owner's equity. The net worth is the book value of the company

The Balance Sheet does not cover a period. The Account amounts listed, for Assets, Liabilities, and New Worth is the value as if the picture was taken at the 'Point in Time' such as mid-night. Many of the amounts change within a few minutes after we took the picture. Accounts such as *Cash in Bank* may change hourly, and other Accounts such as *Vehicles - Car* may not change for years.

If the business could convert all its assets to cash, pay off all debt (liabilities), the remaining money is the New Worth or the actual value of the company at a point in time. It is the same concept as selling your home. When selling your house you pay off the mortgage loan (liability), the cash you have remaining is the actual equity in your home. We can obtain appraisals of our homes, but until we sell a home, it is impossible to determine the true Net Worth or Equity Value. As with all disciplines, accounting has exceptions. Keep it simple and basic.

> ➢ Asset amounts are Debits (+), which is a positive number.
> ➢ Liability amounts are Credits (-), which is a negative number.
> ➢ Net Worth values are Credits (-), which is a negative number.

Assets: Assets are Accounts such as *Petty Cash Fund*, *Cash in the Bank*, *Vehicles*, *Equipment*, *Inventory* and even intangible items such as *Patents*. Assets are listed as a positive number on the Balance Sheet. Each Account has an economic value, is owned by the business and is recorded on the Balance Sheet at the purchase price (Cost).

Note: One trick to understanding and reading financials is Tunnel Vision. The vehicle cost amount is recorded as an asset. Although we may have incurred a 'debt' when we purchased the car, the debt is recorded under the Liabilities section.

Accountants divide a company's Assets into two categories, Current Assets, and Non-Current Assets.

Current Assets: Assets that can be converted to cash faster, quicker and in less than one year are called Current Assets. The current assets are listed in order of the most liquid. Of course, the Account named *Petty Cash Fund* would be the most liquid followed by *Cash in the Bank* (checking accounts), *Accounts Receivable*, *Bonds*, *Stocks*, and Inventory and *Loans Receivable*. Bankers love current assets because they demonstrate liquidly.

Non-Current Assets: These are assets that we expect to keep for a longer period than one year and last longer than one year. My personal definition is that a Non-current asset (1) cost more than $500.00, (2) adds value to the business or to an existing asset and (3) last longer than one year. All three conditions must be met before the asset is recorded on the balance sheet as a Non-Current Asset. A machine or a company vehicle would be a Non-Current Asset. The company could own a patent, or when purchasing a business the purchase price could include Goodwill, and these items would be listed as Non-Current Assets.

Recording Loss of Value in Assets – Contra Account: Assets are listed as a positive number (+). As an example: the company purchases a Truck. The cost was $20,000.00, and this amount is recorded under Non-Current Assets. However, we all know that each year the value of the vehicle decreases. Accountants and bookkeepers have established a formula for recording this decline in value of the vehicle on a Balance Sheet, and it is called Depreciation. Depreciation is a record of the decline in value of an asset or the allocation of the cost of an asset to periods in which the asset is used or consumed. If we determine that the truck has a useful life of five years, we could show Truck Depreciation of $4,000.00 each year. For a period of five years, we would record a $4,000.00 expense in the Profit and Loss statement.

The Non-Current Asset may look as follows:

Truck	20000.00
Depreciation	-4000.00
Book Value	16000.00

The Expenses listed on the Profit and Loss Statement would reflect:

Depreciation Expense	4,000.00

We are demonstrating to the reader of the financial Statement that we have a Truck that we purchased for $20,000.00 and after the first year of using a truck, it has a worth $16,000.00. (Estimate)

Purchase Is An Expense Or An Asset: My clients always had a difficult time determining if an item purchased should be classified as an Asset or should the purchase be recorded as an expense. As stated above, I consider three conditions to determine if a purchase is classified as an asset. (1) Cost more than $500.00, (2) adds value to the business or to an existing asset and (3) last longer than one year. Review the examples below:

Example 1: Fixing a roof on a company owned office building is an expense even if the cost is greater than $500.00. The repair does not add value to the property. Replacing the roof adds value to the property, cost more than $500.00 and last longer than a year; it is a significant purchase. Therefore, the repair is a current expense charged to *Repairs and Maintenance – Building* Account reducing profit this year. Record the cost of a new roof as a Non-Current Asset, *Building Improvement* and reduce profit over a period of year's value declines. .

Example 2: The Company buys a laser printer for $350.00. The printer last longer than a year and adds value to the business. However, the printer cost less than $500.00. Record the printer as a current operating expense, *Office Supplies* Account. It is not a significant investment and is considered immaterial and therefore should be expensed in the year of purchase. Contact your Tax Accountant to determine which purchases should be regarded as insignificant and should be expensed in the year of purchase.

Example 3: The company buys a new Van for $25,000. The company paid $5,000.00 down and borrowed $20,000.00. Record the cost of Van as a Non-Current Asset Account, Transportation Equipment - Truck. The down payment was $5,000.00, and the Account Cash in the Bank Account is credited or reduced by $5,000.00. The company's debt is increased by $20,000.00. A liability is recorded in the Account Bank Loan – Vehicle, a Non-Current Liability. The Van adds value, cost more than $500.00 and last longer than a year. It is a significant purchase.

Liabilities: A Liability is a company's legal debt or obligation that arises during the course of business operations. As an example: a company may use a company credit card (credit card secured by the business) for buying office supplies. The expense Account *Office Supplies* increases. The Account *Credit Card Payable*, a credit also increased as a negative amount. The businesses liabilities increase. Second example: borrowed money at a bank is deposited in the company's checking account. The business checking Account, *Cash in the Bank* is increased. The company creates a debt Account called, *Loan Payable - Bank* in an equal amount. Liabilities are listed on the balance sheet as a negative number.

Accountants divide a company's liabilities into two categories, Current Liabilities, and Non-Current Liabilities.

Current Liabilities: Debts that are due and payable in less than one year. Debts such as credit card obligations or taxes withheld from employees' wages are due and payable in less than a year. If the company owes a bank loan, part of the debt is due in less than twelve months and is listed as a Current Liability. The balance of the bank loan owed after deducting the current portion of the bank debt is a Non-Current Liability.

Bankers hate current liabilities because they are a drain on current assets with-in the next year. Many banks will refuse to make a loan because of high current liabilities even though all other consideration for a loan have been met. Many business attempts to convert Current Liabilities to Non-current Liabilities by borrowing at a local bank, paying off short term debt by replacing the debt with a more manageable long term obligation.

Non-Current Liabilities: Sometimes called Long Term Liabilities, are debts that are due and payable after a year. The amount of a loan that is due within the next year is considered current, and the balance is considered long-term debt because it is due over a period longer than one year. As an example, a car loan is split between current liability and a long term liability. The part of the car loan that is due in the next year is a current liability, and the portion of the vehicle loan due and payable after one year is listed as a long term liability.

Current Ratio: A current ratio is a test of a company's financial strength. The ratio compares the current assets against the current liabilities.

Bankers and investors are very concerned about current liabilities in relation to current assets. A company that has substantial short-term liabilities compared to current assets could be a credit risk. Will the company have sufficient current assets to service the current liabilities? Debts are paid from company profits or by selling assets. A company can borrow additional funds or obtain investors, but if the business is to become successful, liabilities must be paid from profit.

Typically banks and other lending institutions place a lien on major assets to ensure they receive payment before unsecured creditors. As an example: a lien on a vehicle allows the lender to seize and sell the vehicle to pay the car loan before other creditors are paid. You have a lien on your home and if you cannot pay the mortgage the lender has the right to foreclose and take procession of your home, sell the property and receive their loan funds.

Net Worth or Equity: Net worth (Equity) section is also recorded in different categories with different names. Net Worth or Equity is the Fair Market Value of the business at a point in time say 12-31-2012 (Midnight). The next Financial Statement, even a day later reflects a change because of changes in the various assets or Liability <u>Accounts</u>. If you sell the assets, payoff liabilities the remaining cash balance is the true Equity of the business. Assets minus liabilities equal your net worth in the business. Usually, the first transaction to occur in a business is the owner depositing his personal funds into the business checking account. The *Cash in the Bank* Account increases (+) and *owners' equity* Account increases (-). The Balance Sheet would look as follows:

Sample Financial Statement
For XYZ Company

Balance Sheet/Statement of net worth
As of October 31, 2013

Assets

Cash in Bank – Checking (Positive number)   10,000.00

Total Assets   10,000.00

Liabilities

Zero Liabilities

Net Worth

Owner Equity – (Negative Number)   10,000.00

Total Liabilities and Net Worth   10,000.00

Cash was deposited in the bank and the business owner has invested those funds. If this business was a corporation, the owner's equity Account would be called *Capital Stock* because the owner would have purchased stock in his company. If the company was a LLC, we would call it *Members Equity* or *Partners Account*. By any name, it is an investment by the owner or investors into a startup business. Net Worth is a negative number.

Assets Are Positive - Liabilities Are Negative - Net Worth Is Negative.

Asset Accounts are a Positive (+): Negative balances in the asset section could be an error. If the *Cash in the Bank* Account is a negative, it could mean that the company has over-drawn it's checking account or there was an error in posting. Sssets Accounts listed as a negative need to be reviewed. However, contra accounts are a negative in the asset category.

Liability Accounts are a Negative (-): I have reviewed financial statements where the *Bank Loan Payable* Account or *Credit Card Payable* Account is a debit or positive (+) amount. These Accounts are incorrect. Neither the bank or a credit card company owes the company money. A debit (+) in the liability section indicates you may be owed money. You could have a debit (+) in these accounts if the company overpaid the bank or a credit card company. However, a more likely explanation is an error in posting and the account needs to be checked.

Income <u>Accounts</u> are a Negative (-): Years ago I received an income statement reflecting Sales Income as a positive (+) amount of over three-hundred thousand dollars. The bookkeeper had posted the sales income in reverse. Income amounts are posted as a negative (-) amount. In the income section, there could be an <u>Account</u> named *Returns* or *Refunds*, and these <u>Accounts</u> would reflect a positive value demostrating that the company refunded a sale. This is also a Contra <u>Account</u>.

Expense <u>Accounts</u> are a Positive (+): Expenses are recorded as a positive number (+). Anytime you have a negative value reflected in an Expense <u>Account</u> there is probably an error. The company could have returned a purchase, and the refund was posted to a different <u>Account.</u> Any negative balance in an expense <u>Account</u> needs to be checked.

Below is one additional example of a business Balance Sheet for you to review. The business has the following assets and liabilities as of October 31, 2011: (A point in time)

> ➤ Current Asset - *Cash in Checking* - 2,356.98.
> ➤ Current Asset - *Cash in Savings* - 8,325.60.
> ➤ Current Asset - *Accounts Receivable* - 13,890.12.
> ➤ Current Asset - *Inventory* at cost 11,658.42.
> ➤ Non- Current Asset – *Vehicles – Trucks*, 2009 Ford F150 Truck – cost 29,301.20 in 2008.
> ➤ Non-Current Asset, Contra Account – *Accumulated Depreciation* – 6,832.00.
> ➤ Current Liability - *Sales Tax Payable* - 145.36.
> ➤ Current Liability - *Credit Card Debt* Payable - 1,457.36.
> ➤ Current Liability – *Truck Loan Payable*, Current portion of Truck Loan 4,356.60
> ➤ Non-Current Liabilities – *Truck Loan Payable* 16,547.63
> ➤ Net Worth – *Owners Equity* 10,000.00
> ➤ Net Worth – *Profit for the Period* 25,193.37

A balance sheet is simply a recap of the above information. Accountants have designed a statement by placing a company's financial information in an easy to read summation of assets and liabilities and Net Worth. At a glance, anyone can determine the amount of the assets, the amount of debts and of course the amount of the worth (value) of the company.

FINANCIAL STATEMENTS
Balance Sheet

XYZ Company

As of October 31, 2012

ASSETS

Current Assets		
Cash in Bank – Checking	2,356.98	
Cash in Bank – Savings	7,325.60	
Accounts Receivable	13,890.12	
Inventory – Parts & Material	11,658.42	
Total Current Assets		35,231.12
Non-current Assets		
Vehicle – 2009 Ford F150	29,301.20	
Accumulated Depreciation	-6,832.00	
Total Non-Current Assets		22,469.20
Total Assets		57,700.00

LIABILITIES

Current Liabilities		
Sales Tax payable	145.36	
Credit Card Payable	1,457.36	
Current Portion Bank Loan	4,357.00	
Total Current Liabilities	5,959.00	
Non-Current Liabilities		
Vehicle Loan – Bank	16,548.00	
Total Non-current Liabilities	16,548.00	
Total Liabilities		22,507.00

NET WORTH

Owner's Equity	10,000.00	
Profit for the Period	25,193.00	
Total Net Worth		35,193.00
Total Liabilities and Liabilities		57,700.00

The above balance sheet is used by the company owner to make decisions affecting all aspects of the business. If the numbers are incorrect because of

109

errors in posting, it could make a big difference in decisions and for lenders. Remember this is a simple formula. The assets total $57,700.32. The liabilities total $22,506.95. Assets – Liabilities = $35,193.37 (Net Worth)

Profit and Loss Statement or Statement of Income and Expense

The name keeps changing, but accountants use both of the above names. Sales Income minus business expenses are called Net Profit or Net Loss. Unlike the Balance Sheet, the Profit and Loss Statement covers a period, usually a month, quarter or a year. The revenue, sales income, and the operating expenses are a reflection of the entire period. I recommend that you prepare a Statement of Income with three major sections.

> ➤ Sales, Revenue or Income – Posted as a Negative Number – Credit (-).
> ➤ Cost of Sales – Posted as a Positive Number – Debit (+).
> ➤ Expenses – Posted as a Positive number – Debit (+).

Revenue or Sales Income: Revenue is the money received from the sale of services or products. Divide your sales into as many categories as you needed using different Accounts. Point of Sale software programs coupled with your computer or cash register will create sales information into useful Accounts. Also, software programs can divide product sales subject to sales tax, certain Zip code areas or sales to other dealers.

Many small retail and restaurant businesses cannot afford a POS program. However, computers are used for all types of sales postings and information from preparing invoices for services and labor to maintaining a record of retail sales. Computers calculate sales tax collected and payable and inventory control is easier to manage. To save money, you can use a cash box or even a Cash Register, which you can buy at Sam's Club.

I suggest you split up your sales revenue into categories that make sense to you or provide you marketing information . The Income Statement provides management with significant information. I recommend that sales are divided into different Accounts so I can review trends from one month to the next or have information for a year to year analysis. One of the keys to bookkeeping is developing revenue and expense Accounts that provide you with information necessary to make management decisions. You could divide sales into different sections of the city by zip code or even breakdown sales into labor, parts, and specialty items. When you are preparing your advertising budget, you can then place a greater emphasis on the areas that produce most of your sales.

Note: A Point of Sale (POS) system is a system for managing the sales of retail goods. We all see POS systems in our grocery stores, restaurants and just about every business we enter. Using a POS system makes a business efficient, and the system lowers the costs of running a business while improving customer service.

Revenue can be much more complicated than recording money received for sales income. You may offer credit sales and you also may be selling products that you have purchased for resale. If you are selling on credit or have an inventory of products for sale I strongly suggest you contact an experienced bookkeeper or accountant.

Cost of Goods: The old term was Cost of Goods Sold (COGS). Either title is acceptable. The cost of Sales is a section where you record those disbursements (Expenses) that can be directly connected to income. If you were selling books, the cost you paid for the books sold would be recorded under Cost of Sales. A restaurant considers cost food, waitress and cooks as cost of goods sold. These cost are directly related to producing your restaurant income. Again the categories should represent the information you need to make business decisions. You need to know what percent your food cost are to sales income. If you had food cost greater that 19% in a small restaurant you probably need to reduce food expenditures or increase your selling price.

Subtracting Cost of Sales from sales income gives you Gross Profit or in some cases Gross Loss. Gross profit is the amount of profit or loss before considering general operating expenses. I prefer that the Statement of Income includes percent data so the reader can clearly and quickly determine the cost of sales. The percent values are necessary for managing the company operation. As an example: If food cost in a restaurant exceeds 25%, the restaurant will soon be in financial trouble.

There are exceptions and the Statement of Income needs to be studied before percents can be used as a guide. You can go online and review government statistics for just about every business. Operating expense percentages are also available and can provide you information concerning industry averages. Such expenses as labor cost, rent, and operating supplies are measured, and the information provides you a management tool. When preparing financial statements, expenses must be posted consistently in the same categories for the financial statements percentages to be useful.

 The year-end method for calculating Cost of Goods Sold is using the following formula.

> ➤ Beginning Inventory (Actual count using purchase price), as of the start of the year.

> ➤ Record total purchases of inventory for the year. (All purchases for resale items and used to generate sales)

> ➤ Add together the Beginning Inventory and Purchases.

> ➤ Subtract ending Inventory (actual count using purchase price) as of the end of the year.

> ➤ The result is Cost of Goods Sold.

Disbursements or Expenses: Establish business expense Accounts using the Chart of Accounts below. For a small business, I recommend all Expense Accounts are recorded in alphabetical order. Many Accounting Software programs provide sub-totals for Similar Accounts. As an example, all the Expense Accounts totaling the cost of operating the company vehicle could be combined reflecting the total vehicle operating cost. Accounts such as *Vehicle - Gas and Oil*, *Vehicle - Insurance*, *Vehicle - Repairs* and *Vehicle - Registration Cost* would be combined. I do not like combining Accounts for small businesses. The expenses need to be review separately.

Your Income Statement should reveal different management information such as the relationship between sales and advertising cost. Operating cost are tax deductible if the expense is 1) ordinary, common and accepted in the trade and 2) necessary, appropriate and useful in running a business.

Below is a list of expense Accounts that I have determined are very helpful in most companies. Small Businesses should record expenses in alphabetical order. It is just easier to post and review.

Chart of Expense Accounts

- ➤ Accounting
- ➤ Advertising – General
- ➤ Advertising – Web Site
- ➤ Attorney Fees
- ➤ Bank Service Fees
- ➤ Amortization Expense
- ➤ Contract Serv.-Cleaning
- ➤ Contract Services
- ➤ Charity
- ➤ Dues, Subscriptions & Fees
- ➤ Depreciation Expense
- ➤ Employee Business Millage
- ➤ Entertainment – Business Meals
- ➤ Entertainment – Music
- ➤ Insurance – Liability
- ➤ Insurance – Workman's Comp.
- ➤ Insurance – Officer Medical
- ➤ Insurance – Employee Medical
- ➤ License & Inspection Fees
- ➤ Merchant Fees – Credit Cards
- ➤ Miscellaneous Expense
- ➤ Office Supplies
- ➤ Operating Supplies

- ➢ Penalties – Federal and State
- ➢ Postage & Package Mailing
- ➢ Repairs & Maintenance – Building
- ➢ Repairs & Maintenance – Appliances
- ➢ Return Checks
- ➢ Salaries – Officers
- ➢ Salaries – Staff
- ➢ Salaries – Managers
- ➢ Sanitation
- ➢ Taxes – Employer FICA Matching
- ➢ Taxes – Colorado Unemployment
- ➢ Taxes – Federal Unemployment
- ➢ Taxes – Property
- ➢ Telephone – Business Line
- ➢ Telephone – Mobile
- ➢ TV & Cable Service
- ➢ Utilities – Gas & Electric
- ➢ Utilities – Water
- ➢ Vehicle – Gas & Oil
- ➢ Vehicle – License
- ➢ Vehicle – Insurance
- ➢ Vehicle – Repairs & Maintenance.

> ➢ OTHER EXPENSE

- ➢ Interest Expense
- ➢ Sales of Capital Assets
- ➢ Financial Statements

Notes

_____

_____

_____

_____

_____

_____

_____

_____

_____

_____

_____

_____

_____

_____

_____

_____

_____

_____

_____

_____

_____

_____

_____

_____

_____

_____

FINANCIAL STATEMENTS

FOR

John Smith Plumbing, Inc.
For the Period Ending
December 31, 2012

SEE ACCOMPANYING ACCOUNTANTS COMPILATION REPORT

Accountant's Compilation Report

Jordan Bartre, CPA
(Made-up name)
Riverside, NY

January 27, 2013

John Smith Plumbing, Inc.
2500 Any Street
Austin, TX 78734

Dear Client;

I have compiled the Balance Sheet of John Smith Plumbing, Inc. as of December 31, 2013. Included is the related Statement of Income and the Statement of Cash Flows for the twelve-month period ending December 31, 2012. All the statements are in accordance with standards established by the American Institute of Certified Public Accountants.

A compilation is limited to the presenting in the form of financial statements information that is the representation of the company's management. I have not audited or reviewed the accompanying statements, and accordingly I do not express an opinion or any other form of assurance on them.

Management has elected to omit all of the disclosures. If the omitted disclosures were included in the financial statements, they might influence the user's conclusions about the company financial position. Accordingly these financial statements are not designed for those who are not informed about such matters.

Sincerely

Jordan Bartre, CPA

John Smith Plumbing, Inc.
Balance Sheet – As of December 31, 2012

ASSETS

Current Assets

Petty Cash Fund	300.00	
Cash in the Bank-Checking	11,749.63	
Cash in the Bank-Savings	8,760.09	
Inventory - Plumbing Parts	11,344.15	
Accounts Receivable	11,438.63	
Total Current Assets		43,592.50

Non-Current Assets

Office Furniture & Fixtures	842.38	
Computer Equipment	845.83	
Computer Software	761.41	
Company Vehicles	86,093.94	
Accumulated Depreciation	-31,915.99	
Total Non-current Assets		56,627.57

TOTAL ASSETS	100,220.07

LIABILITIES

Current Liabilities

Accounts Payable	1,815.96	
Federal Withheld Payable	3,056.08	
State Withheld payable	517.87	
State Unemploy. Payable	340.97	
Federal Unemploy. Payable	119.97	
Sales Tax payable	366.23	
Visa Credit Card Payable	1,046.83	
MC Credit Card payable	336.22	
Current portion Bank Payable	3,556.03	
Total Current Liabilities		11,155.58

Non-Current Liabilities

Loan Payable – Bank	18,438.98	
Total Non-Current Liabilities		18,438.98

TOTAL LIABILITIES   29,594.23

NET WORTH

Capital Stock	15,000.00
Distribution of Profit	-35,000.00
Retained Earnings	57,225.25
Profit for the Period	33,400.59

Total Net Worth   70,625.84

**TOTAL LIABILITIES &
NET WORTH**   100,220.07

See Accompanying Accountants Compilation Report

John Smith Plumbing, Inc.
Statement of Income
For Period January 1, 2012 through December 31, 2012

Income

Income – Service Sales	141,942.00	
Income – Plumbing Part	122,395.20	
Total Income – Sales		264,337.20

Cost of Goods Sold

Plumbing Parts & Material	29,546.98		11.18%
Plumbing Permits	2,941.02		1.11%
Sub-Contractor Plumbing		14,054.80	5.32%
Salaries – Plumbers	37,805.20		14.30%
Salaries – Plumbers Helper	16,458.98		6.23%
Total Cost of Goods Sold		100,806.98	38.14%
Gross Profit		163,588.22	61.89%

Operating Expenses

Accounting Fees	3,360.00	1.27%
Advertising Expense	4,870.20	1.84%
Attorney Fees	300.00	0.11%
Bank Service Fees	342.58	0.13%
Contract Services	1,950.00	0.74%
Computer Services	1,450.09	0.55%
Dues & Subscriptions	690.00	0.26%
Depreciation Expense	9,458.00	3.58%
Education and Training	798.05	0.30%
Entertainment – Travel	1,245.38	0.47%
Insurance – Liability	6,020.41	2.28%
Insurance – Officer Medical	4,548.30	1.72%
Insurance – Employee Medical	4,902.62	1.85%
Insurance – Workmen's Comp.	8,756.38	3.31%
Interest Expense – Visa Credit Card	245.98	0.09%
Interest Expense – MC Credit Card	95.30	0.04%
Interest Expense – Vehicle Loan	1,331.08	0.50%

Internet Fees & Web Site	8,840.00	3.34%
Lease – Storage Unit	1,044.00	0.39%
License & Fees	302.39	0.11%
Miscellaneous Expense	127.86	0.05%
Office Supplies	1,657.55	0.63%
Operating Supplies	987.52	0.37%
Postage & Freight	360.00	0.14%
Salaries – Officer	48,000.00	18.16%
Taxes – Employee Social Security	6,961.50	2.64%
Taxes – State Unemployment	640.30	0.24%
Taxes – Federal Unemployment	356.89	0.14%
Taxes – Personal Property	1,458.97	0.55%
Telephone – Business Office	491.27	0.19%
Telephone – Mobile	904.89	0.34%
Tools - Consumable	850.20	0.32%
Vehicle Expense – Fuel	4,256.98	1.61%
Vehicle Expense – License	320.12	0.12%
Vehicle Expense – Repairs	608.57	0.23%
Vehicle Expense – Insurance	<u>1,654.25</u>	0.63%

Total Operating Expenses   <u>130,187.63</u>   49.25%

Net Profit   <u>30,400.59</u>   11.50%

See Accompanying Accountants Compilation Report

John Smith Plumbing, Inc.
Statement of Cash Flows
For the period ended December 31, 2012
Increase (Decrease) in Cash or Cash equivalents

Cash Flow from Operating Activities
Net Income (Loss)   33,400.59

Adjustments to Reconcile Cash Flow
Depreciation Expense   9,458.00

Decrease (Increase) in current Assets
Inventory – Plumbing Parts   (1,020.36)
Accounts Receivable   1,020.53

Increase (Decrease) in current Liabilities
Accounts Payable   356.98
Federal W/H & FICA Payable   210.30
State Withholding Payable   58.90
State Unemployment Payable   (24.50)
Federal Unemployment Payable   15.39
Sales Tax Payable   145.89
Visa Credit Card Payable   589.75
Master Card Payable   (265.98)
Current Part of Wells Fargo Loan payable   (289.75)

Total Adjustments   10,255.16

Cash Provided by Operations   43,655.74

Cash Flow from Investment Activities   00

Cash Flow from Financing Activities
Loan Payable – Wells Fargo   (3,020.00)
Dividends Paid to Shareholders   (35,000.00)

Cash Provided (Used) from Financing   (38,020.00)

Net Increase (Decrease) in Cash   5,635.74

Cash at the Beginning of Period   15,173.98

Cash at End of Period   20,809.72

See Accompanying Accountant's Compilation Report

Review of Assets: The Financial Statements of John Smith Plumbing, Inc. for the year ending 12-31-11 are above. Review the Balance Sheet noting the differences between 12-31-10 and 12-31-11, the Current Asset position has improved by $5,635.57 and most of the increases in Current Assets were from Cash in Savings. Fixed Assets has not changed except for the book value. Each year the value of assets usually decrease. Accounts show this decline in value by recording assets at cost when purchased and then reduce the figure by applying depreciation. Depreciation is a drop in value or a reduction in value over time, usually one year.

AICPA (American Institute of Certified Public Accountants) has established GAAP (Generally Accept Accounting Rules). We have pages and pages of rules concerning depreciation. Use the KISS approach; keep it simple stupid. I recommend that your bookkeeper uses straight-line depreciation for all assets and note the information on the Accompanying Compilation Report. Straight-line depreciation is simply dividing the cost of the asset by the number of years of expected useful life. Below are a list of several common Assets and a useful life figure.

> Agriculture Equipment – 7 Years
> Breeding Animals – 5 Years
> Manufacturing Equipment – 7 Years
> Office Related Equipment and Fixtures – 5 Years
> Real Estate – 15 Years
> Land – Zero
> Residential Rental House – 27.5 Years
> Non-Residential Real Property (Commercial) – 39 Years
> > Transportation Equipment – 5 Years

Note: There are many methods used for Depreciating Assets. There are differences between Generally Accepted Accounting procedures and Income Tax Accounting Procedures. Keep your Financial Statements simple. Use straight line depreciation.

Review Liabilities: In our example the current liabilities have increased. One such increase is in credit card debt which usually is a high-interest rate. The amount of debt increase is not sufficient and not a problem.

Long Term Liabilities has decreased because the long-term debt with Wells Fargo has been paid down.

Review Equity (Net Worth): A) the capital Stock Account amount has not changed. The $18,987.60 is the amount Mr. Smith invested into his company when he organized the corporation. B) In 2011 John Smith took distribution of profits in the amount of $ 35,000.00. If we review the 2010 numbers, we can see that Retained Earnings were $13,227.58 as of 12-31-10. After the year ended the 2010 profit of $41,209.82 was converted to additional retained earnings.

Retained Earnings are profits from past years retained in the business and used by the business for operating the company. In this case at the start of 2010, the company had $13,227.58 in retained earnings. The profit for 2010 was $41,209.82 bringing the total retained earnings to $ 54,437.40 as of 1-1-2011. C) In 2011 John Smith took $35,000.00 as a Distribution of Profits. Since Mr. Smith's Corporation elected to be taxed as a Sub-Chapter S corporation the total amount of $54,437.40 has already been taxed. Mr. Smith has decided to take $35,000.00 from his *Retained Earnings*. The withdrawal is considered *Distribution of Profits*. Unlike dividends from a Regular Corporation, there is no additional income tax on distributions of profit.

The distributions of profit amount have no relationship to the amount of retained earnings other than distributions of profit in the amount greater than retained earnings could have taxable consequences. In other words, you should, not take more actual money out of your S Corporation than you have in profit.

Review the Income Statement: Income statements showing two years of values and percent's allows the reader to see the problems develop. Revenues (Income) has increased, but only service income. Part sales income is down. Plumber salary expense has increased but as expected plumbing parts and plumbing material cost is down. Overall gross profit is down by around $ 5,000.00. Your job as the owner/manager is to review these numbers and determine what is happening. Sales of parts is down, do you need sales training. Are you working less because your plumber salaries have increased?

All expenses look average and overall remain at around 50% of sales. Profit is down by over $8,000.00. Of course, this is easy to understand since sales revenue decreased and salaries are up.

Review Statement of Cash Flows: Cash is king. Profits were down, and the shareholder took $35,000.00 in Distribution of Profit from Retained Earnings. 2011 was not a great year. Retained Earnings are down from last year, and that affects the amount of Profits the owner/shareholder can take next year. The changes from 2010 are a warning light for the owner. It is a slow slid down and if sales continue on a downward trend, reversing this decrease will become difficult.

"I spent hours writing down my goals,
reciting my affirmations and visualizing
my success...while my competitors
were out making sales calls."

Notes

_____

_____

_____

_____

_____

_____

_____

_____

Chapter 6
How to Prepare Your Companies Bookkeeping
THE ESSENTIAL SMALL BUSINESS HANDBOOK
The best and most complete handbook for the small business entrepreneur
Essential information for starting, buying, operating and succeeding

The function of bookkeeping is to prepare and generate a financial statement which represents the financial condition of your business. Your Financial Statement is used to prepare your business tax return; it is a tool to secure investors and business loans, and it provides management information when making business decisions. Preparing your company's bookkeeping will require time and effort. However, if you are willing to invest the energy and money into absorbing basic accounting knowledge, it can be done. All Small Businesses Entrepreneurs can prepare their companies bookkeeping.

Three-Step Approach to your Business Bookkeeping

1. **Prepare your Bookkeeping with Professional Help.**
2. **Hire a Professional Bookkeeping Service.**
3. **Hire a Full-time Bookkeeper employee.**

Step 1: Prepare Your Bookkeeping with Professional Help

You can prepare your company's accounting-bookkeeping with training. The training may be as simple as hiring a bookkeeper for a couple of hours to provide you with in-house education, or you may want to take an accounting class at a local college. Also, there are many accounting courses on-line. Any method of training will work, but do not be so arrogant that you believe bookkeeping is simple, and anyone can prepare a double entry set of books. Follow the examples below and you will understand the complexity of preparing financials. Each year Tax Accountants receive financial statements that do not make any sense, and even creative accounting cannot fix. A Tax Accountant can save your business thousands of dollars in tax liability when presented with accurate financial statements. Lenders need correct financial statements to make an informed decision, and investors will not consider investing if they can understand your financials. Do it right from the start and receive basic training.

Single Person Small Business Operation

Many single-person businesses do not need an accounting software program. Using ledger paper or tabloid paper you can post your Income and Expenses.

Income: I recommend using a business checking account. However, if you are a sole proprietorship, you can use one checking account for both personal and business. As a corporation or LLC do not co-mingle personal and commercial transactions in the same account. Always record the basic information on the deposit slip. Record the name, date and why you received the deposited. You may have to prove that each deposit is either personal or business. Unidentified deposits may be reclassified by the IRS as income if audited. A gift from your mother could end up as taxable income.

Usually, an IRS audit includes a review of all checking accounts and even investment accounts for unidentified deposits. Over the years, the IRS has discovered taxpayers may deposit business income into personal checking accounts, money market accounts and even stock broker accounts. I assure you that IRS auditors will check all deposits made in all checking accounts and review the backup for these deposits.

Business Expenses: Clearly identify business expenditures in checking accounts, credit cards or cash with backup information. I file all deductible expense receipts in date order. I know it sounds like overkill but since receipts are different sizes, I created a form on which I tape the receipt and maintain a monthly record in date-order. On the document I record the Date, who paid, amount paid and the business purpose of the expense.

Business expenses can be difficult to find if you use a personal checks, debit cards, credit cards and even cash when purchasing deductible items. Co-mingling business expenses with your personal credit cards and checking account makes the job of organizing your year-end disbursements or expenses difficult. Even if you have a tiny business it could take you hours to prepare the information for your 1040, Schedule C. I recommend all business disbursements be made from one business checking account. The bank statements reflect all your business expenditures. You just record each payment on a columnar pad categorizing each expense.

Business Expenses Paid Directly From Biz Checking Account: Write Checks, pay by checking account Debit Card or Electronic disbursement. File receipts in date order by month or quarter. Post disbursements in a ledger by category. Use the list of expense accounts in Chapter 5 for your expense categories.

Business Expenses Paid from Personal Credit Card, Cash or Personal Checking Account: Prepare a detailed Expense Report, attached receipts and have the business repay you for these expenditures. You must divorce your personal activities for the company. When you were an employee, you did not have access to the firm funds. If you spend personal funds for company business, you filed an expense report with your employer and requested payment. Nothing has changed. You are still an employee, and although you are the owner of the business, you must treat the company as a separate entity. Do not co-mingle funds. The check written by your company to you, for business expenses will be posted in expense Accounts the same as any other business expense.

Business Expense without Receipts: Most small businesses use their personal vehicle for business. The IRS allows entrepreneurs to deduct a flat per mile rate when using a personal vehicle for company business. You must maintain a record of your business miles. One-hundred percent of the car expense; gas, oil, repairs, insurance and registration cost must be paid personally. Do not have the company pay operating cost. You are only allowed to deduct the flat millage rate. See Chapter 7 for detail information for deducting vehicle cost.

Mid-size to larger Small Businesses

For those companies with more complex bookkeeping problems, I recommend that you record all your deposits and disbursements using an accounting software program. Your income and expenses will be the same as above except instead of using a columnar pad you post transactions to an accounting software program. For the business that extends credit there are many programs available that have an Accounts Receivable module, so maintaining your income can be easier than a ledger book. Bookkeeping programs can create Invoices and automatically post to the client's account, and customer deposits are quickly posted to the *Cash in the Bank* Account, and to your *Accounts Receivable* module at the same time.

Some software programs create a check or allow you to use pre-printed checks when paying expenses. The program decreases the Cash in Bank" balance and categorizes each disbursement. Using your business checking account, Debit Card or having automatic payments made from your account will require you to post these transactions manually. However, with some practice you can create financial statements that reflect your income and post your expenses in different categories.

Software Programs and Training

Accounting Software: It is not possible for this Handbook to recommend or review a particular bookkeeping software program. There are many good accounting software programs available. Some programs are specifically designed for different businesses such as contractors, retail stores, bars, and restaurants. There are software programs designed for almost every major segment of our economy. **No accounting program that will train you to be a bookkeeper.** If you are using an Accountant or a Professional Bookkeeper, they will want you to be on the same program. You must receive training in any program you use. Training, training, and training.

For a small business Quick Books is an outstanding product. Intuit has done a masterful job creating a complete system and in marketing their product. I recommend Quick Books. However, there are other dependable and suitable software programs available. Ask your accountant for a recommendation. The key is training. Do not believe the hype that an accounting software program will replace training. Quick Books Software requires training, and there are many Certified Quick book trainers available. Accountants receive financial statements prepared using many different software programs. Some of these statements do not make any sense.

You will be learning two disciplines at the same time; an accounting software program and bookkeeping. Both subjects are difficult, and both will require a learning curve. Below I have considerable information regarding how accounting works, and the beginning steps you will need to prepare your books.

Hire a Bookkeeper Trainer: I strongly suggest you use a qualified professional to prepare your small business tax return. Most accounting firms and CPAs offer bookkeeping services. Many companies have a staff of qualified bookkeepers who will prepare your books monthly or even log on to your computer and correct or post your income and expenses on a monthly basis. Since your goal is to produce an accurate financial statement, training is a requirement.

Step 2: Hire a Professional Bookkeeping Service

Preferred Booking Procedure: A small business needs to either handle directly or closely monitor deposits and disbursements. At all times, you need to be aware of the company's financial position and in order for you do that, you need hands-on financial management. The following is my recommendation for a small business to accomplish the bookkeeping function and process.

1. Hire a local qualified Bookkeeper or a qualified Bookkeeping Service.

2. Receive basic training in the bookkeeping program recommended by a professional bookkeeper. If you have inventory, accounts receivable, accounts payable or accounts payable learn how to post these transactions correctly.

   Learn how to post income, write computerized checks and how to record electronic and debit disbursements with your accounting program. Do not delegate the necessary bookkeeping functions to anyone, including a spouse, until your business obligations require you to transfer portions of the accounting function to an employee.

3. Personally make deposits or create a procedure for employees to handle deposits with checks and balances. Never allow the employee that post the accounts receivable to prepare the deposit slip. Write all disbursement checks including payroll. If needed design a procedure for an employee to handle the expenditures with checks and balances.

4. Once a month your bookkeeper either taps into your accounting program from his or her office or visits your business to finalize the financial statements. Usually, the bookkeeper completes the following tasks:

   a) Balances the checking account to ensure all income and disbursements are included in the books.

b) Reviews and corrects income or disbursements postings as necessary.

c) Creates Federal and State reports such as sales tax and payroll reports.

d) The bookkeeper checks and corrects any sub-ledgers such as Accounts Receivable or Accounts Payable with the owner's help. Usually, the owner is aware of errors and many times accounting programs require a higher level of expertise to correct these balances.

e) Bookkeeper reviews and adjusts all liability balances if necessary. Credit card statements are posted, and monthly loan statements are reviewed and balanced with lender statements.

f) The bookkeeper also handles amortization and depreciation postings. Handling insurance pre-payments and creating the bookkeeper should handle a monthly liability for items such as property taxes.

g) The last interface between the bookkeeper and the owner should be a review of the Financial Statements and complete any corrections needed.

Remember, every line item on the Balance Sheet needs to balance with the backup ledgers. As an example, the Aged Customers Receivable totals, needs to balance with the *Accounts Receivable* Account. The bank loan balance and the interest paid needs to balance with the lenders monthly statements.

I knew a certified bookkeeper who operated a full service bookkeeping business. His clients were trained on Quick Books and daily they posted their income and paid expenses, including payroll. Monthly the bookkeeper visited each client's office and finalized their financial statements. He corrected any posting, balanced the bank account, prepared all required government forms and check each line item on the Balance Sheet and Income Statement. He charged $60.00 an hour, was scheduled 200 hours a month and unless he needed a day off was busy every day. He billed for his travel time and mileage and never had a month below $10,000.00 in income. He required that his clients be present each visit and the two of them review the financials correcting any errors. If you are looking for a business earning $120,000.00 a year you may want to specialize as a Certified Bookkeeper.

Independent Bookkeeping Service: By entering into a contract with a company or an individual to provide bookkeeping services you are hiring an outside service to accomplish an important function for your business. Similar to hiring an employee with accounting expertise, it may be difficult determining if a local bookkeeping company has the qualifications to prepare a true and accurate financial statements, and many do not. Many CPA firms offer bookkeeping service and historically I have found their bookkeepers trained and qualified.

Very few small businesses complete due-diligence when hiring a bookkeeping company. You must conduct an interviewed before entering into a contract, and you need to make sure the accounting company you hire can do the job. I have never been asked to demonstrate my expertise or for that matter no one has presented me with a shopping list of the services needed. Review the bookkeeping procedure above when interviewing an accounting company. Can the company provide training and provide direct services such as reviewing and correcting postings? Does the company have the expertise to balance a checking account, correct *Accounts Receivable* and *Accounts Payable* and review and adjust the monthly Financial Statements? What will this cost?

Step 3: Hire a Full Time Bookkeeper Employee

Hire a Bookkeeper: Ready for a full-time bookkeeper? The American Institute of Professional Bookkeepers offers Certification for Bookkeepers. The difficulty of contracting a bookkeeping service with certification or hiring an employee who is a certified bookkeeper is there are only 30,000 members. Hundreds of thousands are needed. Therefore finding a certified bookkeeper is next to impossible.

Companies continue to use a secretary or receptionist to act as a bookkeeper along with her other duties. Thousands of professionals believe no one could replace their job skills, but they have no respect for the professional bookkeeper's abilities. The mindset concerning the high esteem held for themselves and the little value placed upon a bookkeeper's skills astonishes me. Hundreds of times new clients have told me that their wife can do the books, after all what is so hard about keeping track of a few numbers. She pays the bills at home!

A professional bookkeeper has had years of training and experience and can save you thousands of dollars in taxes. The professional bookkeeper is more important than a CPA. When CPAs receive a year-end financial statement used to prepare your tax return, they have no idea as to what has been posted to any of the Accounts. Financials prepared by unskilled bookkeepers are incorrect, and unless you are prepared to pay thousands of dollars in accounting fees, your tax return will be wrong. An IRS audit could cost you thousands.

There are many knowledgeable and professional Bookkeepers who are experts and probably as many who believe they are bookkeepers, but would not know a debit from a credit. You must weed out those individuals who claim bookkeeping expertise but in reality do not possess accounting knowledge. You need to conduct an extensive interview and test their abilities. Do not disqualify an applicant because they are not proficient in particular bookkeeping software program. A qualified bookkeeper can use any accounting program after a short training period. The key is accounting knowledge.

Test Potential Bookkeepers: I have reviewed a company called Accounting Coach that provides online bookkeeping training and testing. They provide Bookkeeping Exam Questions which you can use to qualify a potential bookkeeper or even a Bookkeeping Service. It appears that the company provides a needed service to the Bookkeeping profession and for selecting a bookkeeper employee. I do not endorse this company only because I have not used their services. As with any on-line company complete your due-diligence before sending anyone money.

If you feel uncomfortable hiring an on-line company, below are ten fundamental bookkeeping questions with answers you can use to test a bookkeeper's abilities. If a more comprehensive test is needed, download a bookkeeping exam from the internet.

Basic Bookkeeping Knowledge

The function of accounting is to prepare and generate a Financial Statement that represents an accurate financial condition of your business. Your Financial Statement is used to prepare your business tax return; it is a tool for securing investors and business loans, and it provides management information when making business decisions. Preparing your company's books will require time and effort. If you are willing to invest energy and dollars into absorbing basic accounting and bookkeeping knowledge, it can be done. All Small Businesses Entrepreneurs can prepare their books.

Understanding Bookkeeping: Chapter 5 tackled the problem of Understanding Financial Statements, and this chapter covers the task of preparing your accounting resulting in a Financial Statement.

Establish a Chart of Accounts: There is a complete Chart of <u>Accounts</u> in Chapter 7.

One Business Bank Checking Account: Once again I suggest only one business checking account. Do not co-mingle business income or business expenses with your personal finances.

What the Hell is Double Entry Bookkeeping: Record every financial transaction in two (or more) Accounts, post one as a negative and the post the other as a positive. Post an equal amount as a plus and a minus, one called a debit and the other a credit.

When you buy office supplies with a company check, the transaction requires a debit (plus) increasing the *Office Supply Expense* <u>Account</u> and a credit (minus) decreasing the *Cash in the Bank* <u>Account</u>. Post the same amount in both <u>Accounts</u>. The disbursement of $20.00 for office supplies lowers the bank balance by $20.00 and the office supply expenses are increased by $20.00. The same amount is posted to two different <u>Accounts</u> – a negative and a positive.

Record Keeping – Receipts and Copies: Maintain a copy of all receipts in date order. My wife who is also an Accountant, files receipts by company. I think a small company deals with far too many suppliers, and you need too many file cabinets. I even tape or attach different size receipts to an 81/2 X 11 inch copy paper noting the date at the top.

Deposits: When recording deposits include detail information on the deposit slip. Include from whom, what for and where the deposit came from on your Deposit Slip in detail. Just recording the customers check number is not adequate information. Record sufficient description on the deposit slip so you can tell two years down the road where the money come from and why you receive the funds. I once had a client that never recorded information on their deposit slip. The IRS audited his business, thousands of dollars of deposits recorded in his personal checking account were reclassified as income by the IRS. He co-mingled his business and personal and compounded the co-mingling by inadequate records. If you cannot verify a deposit as non-taxable income, the IRS will reclassify the deposits as income

Disbursements – Expenses: Keep copies of payment receipts or invoices for all expenditures. I keep receipt copies in date order and use a standard 8 ½ inch by 11 inch paper by taping smaller expense receipts to the paper. Since many receipts are small, I spend the time attaching the receipt to a standard size paper. Many of you are more computer savvy and can scan each document and file in the "Expense" folder within your computer. I'm old fashion and very well-organized so I keep my receipts in date order for easy reference. Record the date paid, who paid, business purpose and the Account name or number on the letter size paper. At any time, your accounting software program can create a list of each posting to any single Account. As an example: Throughout the year you receive the monthly Electric bill. Retain a copy in your paid expense folder. Post Electric cost in an Account Titled *Utilities*. At any time, print a master list of each separate amount posted to the Account named *Utilities.* A cumulative report of the *Utility* Account can be prepared for an IRS audit at moment's notice. The receipts are easily found when filed by date paid. Use the list of expense Accounts in Chapter 5.

Business Expenses Paid Directly From Biz Checking Account: Write Checks, pay by checking account, Debit Card or Electronic disbursement. File receipts in date-order by month or quarter. Post disbursements in a ledger by Account.

Business Expense Paid With Company Credit Card: When using any credit card you are incurring a debt. Buying gas or supplies with a credit card, the Expense Account increases, and the company incurred credit card debt.

Pay Credit Card in Full: Treat the payment as any other checking account disbursement. Divide the expenses into the correct Expense Account.

Pay Credit Card Payment: Purchases on the company credit card is only borrowing money and incurring debt. A) Post the correct expense Account and

Credit Card Payable <u>Account</u> for each charge. B) Pay credit card either with a debit or a business check. The amount is posted against *Credit Card Payable* <u>Account</u> and a decrease in cash.

Business Expenses Paid from Personal Credit Card, Cash or Personal Checking Account: Prepare a detailed Expense Report for any business expenses paid with personal funds or personal credit card. Treat yourself as an employee. Request that your company repay all business expenses you incurred for the business. When you were an employee, you did not have access to the company funds. If you spend personal funds on company business, you filed an expense report with your employer and requested payment. Nothing has changed. You are still an employee, and although you're own a business, you must treat the business as a separate entity. Do not co-mingle funds. The check written by your company to you for business expenses will be posted in cost category <u>Accounts</u>, the same as any other business expense.

Business Expense without Receipts: Most small companies use their personal vehicle for business. The IRS allows entrepreneurs to deduct a flat rate per mile when using a personal vehicle for business. You must maintain a record of your business miles and personal miles. One-hundred percent of the car expense, gas, oil, repairs, insurance and vehicle cost must be paid personally, not by your business. You are only allowed to deduct the flat millage rate. See Chapter 7 for detail information for deducting a business owned vehicle versus a personal vehicle used in your business.

Copyright 2003 by Randy Glasbergen.
www.glasbergen.com

"Billy, you've been a fine son, but it's time for a change. I found a child overseas who can do it cheaper."

Bookkeeping Concepts

My formal education did not include bookkeeping, and I was self-taught. Trying to understand accounting by studying debits and credits was impossible until I learned four basic bookkeeping concepts.

First Concept
Understand the Basic Financial Statement

In Chapter 5 of this manual is a detailed basic structure of a financial statement. To learn basic bookkeeping, you must have a basic knowledge of the structure of financial statements. Let's review: Financial statements are Assets, Liabilities, New Worth, Sales and Expenses. The individual line items are either Debits (Plus) or Credits (Minus).

Assets - Items of Value: Record assets as a debit (+), a positive number. Assets encompass <u>Accounts</u> such as *Cash in the Bank, Inventory* or Fixed Assets <u>Accounts</u> such as *Real Estate* or *Vehicles.*

Liabilities – Listing of Company Debts: Record liabilities as a credit (-), a negative number *Accounts Payable*, *Federal & State Employment Taxes Payable* and *Credit Cards Payable* are Current-Liabilities. Long Term Liabilities are *Vehicle Loans* or *Bank Loan' payable*.

Net Worth – Assets minus Liabilities Equals Net Worth: Record Net Worth Accounts as a credit (-), a negative number. Titles of Net Worth <u>Accounts</u> are *Owner's Equity, Capital Stock* or *Profit for the period*. The <u>Account</u> for maintaining the record of past years profit that was not distributed to the owners is *Retained Earnings*. If you sold all your assets and paid all your debts, the dollar amount realized is the actual Net Worth of the business.

Consider the Net Worth as a category designed to maintain a record of the company's book value. You post assets at cost and record debts at the amount owed. Simplify the equation by applying the same principle to a rental house. Record the house at cost. Record the mortgage you incurred when purchasing the rental house. Cost minus the debt is your Net Worth in the rental.

Sales - Record of Income: Record Sales as a credit (-), a Negative number. This category sign does not make sense. Just accept that *Sales Income* of any type is recorded as a negative. Sales <u>Accounts</u> have titles such *Retail Sales* or *Service Sales*.

Expenses - Record of Disbursements: Record expenses, expenditures or payments under the <u>Account</u> title *Cost of Goods Sold* or *Operating Expenses* as a debit (+), a positive number. There are many different Expense <u>Accounts</u>. *Advertising, Attorney Fees, Office Supplies, Property Taxes* and *Vehicle Expense* are just a few expense <u>Accounts</u>.

Second Concept
Walk-through Each Transaction in Your Minds-Eye

View every financial transaction your minds-eye. As a Quarter-Back, you can plan your next move like a video in your mind. The phrase 'mind's eye' refers to the human ability for visualization. It is the ability to see things with the mind. What happen? How does a single financial transaction change my financial statements by changing my Accounts?

Accounting Terms:

General Ledger: Term for describing the company's accounting records. The General Ledger is a record of all the companies' financial transactions over the life of the company. The General Ledger is *Assets, Liabilities, Net Worth, Income,* and *Expenses.* In Chapter 7 review a complete Account listing within the major categories.

Bookkeeping Financial Transaction: A transaction involves changes to the company's books of Accounts. One or more of the companies Accounts moves up (+), and one or more of the companies Accounts moves down (-) in an equal amount.

Account: The accounting definition of an Account is a 'record' in the general ledger. The categories Assets, Liabilities, Net Worth, Income, and Expenses contain many separate and distinctive Accounts. Each Account is used to collect and store debit and credit values. For example, a company will have *Cash in the Bank* Account in which every transaction involving cash is recorded. If the company buys office supplies for cash, the Cash Account will be credited, and the *Office Supply* Expense Account is debited.

Double-Entry Bookkeeping: A double-entry system of bookkeeping is so named because every entry to an Account requires a corresponding and opposite equal entry to a different Account. For instance, recording sales of $50 would require making two entries, Debit (+) entry of $50 to an Account called *Cash in the Bank* and a credit (-) entry to an Account called *Income*.

Visualize each transaction and the transactions effect on the financial Accounts. We know that every transaction requires two or more off-setting entries. Follow the examples below visualizing the transaction:

Example 1: Employee enters the Post Office with a business package. Hands the post office clerk a package, the clerk weights the package, computes the amount and requests payment. Employee writes a check for the amount, tenders the payment and the clerk gives employee a receipt.

What Happen?

a) The company's *Cash in the Bank* Account decreased (-) by the amount of the check and

b) The amount is recorded in *Postage Expense* Account, The Account increases (+) reflecting the amount of the purchase.

Two things happen; two separate Accounts were affected. Cash was used to buy postage and the business incurred a postage expense.

Example 2: Company employee visits the local gas station to purchase fuel for the company car, using a company business credit card. The card is swiped and approval. The business vehicle is fueled. Usually, a receipt is printed.

What Happen?

a) The gas was purchased using a Business Credit Card. The company's Credit Card debt increases (-) and the amount is posted to an Account named *Credit Card Payable* (-) and

b) The business purchased gas. The Account *Vehicle Expense – Gas* is increased (+). (Liabilities are negative, expenses are a positive). Gas is the same as any other expense. The difference between Example 1 and 2 is that the employee used a company credit card and not cash.

Two separate Accounts were affected. The company increase credit card debt (-), and the company's vehicle operating cost increased (+).

Example 3: The business receives the Credit Card statement. The charges on the statement and the charges and in the *Credit Card Payable* Account are compared. If all the purchases made are record on the statement, including the gas purchase in Example 2, the only charge on the statement not posted, could be interest charged by the Credit Card Company.

The credit card statement must balance with the *Credit Card Payable* Account. Any purchases missed must be posted to the books as in Example 2. One new expense is included on the statement. The Credit Card Company has charged interest. Because I post each new purchase to the books, the companies balance and the credit card agree except for the interest charge. So the first thing I need to do is post the interest charge.

What Happen?

The Credit Card Company charged interest on the outstanding balance and the interest is a business expense. Post the amount of interest charged to the *Credit Card Payable* Account as a negative (-). The Account should reflect the purchases, charges and payments on the Credit Card Statement. The two should be a mirror image of each other. Account *Credit Card Payable* = Credit Card Statement.

a) The Account *Interest Expense – Credit Card* increases (+). Post the amount of interest charged by the credit card company as an expense.
b) A check is written to the Credit Card Company. The company's *Cash in the Bank* Account is reduced (-) by the amount of the check and *Credit Card Payable* Account decreased (+) by the amount of the payment.

The company purchased an item by using a credit card. Therefore, increasing the business liabilities (-) and increasing an expense (+). Business paid the debt by writing a check. Cash decreases (-) and the debt decreases (+). Walk through the transaction in your mind.

Suggestion: When setting up your Account Numbers, I suggest you have an *Interest Expense* Account for each bank, vehicle and credit card debt. At the end of the year lenders and Credit Card companies will send a 1099 Interest Statement; a copy goes to the IRS and is compared to your tax return. If you combine interest expense from several loans, checking the interest paid on various loans or credit cards is difficult.

Third Concept
Use Tunnel Vision

I have impressed upon you that every financial transaction has two sides; a debit and credit. As an example cash goes down in the bank and an expense cost goes up. Many times, when you are posting your computerized accounting program and a particular transaction will seem very confusing, I use the concept of Tunnel Vision. I solve the problem of posting of a transaction by looking at only one side of the transactional at a time.

Consider the Easy Side of the Transaction: If I write a check or use my debit card I know Cash in the Bank decreased. This entry is the easy side of the two posting. Cash in the bank decreased, we spent it.

Next I have to determine what happened to the money. What did I purchase? Did I pay a loan payment, an expense, inventory or wages? Most software programs will not allow you to continue until both sides of the transaction are posted. Using Tunnel Vision, I concentrate on what happen to the money.

If you are using a bookkeeper to help you each month, and you do not know where to post one side of any transaction, post it in an Account called *Suspense*. The bookkeeper or accountant then can correct the entry. If you post a transaction incorrectly, it's hard to track the problem.

If the money in the bank increases, that is the easy side of the entry. What other accounts are effected? Who paid the money and why? Is it income, a payment from a customer or maybe the money is a bank loan. I know my bank account went up, the easy side of the entry.

Do not follow the money: Many times clients attempt to follow the money. They borrow $1,000.00 from the bank to pay $980.00 of expenses.

1. The money from the bank loan is deposited into the company's checking account. *Cash in the Bank Cash* increases (+). The company owes the Bank so the <u>Account</u> *Bank Loan* increases (-). (Liabilities are negative so an increase in liability accounts is a minus (-). Using Tunnel vision – all that happen is the company borrowed money. You walked into the bank, signed a Note Payable and the banker deposited the amount of the loan into your business checking account.

2. The second operation involves paying the expense from your *Cash in the Bank* <u>Account</u>. Cash decreases (-) and an Expense increases (+). You can't follow the money. Two separate transactions occurred: (1) You borrowed money and (2) you paid the expense.

Fourth Concept
All Transactions have Equal Debits (+) and Credits (-).

This concept is simply an application of how Debits (+) and Credits (-) effect your financial Statements.

Use this as a tool for understanding how transactions affect a company's financial Statements. By adding and subtracting all the positive and negative <u>Account</u> balances, the total should be zero. Double Entry Bookkeeping requires that every time I post a debit I must post a credit in an equal amount.

All accounting software programs use the same theory, debits and credits. Some of these programs use 'Name Titles" for <u>Accounts</u>, most use 'Number Titles" for <u>Accounts</u>. However, both use Debits and credits. One major problem exist when the software program does not force the bookkeeper to pick the two separate <u>Accounts</u>, in other words posting your transactions 'Unbalanced'. Unbalanced postings are forced into a *Suspense* <u>Account</u>. Quick books titles this <u>Account</u>, *Owners Equity, I call it Suspense.* The <u>Account</u> is just a place where your software program forces a balancing entry. I have received Financial Statements prepared on Quick Books with thousands of dollars in this <u>Account</u>. Creative accounting cannot solve this problem.

As an example, the business buys office supples. The *Cash in the Bank* decreases (-). However, unless your software program is programmed correctly, the Debit (+) will be posted automatically to an Account named *Owners Equity,* or an Account named *Suspense*. If this condition continues your financial statements are useless, and an accountant must correct your transaction posting.

The first step of preparing your books requires hiring an experienced bookkeeper to set-up your books and provide training.

Example Transactions

Included below are nine financial transactions. Each transaction is reviewed three ways.

1. The financial transaction is described in detail. What happen?

2. Your entry into the bookkeeping system. The Accounts are affected either with a Debit or a Credit.

3. The Financial Statement is prepared after each example to demonstrate the effect the transaction has on the financial statement. The reader can see the changes as each transaction is posted.

Example 1

Opening a business checking account. Your first order of business is to open a business checking account. You need to transfer money from your personal account or record a bank loan into your new business checking account. Focus on the Business checking account. You deposit personal funds into your business checking account. You secure a bank loan, and those funds are deposited into your bank account.

Cash in the Bank is an Asset Account, a Debit (+). A Debit (+) to this Account increases the cash in the company checking account.

Owners' Equity is a Net Worth Account, a Credit (-). A Credit (-) to this Account increases the amount of equity (Value) the owner has in the company. You simply transferred your personal funds into the business checking account and created an equity position in the company.

Bank Loan Payable is a Liability Account, a Credit (-). Let's assume that you deposited $1,000.00 from your personal account and borrowed $2,500.00 from your bank. A Credit (-) to this Account increases the company's debt by $2,500.00.

Journal Entry Used to Post Transaction – Example 1

	Debit	Credit
Cash in Bank	3,500.00	
Bank Loan		2,500.00
Owners' Equity		1,000.00

Accounting instructors insist that you always record Debits first. What a bunch of crap! Record the easiest side of your entry first and then figure out the difficult side. Cash in Bank, Debit or Credit, is usually the easiest, so I usually start with the cash as my first entry.

Financial Statement after Posting Example 1 Transaction

BALANCE SHEET

Assets

Cash in Bank   3,500.00 (Debit)

TOTAL ASSETS   <u>3,500.00</u> (Debit)

Liabilities

Bank Loan Payable   2,500.00 (Credit)

TOTAL LIABILITIES   2,500.00 (Credit)

Net Worth or Equity

Owners' Equity   <u>1,000.00</u> (Credit)

TOTAL NET WORTH   <u>1,000.00</u>(Credit)

TOTAL LIABILITIES AND NET WORTH   <u>3,500.00</u> (Credit)

****

Example 2

Write a company check or present a company Debit Card for office supplies. Either payment reduces the cash in the business checking account. The office supplies will be consumed which creates an expense for the company.

Cash in Bank is an Asset <u>Account,</u> a Debit (+). A credit (-) to this <u>Account</u> reduces the amount in the bank. A check or debit card disbursement results in a decrease in *Cash in the Bank* <u>Account</u>.

Office Supply Expense is an Expense <u>Account,</u> a Debit (+). A Debit (+) to this <u>Account</u> increases the amount spent on office supplies.

Sometimes I tack on the word *Expense* when creating my General Ledger Expense <u>Accounts</u> because the word quickly denotes an expense. I have also been known to use the word Payable for liabilities. An <u>Account</u> located in the Liability section of the Financial Statement is a Liability automatically and therefore a payable because of the placement of the <u>Account</u>.

Journal Entry Used to Post Transaction – Example 2

	Debit	Credit
Cash in Bank		87.00
Office Supplies Expense	87.00	

Financial Statement after Posting Example 2 Transaction

BALANCE SHEET

Assets

Cash in Bank   3,413.00 (Debit)

TOTAL ASSETS   3,413.00 (Debit)

Liabilities

Bank Loan Payable   2,500.00 (Credit)

TOTAL LIABILITIES   2,500.00 (Credit)

Net Worth or Equity

Owners' Equity   1,000.00 (Credit)
Current Profit (Loss)   (87.00) (A Debit in a Credit section-Loss)

TOTAL NET WORTH   913.00(Credit)

TOTAL LIABILITIES AND NET WORTH   3,413.00 (Credit)

PROFIT AND LOSS STATEMENT

Sales

No Sales

Operating Expenses

Office Supplies Expense   87.00 (Debit)

TOTAL OPERATING EXPENSE   87.00 (Debit)

NET PROFIT (LOSS)   (87.00) (Debit)

Note: Did you notice that the Profit (Loss) is recorded in the Net Worth Section so the Balance Sheet
Balances? Remember when you total all the pluses (+) and minuses (-) in the General Ledger the total must be zero. However, in order for the Balance Sheet to 'Stand Alone,' you must include the Income Statement Profit or (Loss). Many times a Balance Sheets can provide more evidence as to the company's financial condition than the Income Statement. Cash or cash equivalents are so important for a company to survive if there are losses.

∗∗∗

Example 3

Purchasing a Business Vehicle. The business vehicle cost $12,500.00. The company makes a down payment of $1,000.00 and secures a loan for $11,500.00, you have an asset worth $12,500.00, a liability of $11,500.00 and your cash is decreased by $1,000.00. Three accounts are changed.

Cash in Bank is an Asset <u>Account</u>, a Debit (+). A Credit (-) to this <u>Account</u> reduces the amount in n the bank.

Transportation Equipment is an Asset <u>Account</u>, a Debit (+). This <u>Account</u> increases by the total cost of the Vehicle including sales tax and dealer fees. Since we are purchasing an Asset, the *Transportation Equipment* Asset <u>Account</u> increases by $12,500.00.

Vehicle Loan Payable is a Liability <u>Account</u>, a Credit (-). The company owes $11,500.00 which is recorded as a credit under liabilities. A credit to this <u>Account</u> increases the company's debt payable.

Journal Entry Used to Post Transaction – Example 3

	Debit	Credit
Cash in Bank		1,000.00
Transportation Equipment	12,500.00	
Vehicle Loan Payable		11,500.00

Financial Statement after Posting Example 3 Transaction

BALANCE SHEET

Assets

Cash in Bank	2,413.00	
Transportation Equipment	<u>12,500.00</u>	
TOTAL ASSETS		<u>14,913.00</u> (Debit)

Liabilities

Bank Loan Payable	2,500.00	
Vehicle Loan Payable	<u>11,500.00</u>	
TOTAL LIABILITIES		14,000.00 (Credit)

Net Worth or Equity

Owners' Equity	1,000.00
Current Profit (Loss)	(87.00)

TOTAL NET WORTH   913.00(Credit)

TOTAL LIABILITIES AND NET WORTH   14,913.00 (Credit)

Profit and Loss Statement

Sales

No Sales

OPERATING EXPENSES

   Office Supplies Expense   87.00 (Debit)

TOTAL OPERATING EXPENSE   87.00 (Debit)

NET PROFIT (LOSS)   (87.00) (Debit)

****

Example 4

Company makes a payment on the Bank Loan. A check is prepared, or the funds are electronically transferred to the lender. Bank balance will decrease. Loan payments involve paying principal and interest. Payment on the principal reduces the amount owed on the bank loan. Interest on a company loan is an expense therefore interest expense increases. The payment is divided between principal and interest. The monthly loan payment is $300.00. Principal is $262.00 and Interest is $38.00 as detailed from the lender's monthly invoice statement.

Cash in Bank is an Asset Account, a Debit (+). A credit to this Account reduces the amount in the bank.

Bank Loan Payable is a Liability Account, a Credit (-). A Debit (+) to this Account decreases the amount owed on the bank loan.

Interest Expense is an Expense Account, a Debit (+). A Debit (+) to this Account increases the businesses interest expense paid for the year.

Many times students have difficulty when posting loan payments. Loans are created when the lender deposits funds into the company's bank account or the lender pays a third party for a large purchase such as vehicles or equipment. Using Tunnel Vision I post the loan payable when the debt is incurred. Payment of the debt usually requires paying the principle and interest charged. For both

Journal Entry Used to Post Transaction – Example 4

                         Debit   Credit

143

Cash in Bank		300.00
Bank Loan Payable	262.00	
Interest Expense	38.00	

Financial Statement after Posting Example 4 Transaction

BALANCE SHEET

Assets

Cash in Bank	2,113.00	
Transportation Equipment	12,500.00	
TOTAL ASSETS		14,613.00 (Debit)

Liabilities

Bank Loan Payable	2,238.00	
Vehicle Loan Payable	11,500.00	
TOTAL LIABILITIES		13,738.00 (Credit)

Net Worth or Equity

Owners' Equity	1,000.00	
Current Profit (Loss)	(125.00)	
TOTAL NET WORTH		875.00 (Credit)

TOTAL LIABILITIES AND NET WORTH   14,613.00 (Credit)

PROFIT AND LOSS STATEMENT

Sales

No Sales

OPERATING EXPENSES

Office Supplies Expense	87.00	
Interest Expense	38.00	
TOTAL OPERATING EXPENSE		125.00 (Debit)

NET PROFIT (LOSS)   (125.00) (Debit)

****

Example 5

The company has Service Sales of $5,000.00. $3,000.00 is received, and the company extends credit to the customer for $2,000.00, payable in 30 days. Sales income increases. We received $3,000.00 so our bank balance increases. The customer owes the company $2,000.00, the accounts receivable. (A record of money owed the company for credit sales)

Cash in the Bank is an Asset Account, a Debit (+) Account. A Debit (+) to this Account increases the amount in the bank.

Income – Professional Services is an Income Account, a Credit (-). A credit (-) to this Account increases your sales income.

Accounts Receivable is an Asset Account, A Debit (+). A Debit (+) to this Account increases the amount of customer due from customers.

The Income Account is a negative number. Does not make sense but must be accepted. Within the Income Statement, Income is a negative and Customer Refund is a positive resulting in net income.

Journal Entry Used to Post Transaction – Example 5

	Debit	Credit
Income – Professional Services		5,000.00
Cash in the Bank	3,000.00	
Accounts Receivable	2,000.00	

Financial Statement after Posting Example 5 Transaction

BALANCE SHEET

Assets

Cash in Bank	5,113.00
Accounts Receivable	2,000.00
Transportation Equipment	12,500.00

TOTAL ASSETS   19,613.00 (Debit)

Liabilities

Bank Loan Payable	2,238.00
Vehicle Loan Payable	11,500.00

TOTAL LIABILITIES   13,738.00 (Credit)

Net Worth or Equity

Owners' Equity	1,000.00	
Current Profit (Loss)	4,875.00	

TOTAL NET WORTH   5,875.00 (Credit)

TOTAL LIABILITIES AND NET WORTH   19,613.00 (Credit)

PROFIT AND LOSS STATEMENT

Sales

Sales – Professional Services   5,000.00 (Credit)

Total Income   5,000.00 (Credit)

Operating Expenses

Office Supplies Expense	87.00	
Interest Expense	38.00	

TOTAL OPERATING EXPENSE   125.00 (Debit)

NET PROFIT (LOSS)   4,875.00 (Credit)

✱✱✱

Example 6

Purchasing gas for the company car with the company credit card. Cost the Gas is $92.50. Vehicle Expense–Gas increases. Credit Card Payable increases. Also purchased are pens (office supplies) for the office. Cost of the pens is $7.22. Office supply expense increases.

Credit Card Payable is a Liability Account, a Credit (-). A Credit (-) to this Account increases the debt owed to the Credit Card Company (A lender). You Credit (-) this Account for $99.72.

Vehicle Expense-Gas is an Expense Account, a Debit (+). A Debit (+) to this Account increases the amount the business has spent for vehicle cost. Debit (+) this Account for $92.50.

Office Supply Expense is an Expense Account, a Debit (+). A Debit (+) to this Account increases the amount the business has spent for office supplies. Debit (+) this Account for $7.22.

Usually, amounts charged to the company credit card are posted when the Credit Card Statement is received. A credit card company similar to Visa or

Master Charge is simply a lender, extending credit to the firm. Credit card purchases are usually expensed and the credit extended by the Credit Card Company is a liability thus *Credit Card Payable*. The monthly interest charge is another expense.

As we review each finished financial statement, you should realize that each Account starting with the *Cash in the Bank* Account through the *Owner's Equity* Account matches outside information. The account balances reflect exactly the correct balances on supporting documents. When reviewing a Balance Sheet check the following supporting documents:

➢ *Cash in the Bank* Account balances with Bank Statement. Balance this Account once a Month.

➢ *Accounts Receivable* Account balances with Sub-Ledger of customer aging Accounts Receivable. Software program prints an aging report of customer balances.

➢ *Transportation Vehicles* Account balances with Vehicle purchase documents.

➢ *Bank Loan Payable* Account balances with monthly loan invoice or statement received from the lender. The monthly statement reflects the loan balance and monthly or yearly interest amount.

➢ *Credit Card Payable* Account balances with monthly Credit Card Statements. Each month post any line items not included in expense Accounts. Interest is calculated by the Credit Card Company and needs to be posted.

Receiving a Financial Statements that the Accounts do not balance with the supporting documents is useless. Many year-end statements I receive from bookkeepers and owners are not balanced against supporting documents.

Every month the business owner should demand that the Balances Sheet Accounts balance.

Journal Entry Used to Post Transaction – Example 6

	Debit	Credit
Credit Card Payable		99.72
Vehicle Expense - Gas	92.50	
Office Supplies	7.22	

Financial Statement after Posting Example 6 Transaction

BALANCE SHEET

Assets

Cash in Bank	5,113.00
Accounts Receivable	2,000.00
Transportation Equipment	12,500.00

TOTAL ASSETS   19,613.00

Liabilities

Credit Card Payable	99.72
Bank Loan Payable	2,238.00
Vehicle Loan Payable	11,500.00

TOTAL LIABILITIES   13,837.72

Net Worth or Equity

Owners' Equity	1,000.00
Current Profit (Loss)	4,775.28

TOTAL NET WORTH   5,775.28

TOTAL LIABILITIES AND NET WORTH   19,613.00

PROFIT AND LOSS STATEMENT

Sales Income

Income – Professional Services   5,000.00

TOTAL INCOME   5,000.00

OPERATING EXPENSES

Office Supplies Expense	94.22
Interest Expense	38.00
Vehicle Expense – Gas	92.50

TOTAL OPERATING EXPENSE   224.72

NET PROFIT (LOSS)   4,775.28

✱✱

Example 7

Employee prepares an expense report for business expenses personally. The company writes a check to the employee for the business expenses. Cash in the bank decreases and the various expenses accounts are increased.

148

Included are business Millage for the business use of the employee's personal vehicle, office supplies purchased with employee's personal credit card and for a lunch the employee paid for with cash. The checking account, the credit card and of course the cash are the employee's money. He is responsible for paying these amounts. The employee request payment for the following expenses: Use of personal vehicle, company business at 56.5 cents a mile (2014 IRS amount allowed) for 683 miles or $385.90, Office supplies purchased for the company in the amount of $114.00 and client entertainment of $56.31 for a total of $556.21.

Cash in the Bank is an Asset Account, a Debit (+). A Credit (-) to this Account reduces the amount in the bank.

Employee Millage Expense is an Expense Account, a Debit (+). A Debit (+) to this Account increases the amount the company has paid to any employee, including officers, for the business use of a personal vehicle.

Office Supplies Expense is an Expense Account, A Debit (+). A Debit (+) to this Account, increases the business office supply cost.

Entertainment Expense is an Expense Account, A Debit (+). A Debit (+) to this Account increases the amount the company has spent on business entertainment.

Journal Entry Used to Post Transaction – Example 7

	Debit	Credit
Cash in Bank		556.21
Employee Millage Expense	385.90	
Office supplies Expenses	114.00	
Entertainment Expense	56.31	

Financial Statement after Posting Example 7 Transaction

BALANCE SHEET

Asset

Cash in Bank	4,556.79
Accounts Receivable	2,000.00
Transportation Equipment	12,500.00

TOTAL ASSETS   19,056.79

Liabilities

Bank Loan Payable	2,238.00
Vehicle Loan Payable	11,500.00

149

TOTAL LIABILITIES   13,738.00

Net Worth or Equity

Owners' Equity   1,000.00
Current Profit (Loss)   4,219.07

TOTAL NET WORTH   5,219.07

TOTAL LIABILITIES AND NET WORTH   19,056.79

PROFIT AND LOSS STATEMENT

Sales Income

Income – Professional Services   5,000.00

TOTAL INCOME   5,000.00

Operating Expenses

Entertainment Expense   56.31
Office Supplies Expense   208.22
Interest Expense   38.00
Vehicle Expense – Employee   385.90
Vehicle Expense – Gas & Oil   92.50

TOTAL OPERATING EXPENSE   780.93

NET PROFIT (LOSS)   4,219.07

Note: Business charges to a personal credit card must be recorded on an employee expense report for reimbursement. The credit card liability is the employee's responsibility and not a business liability. Do not pay an employee's Credit Card Expenses. Only pay an expense report. Remember do not charge personal expenses on a business credit card. The bookkeeping becomes almost impossible when you co-mingle personal and business charges on a business credit card. Business expenses charged on a business credit and Credit Card Interest are 100% deductible. A credit card is nothing more than borrowing money to buy and pay business expenses.

****

EXAMPLE 8

Bookkeeping for wages or salaries paid can be confusing. The IRS has determined that preparing payroll checks and completing the tax forms you are required to file can take 27 hours per month. Unless your hire an outside bookkeeping service or a payroll service, you must learn how wages are posted to your books. As an S-Corporation you are required to take a salary or wages. Let's walk through a simple payroll bookkeeping process. In this example, we are paying an employee monthly the amount of $3000.00. Usually, you need to withhold from these wages (A) Federal Income Tax, (B) Social Security Taxes, (C) Medicare Texas and (D) State Income Taxes.

The IRS provides withholding tables for all employees either single or married, by the week, semi-monthly or monthly. Review the charts and determine the Federal Tax to withhold from the employee's pay. The Table for this employee requires us to withhold $282.00 in Federal Income tax. Withhold 6.2% of the wages for Social Security Tax or $186.00. Withhold Medicare - 1.45%, $43.50 and Withhold State Income Tax (If it applies) per the State furnished Tables. We have determined that the Tables require us to withhold $184.00 for State Income Tax.

Gross Wages	3,000.00	
Federal Withholding For Income Tax	282.00	
Social Security Tax Withheld 6.2%	186.00	
Medicare Tax Withheld	43.50	
State Income Tax Withheld	184.00	
Total Withheld		695.50
Net Payroll		2,304.50

Note: Special rules exist for employee's receiving TIP income. Contact you accountant.

Note: Remember the amounts withheld from an employee wages are considered 'Trust Funds' and you are the trustee responsible for transferring these amounts to the IRS as the IRS requires. (See IRS deposit requirements)

As an employer, you are required to match amounts withheld from an employee's wages for Social Security and Medicare. In this example, Social Security and Medicare total $229.50. You are required to make an IRS deposit of $282.00 (Federal Tax Withheld) and $459.00 (Social Security and Medicare withheld and the matching amounts) for a total IRS deposit of $$741.00.

Cash in Bank is an Asset Account, a Debit (+). A credit (-) to this Account reduces the amount in the bank. Net wages paid is $2,304.50.

Federal Income Tax Payable is a Liability Account, a Credit (-). A credit to this Account increases the amount the company owes the IRS for withholding income tax of $282.00.

Social Security Tax & *Medicare Tax Payable* is a Liability Account, a Credit (-). A credit to this Account increases the amount the company owes the IRS for withholding Social Security Tax and Medicare Tax from the employee's wages of $229.50.

State Income Tax Payable is a Liability <u>Account</u>, a Credit (-). A credit to this <u>Account</u> increases the amount the company owes the State for withholding State income of $184.00. You are also a trustee for the State Income Tax Withheld.

Wage Expense – Staff is an Expense <u>Account</u>, a Debit (+). A Debit (+) to this <u>Account</u> increases the amount of total wages paid to an employee of $3,000.00.

Note: As an employer you are required to match the Social Security Tax, and Medicare Tax withheld from an employee's wages. In this example, the amount of $229.50 is due the IRS as a matching amount. This amount is a legal obligation to the company. The amount owing is not a Trust Amount nor is it a payroll roll amount. It is an expense to the company. Social Security and Medicare is a total of 7.65%. This expense is posted to an <u>Account</u> called *Payroll Tax Expense*. At any time, you can check the balance of this account by multiplying 7.65% times gross wages paid.

Social Security Tax & Medicare Tax Payable is a Liability <u>Account</u>, a credit (-). A credit to this <u>Account</u> increases the amount the company owes the IRS for the requirements of matching withheld Social Security Tax and Medicare Tax from an Employees Wages. In this example, the amount of $229.50 was withheld, and the company must match that account.

Payroll Tax Expense is an Expense <u>Account</u>, a Debit (+). A Debit to this <u>Account</u> increases the company costs. The ccompany must match the payroll taxes for Social Security and Medicare withheld. $229.50 must be matched by the company.

Journal Entry Used to Post Transaction – Example 8

	Debit	Credit
Wage Expense – Staff	3,000.00	
Cash in the Bank		2,304.50
Federal Income Tax Payable		282.00
Social Security Tax and Medicare Tax Payable		229.50
State Income Tax Payable		84.00
Payroll Tax Expense	229.50	
Social Security Tax and Medicare Tax Payable		229.50

Financial Statement after Posting Example 8 Transaction

BALANCE SHEET

Assets

Cash in Bank	2,252.29

152

Accounts Receivable	2,000.00	
Transportation Equipment	12,500.00	
TOTAL ASSETS		16,752.29

Liabilities

Federal Tax Withheld Payable	282.00	
Soc. Sec & Med Withheld Tax Pay	459.00	
State Tax Withheld Payable	184.00	
Credit Card Payable	99.72	
Bank Loan Payable	2,238.00	
Vehicle Loan Payable	11,500.00	
TOTAL LIABILITIES		14,762.72

Net Worth or Equity

Owners' Equity	1,000.00	
Current Profit (Loss)	989.57	
TOTAL NET WORTH		1,989.57
TOTAL LIABILITIES AND NET WORTH		16,752.29

PROFIT AND LOSS STATEMENT

Sales Income

Income – Professional Services	5,000.00	
TOTAL INCOME		5,000.00

Operating Expenses

Entertainment – Business	56.31	
Interest Expense	38.00	
Office Supplies Expense	208.22	
Salaries – Staff	3,000.00	
Taxes – Employer Payroll	229.50	
Vehicle Expense – Employee Miles	385.90	
Vehicle Expense – Gas & Oil	92.50	
TOTAL OPERATING EXPENSE		4,010.43
NET PROFIT (LOSS)		989.57

****

Example 9

Inventory is purchased at wholesale or dealer cost. A retail business or a restaurant accumulate inventory and the cost is recorded in an Asset <u>Account</u> named *Inventory-food* or *Inventory-Merchandise.* Inventory is expensed as sold or as with a restaurant, as consumed. The inventory Account reflects the dollar cost of inventory available for sale. As sales occur the cost of inventory sold is transferred from the Inventory Account, an asset account, to cost of goods sold and expense account. In this example, the company purchases T-Shirts with the companies logo. 100 T-Shirts are purchased for $2.00 each. 12 T-Shirts are sold for $6.00 each.

Cash in Bank is an Asset <u>Account,</u> a Debit (+). A credit (-) to this <u>Account</u> reduces the amount in the bank.

Inventory - T-shirts is an Asset <u>Account,</u> a Debit (+). A Debit (+) to this <u>Account</u> increases the dollar amount of T-Shirt inventory available for sale.

Note: The accounting concept called 'Matching,' is defined as matching the cost of goods sold or consumed (as in a restaurant or a retail outlet) against sales income received. The cost of inventory sold is transferred to an Expense <u>Account</u> named *Cost of Goods Sold*. In this example, 100 T-Shirts were purchased at a cost of $2.00 each. The 12 T-shirts sold cost $2.00 times 12 or $24.00. The T-Shirts were sold for $6.00 each.

Income – T-Shirt Sales is an Income <u>Account,</u> a Credit (-). A Credit to this <u>Account</u> increases sales income.

Cash in the Bank is an Asset <u>Account,</u> a Debit (+). A Debit (+) to this <u>Account</u> increases the bank balance.

Inventory – T-Shirts is an Asset <u>Account,</u> a Debit (+). When inventory is sold or consumed, the cost amount of the item sold or consumed is transferred to *Cost of Goods Sold*. When this <u>Account</u> is credited (-), inventory available is reduced. A Credit to this <u>Account</u> decreases the Inventory Balance.

Cost of Goods Sold is an Expense Account, a Debit (+). A Debit (+) to this <u>Account</u> increases the cost of inventory sold expense. Cost of Goods Sold is expense <u>Accounts</u>.

Journal Entry Used to Post Transaction – Example 9

	Debit	Credit
Cash in Bank		200.00
Inventory – T-Shirts	200.00	
Cost of Goods Sold	24.00	
Inventory – T-Shirts		24.00
Cash in Bank	72.00	

Income – T-Shirt Sales   72.00

Financial Statement after Posting Example 9 Transaction

BALANCE SHEET

Assets

Cash in Bank	2,124.29
Inventory – T-Shirts	176.00
Accounts Receivable	2,000.00
Transportation Equipment	12,500.00

TOTAL ASSETS   16,800.29

Liabilities

Federal Tax Withheld Payable	282.00
Soc. Sec & Med Withheld Payable	459.00
State Tax Withheld Payable	184.00
Credit Card Payable	99.72
Bank Loan Payable	2,238.00
Vehicle Loan Payable	11,500.00

TOTAL LIABILITIES   14,762.72

Net Worth or Equity

Owners' Equity	1,000.00
Current Profit (Loss)	989.57

TOTAL NET WORTH   1,989.57

TOTAL LIABILITIES AND NET WORTH   16,752.29

PROFIT AND LOSS STATEMENT

Sales Income

Income – Professional Services   5,000.00

TOTAL INCOME   5,000.00

Operating Expenses

Entertainment – Business	56.31
Interest Expense	38.00
Office Supplies Expense	208.22
Salaries – Staff	3,000.00

Taxes – Employer Payroll	229.50	
Vehicle Expense – Employee Miles	385.90	
Vehicle Expense – Gas & Oil	92.50	

TOTAL OPERATING EXPENSE   4,010.43

NET PROFIT (LOSS)   989.57

Inventory and Cost of Goods Sold

The actual cost of the item sold can be determined by the cost of each item sold. However, many times it is impossible to determine the exact cost of the inventory consumed or products sold, mainly for a restaurant or a bar. The following formula is used to prepare your business tax return, Schedule C, Corporation or LLC. to determine the exact cost of *Cost of Goods Sold*.

Each year, on the 1st of January count and price the inventory. Cost may be difficult for some items because of replenishing the inventory throughout the year. Use the last purchase cost basis which is considered "Last-in and first-out" inventory valuation.

Post your inventory purchases into an *Inventory* Account. The starting inventory at cost plus new inventory purchased would be 100% of the inventory that was or is available for sale, throughout the year.

Instead of taking a physical inventory each month, use an estimated Cost of Goods Sold, based upon sales. Each month this calculated amount reduces the physical inventory and increases the Cost of Goods sold Account.

At the end of the year prepare a complete inventory at cost. Count and price out each inventory item. Again use the last-in and First-out as the cost basis.

Use the December 31 inventory basis to correct the *Cost of Goods Sold* Account. Throughout the year, the inventory was adjusted, and cost of goods sold was computed using the estimated value. Once the final inventory is available you can compute a corrected *Cost of Goods Sold*.

Starting Inventory- January 1	2,500.00	
Total yearly Purchases	3,580.00	
Total Inventory Available For Sale		6,080.00
Ending Inventory – December 31		3,640.00
Cost of Goods Sold for the year		2,440.00

For the determination or the monthly Cost of Goods Sold amount, usually a percent of sales is used. If the sales for the above equation are $9,272.00 the percent would be $2,440 (divided by) $9,272 = 26.316%. Each month the amount of 26.316% of the gross sales income would be used as Cost of Goods

Sold. The actual Cost of Goods Sold would be corrected when an actual inventory is taken at year end.

Accounting Operating Procedures

Bookkeeping is a system which accounts for Deposits and Disbursements. Internal operating procedures provides business owners a formal structure within the organization that protects the company's assets and creates confidence in the Financial Statements. If the accounting procedures are trusted, the business's Financial Statement is trusted. Contrary to belief, a CPA audit is conducted to determine if the accounting procedures can be trusted. A CPA audit is not completed to discover a crime. Special test are performed on the accounting procedures to identify problem areas or determine that the Financial Statements represent the financial position of the company.

Although it is preferred that business owners personally handle deposits and disbursements, the operating procedures must be established which will allow the owner to delegate specific tasks and still maintain control of the company's finances. Protecting your assets is only one-half of the job required of good operating procedures. A primary ingredient of any operating system is the organized flow of financial documents such as checks, deposit slips, invoices and record keeping to ensure that your financial statements are accurate. This handbook cannot provide you with an internal operating system and procedure which will protect your money and provide you with correct and current financial information. You and your bookkeeper, accountant and CPA should set up your internal operating procedures to protect your money from thief and embezzlement and provide you with the financial information you need to make the day to day business decisions.

Business owners use accounting to record and report various pieces of financial information. Accounting procedures are also designed to create Internal Control of the company's assets by providing guidelines and procedures for business owners and employees. Internal controls are another important small business function by creating safeguards to protect the assets and financial information.

Hiring Bookkeepers

One of the fastest and easiest way to determine the competency when interviewing a qualified bookkeeper is to use a short test. You do not need a test with a 100 questions because ten questions will weed out the poorly trained applicants.

Test Potential Bookkeepers: I have reviewed a company called Accounting Coach that provides online bookkeeping training and testing. They provide Bookkeeping Exam Questions which you can use to qualify a bookkeeper applicant or even test the knowledge of a Bookkeeping Service. It appears that the company provides a needed service to the Bookkeeping Profession and for selecting an employee. I do not endorse this company only because I have not used their services. As with any on-line company complete your due-diligence before sending anyone money. I always use a Credit Card, not a Debit Card when making purchases on-line. Several times I have requested my credit card company to reverse a charge.

If you feel uncomfortable hiring an on-line company, below are ten basic bookkeeping questions with answers you can use to test an applicant. A more comprehensive test should be added.

Bookkeepers Test

One of the fastest and easiest way to determine the competency when interviewing a bookkeeper applicant is to require a test. You do not need a test with a 100 questions because the ten questions below will weed out the poorly trained accountants.

1. How do you post a loan payment for a company owned vehicle? (Pick One)

   A. Debit - *Loan Payable*, Credit - *Cash in the Bank* and Credit - *Vehicle Expense*.

   B. Debit - *Loan Payable-Vehicle*, Credit - *Cash in the Bank* and Debit - *Interest Expense*.

   C. Credit - *Cash in the Bank*, Debit - *Vehicle Expense* and Debit - Interest Expense.

   D. Credit - *Loan Payable - Vehicle*, Credit - *Cash in the Bank* and Debit - *Loan Cost*.

2. Prepare a Journey Entry for the following: Wages - $1,000.00, Federal Tax Withheld - $158.00, Social Security withheld - $ 62.00, Medicare withheld - $14.50, Payroll Garnishment for IRS - $82.00, State Tax withheld - $55.00. Net check amount: 645.50. Employer Social Security expense - $62.00 and Employer Medicare expense - $14.50.

Account Name	Debit	(Credit)
Cash in the Bank	_____	_____
Social Security Expense	_____	_____
Medicare Expense	_____	_____
Social Security Payable	_____	_____
Medicare Payable	_____	_____

Federal Income Tax W/H Payable   _____   _____

IRS Garnishment Payable   _____   _____

Wages Expenses – Employee   _____   _____

State Income Tax WH. Payable   _____   _____

3. How do your post an owner's expense report with business entertainment, motel expense and Airline Expense. Company issued a check to the owner. (Pick one)

   A. Post 50% business entertainment expense because the IRS only allows 50% of business entertainment as an expense.

   B. Credit - *Owner Payable*, Credit – *Travel-Lodging Expense*, Debit – *Employee Expense* Account, Debit – *Entertainment & Meal Expense.*

   C. Debit - *Entertainment & Meal Expense*, Debit - *Travel-Lodging Expense*, Debit – *Travel - Transportation Expense*, Credit - *Owner Payable.*

   D. Debit - 50% Entertainment & Meal Expense, Debit Owners Payable, Credit - Travel Expense, and Debit - Travel-Lodging Expense.

4. Health Insurance is deductible for the 100% owner/officer of a qualified S-Corporation.

   TRUE   FALSE

5. Prepare Journal Entry for a cash sale of a company computer. Cost of Computer - $800.00, Sales price and cash received - $300.00, Accumulated depreciation – 250.00

Account Name	Debit	Credit
Cash in the Bank	_____	_____
Capital Equipment Sale	_____	_____
Cost of the Computer	_____	_____
Equipment – Office	_____	_____
Depreciation taken on Computer	_____	_____
Accumulated Depreciation	_____	_____

6. Employee Medical, liability and vehicle insurance should be posted to one expense account. (Circle True or False)

TRUE   FALSE

7. How do you post a payment for liability insurance paid one year in advance? When paid and when expensed. (Pick one)

A. **Paid:** Credit - *Cash in Bank*, Debit - *Insurance Expense–Liability*, **Expensed:** Debit - *Pre-Paid Insurance*, Credit - *Cash in the Bank*.

B. **Paid:** Debit - *Cash in the Bank*, Credit - *Insurance Expense–Liability*, **Expensed:** Debit - *Pre-Paid Insurance*, Credit - *Cash in the Bank*.

C. **Paid:** Credit - *Cash in the Bank*, Debit - *Pre-paid Insurance–Liability*. **Expensed:** Credit - *Pre-Paid Insurance*, Debit - Insurance Expense – Liability.

D. **Paid:** Debit - *Cash in the Bank*, Credit - Insurance Expense-Other, **Expensed:** Debit -*Insurance Expense – Liability*, Credit – Pre-Paid Insurance.

8. The IRS requires payments to any sub-contractor in excess of $600.00 in one year to be sent a W-1099 Misc. (Circle True or False)

TRUE   FALSE

9. *Owners' Equity* and *Profit for the Period* are what type of Accounts?

A. Assets
B. Net Worth
C. Liability
D. Expenses

10. Assets are always posted at Cost?

TRUE   FALSE

Answers to the bookkeepers Test

1. How do you post a loan payment for a company owned vehicle? (Pick One)

B. Debit - *Loan Payable-Vehicle*, Credit - *Cash in the Bank* and Debit - *Interest Expense*.

2. Prepare a Journey Entry for the following: Wages - $1,000.00, Federal Tax Withheld - $158.00, Social Security withheld - $ 62.00, Medicare withheld

- $14.50, Payroll Garnishment for IRS - $82.00, State Tax withheld - $55.00. Net check amount: 645.50. Employer Social Security expense - $62.00 and Employer Medicare expense - $14.50.

Account Name	Debit	(Credit)
Cash in the Bank		628.50
Social Security Expense	62.00	
Medicare Expense	14.50	
Social Security Payable		124.00
Medicare Payable		29.00
Federal Income Tax W/H Payable		158.00
IRS Garnishment Payable		82.00
Wages Expenses – Employee	1,000.00	
State Tax Payable		55.00

3. How do your post an owner's expense report with business entertainment, motel expense and Airline Expense. Company issued a check to the owner. (Pick one)

C. Debit - *Entertainment & Meal Expense*, Debit - *Travel-Lodging Expense*, Debit – *Travel - Transportation Expense*, Credit - *Owner Payable*.

4. Health Insurance is deductible for the 100% owner/officer of a qualified S-Corporation.

   TRUE   FALSE

5. Prepare Journal Entry for a cash sale of a company computer. Cost of Computer - $800.00, Sales price and cash received - $300.00, Accumulated depreciation – 250.00

Account Name	Debit	Credit
Cash in the Bank	300.00	
Capital Equipment Sale		300.00
Cost of the Computer (Expense)	800.00	
Equipment – Office		800.00
Accumulated Depreciation	250.00	
Depreciation taken on Computer (Expense)		250.00

6. Employee Medical, liability and vehicle insurance should be posted to one expense account. (Circle True or False)

   TRUE   ***FALSE***

7. How do you post a payment for liability insurance paid one year in advance? When paid and when expensed. (Pick one)

   C. <u>Paid</u>: Credit - *Cash in the Bank*, <u>Debit</u> - *Pre-paid Insurance–Liability*. Expensed: <u>Credit</u> – *Pre-Paid Insurance*, <u>Debit</u> - Insurance Expense – Liability.

8. The IRS requires payments to any sub-contractor in excess of $600.00 in one year to be sent a W-1099 Misc. (Circle True or False)

   TRUE   ***FALSE***

9. *Owners' Equity* and *Profit for the Period* are what type of <u>Accounts</u>?

   B. Net Worth

10. Assets are always posted at Cost?

   TRUE   ***FALSE***

© Randy Glasbergen
glasbergen.com

"The government is doing you a favor. If they didn't
take most of your money, you'd have to find time
in your busy schedule to spend it yourself."

Chapter 7
BUSINESS INCOME,
DEDUCTIONS & TAX TIPS
The Essential Small Business Handbook
The best and most complete handbook for the Small Business Entrepreneur
Essential information for starting, buying, operating and succeeding

Basic Financial Statements
Recap

<u>Accounts</u> - Different classifications of Products or Services sold

Operating Expenses – (Category)
<u>Accounts</u> - Different classifications of the companies Expenses

Each <u>Account</u> in the <u>Chart of Accounts</u> is assigned a name or a number by which it can be identified. Some bookkeeping software use only a "Name" recognition and other accounting programs allow the used to assign <u>Account</u> Numbers for each <u>Account</u>. Below is a standard <u>Chart of Accounts</u>:

CHART OF ACCOUNTS

Current Assets - Account Numbers 10000 - 14999

10050 - Petty Cash Fund
10100 - Cash in the Bank – Checking
10150 – Cash in the Bank - Savings
12100 - Accounts Receivable
13100 - Inventory

Non-Current Assets – Account Numbers 15000 - 19999

15100 - Land
15100 - Buildings
15500 - Equipment
16000 - Vehicles
16500 - Trucks
18100 - Accumulated Depreciation - Buildings
18300 - Accumulated Depreciation - Equipment
18800 - Accumulated Depreciation - Vehicles

Current Liabilities - Account Numbers 20000 - 24999

20100 - Accounts Payable
20300 – Federal W/H & Payroll Tax payable
20400 – State Withholding Payable
20500 – Sales Tax Payable
20600 – State Unemployment Payable

Copyright ©

20700 – State Unemployment payable
21200 - Notes Payable (Current Amount)
22600 – Officer/Owner Note Payable

Long-term Liabilities - Account Numbers 25000 29999

25100 - Mortgage Loan Payable
25600 – Note payable
25650 – Office/Owner Note Payable

Net Worth - Equity - Account Numbers 30000- 39999

30100 - Distribution of Profit (S-Corporation)
30200 – Owners Equity (Sole Proprietorship)
30300 – Partners/Members Equity (Partnership or LLC)
30400 – Shareholders Equity (C Corporation)
31000 – Common Stock
27500 Retained Earnings

Operating Revenues -Account Numbers 4000-49000

40100 - Sales Revenue – Product or Category #1
40200 – Sales Revenue – Product of Category #2

Cost of Goods Sold (COGS) - Account Numbers 50000 - 59999

41010 COGS - Division #1,
41022 COGS - Division #1,
42015 COGS – Product or Category
43110 COGS – Product or Category

Operation Cost – Account Numbers 6000 – 79999

60100 - Accounting & Bookkeeping Expense
60200 - Advertising Cost
60250 - Answering Service
61000 - Attorney Fees
61100 - Bad Debt Expense
61500 - Bank Service Fees
60650 - Bribes, Illegal Acts & Kickbacks
60700 - Casualty Losses
60800 - Cell Telephone
61000 - Charitable Contributions – Business
61050 - Cleaning, Cleaning Supplies & Janitorial Cost
61100 - Club Dues
61200 – Commissions & Fees
61500 - Contract Services
61550 - Dues & Subscriptions
61600 - Educational Expenses

61660 - Employee Awards, Bonuses & Gifts
61700 - Employee Benefits Plans
61800 - Employee Expense – Vehicle Millage
62000 - Entertainment – Business
62100 - Gifts – Employees & Clients
62200 - Home Office Expense
63000 - Insurance Expense – Liability
63050 - Insurance Expense – Medical
63100 - Insurance Expense - Officer Medical
63150 - Insurance Expense - Workers Compensation
63300 - Interest Expense – Credit Cards
63400 - Interest Expense – Lender Loans
64000 - Internet Fees
64100 - Lease – Equipment & Tools
64200 - Lease – Office
64250 - Lease - Warehouse & Storage Facilities
64500 – Miscellaneous Expense
64600 - Office Supplies
64800 - Operating Supplies
65000 - Parking & Tolls
65100 - Pest Control
65200 - Postage, Freight & Delivery
65300 - Printing & Reproduction
65500 - Repairs & Maintenance
68000 - Salaries – Officers
68500 - Salaries – Staff
70000 - Sanitation – Trash Removal
70100 - Security Systems
71000 - Taxes – Employer FICA & Medicare Cost
71200 - Taxes – Federal Unemployment:
71250 - Taxes – Property
71300 - Taxes – State Unemployment
72000 - Telephone Expense
73000 - Travel – Lodging
73050 - Travel – Meals & Tips
73070 - Travel – Transportation
74000 - Utilities
75000 - Vehicle – Gas, Oil
75040 - Vehicle – Insurance
75080 - Vehicle – Repairs & Maintenance
75100 - Vehicle – Wash & Wax

Other Income and Expense – Account Numbers 80000-89999

80100 – Interest Income
80500 – Gain (Loss) - Sale of Asset

The above Chart of Accounts is a sample of many Accounts you will need posting your bookkeeping. Many times accountants create Sub Accounts.

Basic Accounting and Bookkeeping Information

Cash Method of Accounting: I recommend that the Small Businesses use the Cash Method for internal bookkeeping. The Cash Method of Accounting can be viewed as money-in and money–out. If the Small Business sells merchandise requiring an inventory use the Hybrid Method of Accounting for Financial Statements and Cash Accounting for the preparation of the Business Tax Return.

Accounting Method for Small Business Tax Returns: Usually, a Small Business will prepare their tax return using the Cash Method of Accounting. A Small Businesses with gross receipts less than one-million can prepare their Business Tax Return using the Cash Accounting Method.

The Cash method of accounting is money-in and money-out. Post deposits when received and post disbursements when made. There are special IRS rules and regulations concerning Cash Accounting versus Accrual Accounting depending upon gross receipts and if the company maintains an inventory of merchandise for sale.

Accountable Plan: Reimbursements received by an employee for travel, meals or entertainment expenses, are receipted under an Accountable Plan and the amount received is not includable in the employee wages. However, the ordinary and necessary expenses are fully deductible by the employer. The term "Accountable" merely requires that the employee to detail the business expenses and support such costs with backup receipts or some other form of proof. If the business expense meets the definition of ordinary and necessary, those expenses can be reimbursed to an employee under an Accountable Plan. An ordinary expense is one that is common and accepted in your trade or business.

The IRS has three rules regarding a qualified Accountable Plan:

➢ Your expenses must have a business connection; you must have paid or incurred deductible expenses while performing services as an employee of their company.
➢ You must account to your employer for expenses within a reasonable period.
➢ Excess cash advance allowance must be returned within a reasonable time.

Non-Accountable Plan: Business expenses reimbursed under a Non-accountable plan are treated as taxable wages or treated as contract services to the employee or independent contractor. As an example: If your company pays you a flat $500.00 per month for 'business travel', the yearly amount of $6,000.00 will be included in the W-2 as employee's wages. Of course, wages are subject to Social Security, Medicare, and payroll taxes. Wages are subject to matching Social Security and Medicare taxes by the employer. An employer

166

may be responsible for worker's compensation insurance cost on the Non-accountable amounts paid when the payment is converted to wages.

TAX TIP

Use an Accountable Plan. The employee receives reimbursement for all ordinary, and necessary expense items. The amount is not taxable to the employee and is fully deductible to the employer within IRS limits. (Meals and Entertainment expenses are 50% deductible.)

TAX TIP

Employee Tip: When an employee receives Non-accountable payments for reasonable and ordinary business expenses, the costs are included in his wages. Wages are subject to payroll taxes and Social Security Taxes and Medicare at 7.65%; the amounts are also subject to income taxes. Non-accountable reimbursed employee business expenses are deductible as an Itemized Deduction by the employee. However, many employees are unable to take advantage of this deduction.

TAX TIP

Employer Non-accountable amounts recorded as earnings are subject to employer matching Social Security and Medicare taxes at 7.65%. An employer may be subject to additional workers compensation insurance premiums since this insurance is based upon gross wages paid in most states. Once again, it is clearly advantageous for a company to institute an Accountable Plan.

If the employer's concerns are excessive employee costs, the employer can cap the amounts of reimbursed expenses for any single expense item. The company could restrict the vehicle standard mileage rate or limit the gross amount the employer is willing to reimburse for vehicle business miles.

TAX TIP

The IRS does allow Per Diem Rates under an Accountable Plan. The per-diem rate for Meals and Incidental Expenses is only 50% deductible for an employer that is the same treatment as meals and entertainment using actual receipts. The per-diem method of reimbursements is easier for both employer and employee, and I prefer using a method called the 'High-Low Per-diem Method.' The High-Low method is not a complicated deduction. However, employee and employer training is necessary, and there are many exceptions and regulations

TAX TIP

Sole Proprietors and employees of the sole proprietors cannot use the per diem rate for lodging; actual receipts are required. However, they are allowed to use the per diem rate for meals and entertainment. The entity that is paying the cost and deducting the expense is limited to a deduction of 50% of the amount paid.

TAX TIP

Every Proprietorship, Corporation, LLC or Partnership needs to treat the owner(s) as an employee when paying ordinary and necessary expense reimbursements. Prepare an Expense Report as if you were an employee. Using your vehicle for business should be paid by the company as if you were and employee. Treat yourself as an employee and submit an expense report. The company should never pay personal credit card debt directly.

Capitalizing an Expenditure versus Expensing: We need to understand that almost everything you own and use for business purposes, pleasure, or investment is a capital asset. However, the IRS has established guidelines to help taxpayers determine those expenditures that you can classify as a current operating expense and those expenditures that must be capitalized. Capitalizing is defined as expensing a Capital Asset over a period of years. As an example, the cost of a company vehicle could be expensed over five years. Each year one-fifth of the total cost is deducted as an expense.

Determining which business purchases can be expenses and which must be capitalized is difficult. The IRS has established guidelines help taxpayers determine what expenses can be fully deducted in the year of purchase versus those expenditures that are deductible over a period of years. Consider the following guidelines:

> ➢ Costs that produce a benefit that will last substantially beyond the end of the taxable year.
> ➢ New assets that have a useful life substantially beyond one year.
> ➢ Improvements that prolong the life of a property, restore property to a 'like-new' condition, or add value to the property.
> ➢ Changes to a property that permits the property to be used for a new or different purpose.

If companies followed the above guidelines to the letter, almost every asset purchased requires capitalized. There are thousands of small purchases that cost less than a few dollars. However, they have a useful life beyond one year. Companies would be required to capitalize a $10.00 pen or an $89.95 calculator. Clearly this is ridicules. Checking Generally Accepted Accounting Principles further adds to the confusion. GAAP requires that anything that produces a value beyond a year is considered capital and must be capitalized. It is interesting to note that all large companies and even the IRS use the term 'Immaterial' to determine if an asset should be expensed or capitalized. Immateriality in accounting refers to amounts that do not significantly impact financial statements. Because the IRS and GAAP have not provided us with a definition of immaterial, accountants make judgment calls to decide whether the amount is immaterial or not.

All the above is Greek to the small entrepreneur. The current regulation allows the IRS to reclassify any purchase as a capital item. Taxpayers are at the whim of an IRS auditor. Once again, our tax system throws taxpayers under the bus even if there is no intent to do so. Below I have detailed the procedure I have used for over 30 years in determining immaterial purchases. The amount has changed, but the same idea prevails. I take the position that the tax regulations should be equally applied to all taxpayers, not just the rich taxpayers who can afford a team of tax accountants. As a small business, we do not have the money to undertake a long drawn-out court case with the IRS. However, large corporations use a preset dollar amount when determining an item is immaterial or not, and I recommend you do the same.

My personal definition of a Capital Asset is as follows:

- ➢ Cost is more than $500.00 and cost less than 5% of your total disbursements for one month.
- ➢ Adds a value to the business or to an existing capital asset and
- ➢ Has a useful life longer than one year.

All three conditions must be present in order for a purchase to be recorded on the balance sheet as a non-current capital asset and be depreciated over the life of the asset. Many items meet the criteria for (2) and (3). However, the amount of $500.00 or 5% of monthly disbursements is important and is considered low for most companies. Many businesses believe an immaterial purchase is any purchase of less than $1,000.00 and expense the item in the year of purchase. The amount of $500.00 or 5% of the monthly disbursements should only be used as a guide. IRS Code and IRS regulations do not specify any value as immaterial. Also, contact your CPA for his opinion of the dollar amount to be considered immaterial for your company.

TAX TIP
Review the information concerning 179 Depreciation Expense below. Simply, 179 is the IRS regulation allowing a company to deduct a capital asset in the year purchased. The IRS has established a yearly maximum dollar amount allowable for 179 depreciation. Many Small Businesses do not reach the 179 limit, therefore treating items purchased as an expense may be unnecessary. The amount of 179 depreciation is available up to the amount of profit. A company cannot create a loss using 179 depreciation.

Depreciation: Assets such as automobiles, business equipment, machinery and even real estate lose value over time. Over time, assets become worthless. Depreciation in accounting terms is the reduction of the property's cost over a pre-determined period, in a systematic formula. Record the cost of a capital expense in the balance sheet as a Non-Current Asset. Each month a percent of the cost is expensed to the income statement.

As an Example: Your Company purchases a copy machine for $2,000.00. The IRS has determined that this type of asset has a useful life of five years. The simplest depreciation method is Straight Line Depreciation. Over five years, you would deduct $400.00 each year as an expense against income. Each year the depreciation journal entry is a debit to Depreciation Expense of $400.00 and a credit to Accumulated Depreciation of $400.00, a contra asset Account. After the first full year, your Office Equipment Account indicates the amount of + $2,000.00 and Accumulated Depreciation Account reflects the amount of - $400.00. The book value of the copy machine is $1,600.00. This systematic method of expensing the copy machine is not a valuation process. Depreciation is a procedure established by the IRS and GAAP to expense the cost of assets over time.

Listed property: Listed Property is a distinct class of capital assets subject to a particular set of tax rules. Listed property is defined as a capital asset used for a business purpose no more than 50% of the time. The asset has both business and personal use. Listed property includes such items as vehicles, computers, some equipment, and cell phones. Listed-property rules limit the dollar amount deductible each year. The cost of an asset is divided between personal and business use.

As of January 1, 2010, cell phones and other similar personal telecommunications devices are no longer considered " listed property." Listed property includes automobiles weighing less than 6,000 pounds and computers.

179 Depreciation Deduction: Section 179 Depreciation for small businesses is an essential tax planning tool. You can elect to expense (Depreciate) all or part of the cost of certain qualifying property in the year the property placed in service. As an example if you purchase a qualifying property such as equipment, you may be able to deduct the total cost in the year placed in service. Purchasing and placing an asset in service in December will allow you to take 100% of the cost in the current year.

TAX TIP
Congress established Section 179 Depreciation as an economic stimulus. Section 179 of the IRS tax code allows businesses to deduct the full purchase price of qualifying equipment and software purchased or financed during the tax year. Section 179 is a business incentive that helps small businesses.

The tax savings could be as high as 39% in federal tax and could result in a potential savings of over 50% in federal taxes and state taxes. (Some states limit the amount of Section 179 deduction)

TAX TIP
Buy a qualifying property before the end of the year and not in January. Consider the tax implications of the purchase. The amount of 179 Depreciation is limited to profit of $250,000.00. The list of qualified property and property not eligible is extensive and if you are planning a purchase, review IRS regulation first.

TAX TIP
Section 179 expense is limited to the total taxable income from any single business activity. IRS code prevents a taxpayer from creating a loss in one company by using 179 depreciation for the expressed purpose of using the loss against a profit of another company. Active trade or business income is wages, salaries, proprietorship net income, partnership and S-corporation

pass-through income. If your 179 loss is greater than your income, you are allowed to carry over the unused 179 deduction with limits.

Income

Income Constructively Received: Business income is income received from the sale of products or services. For example, fees received by a professional person are considered business income. Rents received by an individual in the real estate business is business income. Payments received in the form of property or services must be included in income at their fair market value (IRS Topic 407 – Business Income).

Under the Cash Method of Accounting, you include in your gross income you actually or constructively receive during your tax year. If you receive property or services, you must include their fair market value in income.

The amount of your business income should be as simple as totaling all your deposits and recording that amount as gross revenues for the year

NON-CASH INCOME: Bartering occurs when you exchange goods or services without exchanging money. You must include in gross income the Fair market Value of products and services received in exchange for goods or services you provided

Deductible Expenses

Expense must be Ordinary & Necessary: There are hundreds of business expenses that are deductible. Again the maze of Income Tax Rules and Regulations is almost impossible to follow but in general a business expense must be both ordinary and necessary. An ordinary expense is one that is common and accepted in your trade or business. A necessary expense is one that is helpful and appropriate for your trade or business. An expense does not have to be indispensable to be considered necessary

The IRS code is over 72 thousand pages long and includes rules and regulations for every deduction. There are court cases where the taxpayer has won the deduction, and the IRS refuses to acquiesce to the court decision for other taxpayers. This refusal is because every taxpayer is deducting an expense based upon his circumstances which may or may not be similar to other taxpayers. Tax Laws change every year and they are interpreted differently by the IRS, by individual Tax Accountant's and even within our courts. Every situation is different. Seek information and advice from the IRS, a qualified Tax Accountant or a tax attorney if you have a particular question or problem. Use the tax tips and list of expense deductions in this handbook as a guide posting your bookkeeping and when meeting with your tax consultant.

For a more detailed explanation of any IRS Code or Regulation, please review IRS Publication 535 (2013), Business Expenses.

Cost Of Goods Sold: Cost of Goods Sold are those business expenses directly associated with the sales income produced. This cost includes the cost of production or manufacturing and the direct cost of the product sold. If the organization is service orientated the direct cost are wages and salary, payroll taxes and employee benefits cost.

> **As an Example:** Operating a hardware store requires selling merchandise but may also include a department for engine repairs. The cost of goods sold could be cost of merchandise sold and the direct labor cost associated with the repair department. Of course, you can have any categories you want in order for you to analysis sales versus expense percent. If you make too many sub-categories such as dividing your building heating cost between the hardware store and the service department, the bookkeeping becomes increasingly more difficult and expensive. Keep it simple.

"We've got to draw the line on unethical behavior.
But draw it in pencil."

Operational Expense Listed In Alphabetic Order

Accounting and Bookkeeping Expense: Fees for Bookkeeping, Income Tax Preparation, Tax advice and Tax education are deductible. Accounting and bookkeeping costs are necessary to calculate income and taxes due. Therefore, such costs are necessary to report a true and accurate income tax return and are a business expense.

TAX TIP

The costs of travel to visit your bookkeeper, attorney (See Attorney Expense below for details of deductibility of legal fees and travel to your lawyer) or accountant are tax deductible expenses.

TAX TIP

Deducting tax preparation fees as a Miscellaneous Deduction on an individual tax return, Schedule A, usually, results in zero tax benefits because miscellaneous deductions must exceed two percent of the taxpayer's adjusted gross income. In addition, many taxpayers do not itemize their personal deductions because the standard deduction would be greater than the total itemized deductions. The IRS allows taxpayers to deduct tax preparation fees related to business, a farm, or rental property directly on the schedules where the taxpayer reports such income.

Advertising Cost: Advertising and marketing cost are ordinary and necessary business expenses and are fully deductible. Such costs as public relations, promotional activities are also an expense. The cost must be reasonable and related to your company. Advertising to influence legislation is not deductible.

TAX TIP

Most expenses related to customer appreciation are a deductible expense. Having a large dinner, conference, product meeting or even a get-together of all your clients as an appreciation get-to-gather, is deductible. Inviting customers to a function such as a birthday or a wedding will not be tax deductible. The general rule that you should always apply is to conduct business on any client or employee gatherings. The purpose of the gathering is to secure or maintain customer loyalty. Many clients have open houses at their office or even at a manufacturing facility, and these functions are also deductible.

Answering Service: The cost of hiring an outside answering service for your business phone is allowable. The cost of purchasing an answering machine for your business phone is also deductible as is the cost of a particular telephone line in your home for business. The cost of a basic local telephone service into your home is never deductible, and you are not allowed to pro-rate such cost between the business and personal use.

TAX TIP

The cost of an answering machine or even an answering service used on the primary phone line is deductible provided you can prove business purpose and that such a service is an ordinary and necessary expense for your company.

TAX TIP

The IRS has changed its standards concerning Cell phone use by allowing an employer to furnish employees a Cell phone without accounting for personal use. It would follow that an answering service or an answering machine would qualify under the same standard as a Cell Telephone.

Attorney Fees: The tax law does not mention legal fees as a deductible item. The deductibility of legal fees depends upon the situation they are incurred. Legal fees that are ordinary and necessary in the operation of your business are fully deductible. Also, legal fees for the protection of income are allowed.

Legal Fees paid for purchasing and selling a business are considered allowable by adding such costs to the purchase price of a company or as a selling cost. Legal fees for the preparation of contracts and agreements, business lawsuits and even legal fees to protect a patent are deductible. Legal fees to organize an LLC or a corporation are deducted as a current operating expense.

Individual taxpayers can only deduct their attorney fees for tax or alimony related advice. Such legal cost as a divorce or a civil lawsuit would not be deductible unless it is related to the protection of taxable income. A couple splitting assets is not protecting taxable income. Taxpayers need to retain the records for any attorney cost to demonstrate the connection to taxable income.

TAX TIP
Request your attorney to allocate legal fees between deductible and non-deductible services. A receipt will provide written evidence for any deduction question by the IRS. The IRS will accept a lawyer's allocation between tax and non-tax matters.

TAX TIP
Income from an illegal activity is taxable. Because the income is taxable, ordinary and necessary legal costs related to this criminal activity could be deductible. All businesses are allowed to deduct ordinary and necessary operational expenses. Contact your CPA or Tax Attorney for your circumstances.

However, deductions for fines or similar penalties paid to a government agency for the violation of any law are not deductible. Congress has specifically earmarked some criminal activities that deductions are not allowed. I strongly suggest you contact a qualified Tax Accountant if you intend to deduct expenses related to any illegal activity.

TAX TIP
The United States Supreme Court has ruled that requiring a person to declare income on a federal income tax return does not violate an individual's right to remain silent. The privilege may allow a person to refrain from revealing the source of the income. The Tax Code is not and cannot be a conduit to pursuing illegal activities. Prosecutors have been successful convicting individuals for failure to report income. However, prosecutors are barred from prosecuting criminal activity that generated the income, whatever the source when such activity is discovered on an individual's tax return.

TAX TIP

I had a client who owned a local tavern. He consumed a considerable quantity of his inventory and as a result; he has arrested for DUI. He was convinced that his legal fees were a deductible business item. He cited several arguments that drinking with customers was a business activity and his business caused him to drink. Of course, legal cost related to personal conduct are not deductible, and his request denied.

Bad Debt Expense: A bad debt occurs when you're owed money you are unable to collect. There are both business bad debt and non-business bad debts.

A Non-Business bad debt can be deductible if the debt is:

> ➤ A legal obligation for a fixed amount of money.
> ➤ The debt is entirely worthless.
> ➤ The debt result from the loan of amounts previously taxed.

You must be able to show that the funds were not a gift and that attempts were made to collect a debt. Loans to relatives including children are difficult to prove unless you can provide proof of the loan, and you have formally demanded payment in writing. Receiving a statement from the debtor that he cannot repay the loan or that he has declared bankruptcy is an acceptable reason for not making repayment and the debt is deductible.

A business bad debt is deductible as an expense provided the following conditions are present:

> ➤ There must be a legal obligation to pay a fixed sum.
> ➤ You have a basis in the debt. Must be an actual loss of money.
> ➤ The debt is uncollectible.
> ➤ The debt must have occurred within a business relationship.

TAX TIP
Loss of time spent rendering service is not a loss of money unless the uncollected fee for services included as income on a prior tax return as taxable income.

TAX TIP
A business debt becomes worthless when you realize the debt is uncollectible. You must take reasonable action to collect debts before the debt is an expense. Legal action is not necessary. However, you must be able to demonstrate that the debt is uncollectible. A borrower bankruptcy, clearly proves the debt is uncollectable.

TAX TIP
Declaring loans to family members and friends as a deducted bad debt is tricky. You must prove that you made a loan and it was not a gift; you must provide evidence that the debtor stopped paying, and he is unable to pay. Bad Debts incurred with family members will require proof of collection

attempts. Again this deduction is complicated, and you should consult a Tax Accountant for advice.

Bank Service Fees: Have a separate business checking account. Do not co-mingle personal, business income and expenses in a single checking account. Bank Fees on a company checking account are fully deductible. If you insist on co-mingling personal and business funds, you must prorate the bank service charges between the company use and personal use which is almost an impossible task.

Bribes, Illegal Acts, and Kickbacks: Any payment made directly or indirectly to a government official or employee is not deductible if in violation of the law. You cannot deduct payments or gifts of products or services if such payment is given to induce another to commit a criminal act. Providing a government inspector goods or services for a favorable inspection is clearly illegal.

Capital Expenses: (See Capital Assets above) Real Estate, Equipment, Fixtures and even remodeling and some repairs are considered Capital purchases. The cost of such expenditures should be deducted over its useful life while the asset is being used in the business to create income.

Casualty Losses: One-hundred percent of business casualty losses are allowed as a deduction against business income. If you have uninsured equipment that is destroyed in fire, you will be able to deduct any remaining book value as a business expense at the time of the fire.

TAX TIP

Consider the following example:

> Capital Asset Cost $15,000.00
> Depreciated over five years.
> Each year $3,000.00 of the cost is a Business Expense.
> After two years, the asset has a Book-Value of $15,000 -
> $6,000.00 = $9,000.00.
> Asset is destroyed by fire and insurance is available.

A. Insurance company offers the company $8,000.00, and the company would take a $1,000.00 loss as a Business Expense.

B. Insurance company offers the company $10,000.00, and the company has to declare income of a $1,000.00

The book value is the tax value. Dollars disbursed at purchase less the amounts (Depreciation) taken as a business expense, results in book value and tax value. The purchase was made with taxable dollars, and the depreciation deduction reduces taxable profit. Both affect the 'Tax Value' of Capital Asset.

TAX TIP

176

Casualty losses incurred by an individual taxpayer are deducted on Schedule A, Itemized Deductions. There are limits. The benefits of deducting casualty loss as a business expense are many. The deduction on the Schedule A is limited both in amount and location.

Cell Phone: To be considered a business expense, it must be ordinary and necessary. Ordinary means that it is common and accepted in your business. In almost every business, a cell phone is standard and necessary. However is a mobile phone standard and necessary?

Necessarily does not mean indispensable. Personal cell phones are not deductible. Many small business owners routinely provide cell phones to their family members and of course; they deduct the total cost as a company expense. Family members are not furnished a mobile phone for ordinary and necessary business purposes, therefore, such personal costs associated with a mobile telephone is not allowable.

TAX TIP
The IRS has softened its rules concerning business versus personal use for mobile phones. In September 2011, the IRS issued new regulations on the treatment of employer-provided cell phones. The Notice provides that when an employer gives an employee with a cell phone primarily for business reasons, the business and personal use of a cell phone is nontaxable to the employee. The IRS will not require recordkeeping of business use in order to receive this tax-free treatment.

Charitable Contributions: Business: Charitable contributions made by a Proprietorship, Partnership and "S" Corporations are deductible on the owner's, (proprietor, shareholder or partner) individual tax return. "C" Corporation can deduct charitable contributions but are limited to a percent of profit. Contributions made by an "S" Corporation, LLC or a Partnership flow through to the owner's individual Tax return.

TAX TIP
In order for pass-through contributions to be deductible, they must meet the same IRS code standards as contributions made individually. These pass-through contributions are subject to the same limits as any other contributions.

TAX TIP
When purchasing an ad in a church bulletin, the cost is considered an advertising expense. Buying an ad in a newsletter or a special event program for a charitable organization is also an advertising expense. Cost to sponsor baseball or soccer team is a business expense. Sponsorship cost can be considered a company expense provided your business received a benefit that is considered 'of value.'

TAX TIP
Donations of time and services are not a deduction on your personal return or as a business expense.

Cleaning, Cleaning Supplies, and Janitorial Cost: One-hundred percent deductible for your place of business either an office, retail store, warehouse or restaurant.

TAX TIP

Cleaning cost for an 'Office in the Home' is an indirect expense split between personal and business by square footage of the home and office. See Office in the Home deduction.

Club Dues and Social Memberships: Fees and membership cost for clubs that are primary for the purpose of providing entertainment activities for members or their guests are not deductible. Even if you use the club consistently for the entertainment of clients the membership fees are not a deductible business expense. However, direct expenses such as business entertainment and meals occurred at the club are considered allowable with limits.

TAX TIP

The cost associated with entertaining a client at a golf club, sporting event or private club are deductible if such entertainment is ordinary and necessary in your business. However, excessive charges may be denied if your tax return is subject to and IRS audit. Keep your entertainment reasonable.

Commissions, Fees, and Contract Services: The IRS requires that a company maintains a record of business expenses for at least three years. One document that confirms the identity of a product or service vendor is the Form W-9 – Request for Taxpayer Identification Number and Certification. The W-9 provides documentation for vendor identification.

W-9; Request for Taxpayer Identification Number and Certification requirements: The IRS requires that you obtain a completed W-9 for every vendor paid $600.00 or more for labor and services rendered. The IRS Form W-9 is the IRS document acceptable as backup supporting vendor deductions. The IRS requires that any person who is required to file an information return (Tax Return) must get a correct identification number supporting expenses paid. It is common practice for businesses to require a W-9 for individuals (proprietorships), LLC and Partnerships. Because of complex IRS regulations, your company is also expected to request a W-9 from individual corporations.

Nothing is simple. I realize it is difficult to obtain W-9s for companies and many times a company will refuse to provide such information. Always get W-9s from individuals providing labor and services and use your best efforts and common sense.

Form 1099 Requirements: The IRS uses this form to ensure companies report all their income received and to monitor expenses paid without documentation. Copies need to be sent to the vendor and to the IRS. There are 1099s used to report Dividends, Interest, retirement amounts, rents and a long list of other income items paid and received by individual and businesses.

Prepare Forms 1099-MISC yearly. Mail a copy to the recipient by the first of February each year and mail a copy to the IRS by the first of March each year. Form 1099-Misc required when payments to individuals, LLCs or partnerships are made, and the amount of the payments exceed $600.00 in a single year. There are some exceptions for LLCs, but it is strongly suggested you prepare Form 1099s for all vendors of services and labor unless such vendor is a corporation. Form 1099 is not required for a corporation supplier.

TAX TIP

Many businesses pay plumbers, bookkeepers and other contract services individuals more than $600.00 a year. At the end of the year, the business does not have the necessary tax ID information to complete the Form 1099. Even payments to a landscaper, a pest control individual or an independent plumber may require a 1099.

TAX TIP

If the payee on your check is to an individual, complete the W-9. You are not required to send 1099s to corporations, however, make the check is payable to the corporate entity and not to an individual. Any payments to a proprietorship (individual), LLC or Partnership, require a W-9 followed at year-end with a 1099. Many business will issue checks payable to an individual. If the work performed was by a business entity make the check payable to the business name not an individual. The general rule is to demand a W-9 unless the payee on your check is a Corporation such as Jim Smith, Inc.

Contract Services V's Employee classification. One-hundred percent of my business clients were tempted to classify an employee as an independent contractor. It is one of the most abused deductions for small enterprises. The employer's share of Social Security and Medicare Costs and Federal and State Unemployment cost can cost an organization up to 10% of gross wage expense. Most states require employers to pay Worker Compensation Insurance for any employee and for independent contractors who do not have such insurance. Therefore, there may or may not be a saving by classifying an employee as a contractor for worker's compensation cost.

One of the largest areas of abuse is in the construction and manufacturing industry. Our country has a large population of untrained and uneducated illegal immigrants. Of course, I'm not tackling the solution to this problem, I'm only concerned with the effect such a condition has on small business. Contractors who incorrectly classify workers have a financial advantage over contractors who follow the law. If I were in competition against these contractors, I would be standing on my Representative's doorstep until the practice is stopped.

TAX TIP

The IRS assumes that all workers are employees unless you prove they are independent contractors. With that in mind, you should prepare a written agreement covering the worker's status. The IRS reviews three primary areas:

> ➢ Financial Control: How is the worker paid, is he reimbursed for expenses and who provides   products, material, and tools.
> ➢ Behavioral Control: Who controls what the worker does and how the worker completes his work.
> ➢ Nature of the Relationship: Are there written contracts or employee type benefits

Businesses must weigh all these factors when determining whether a worker is an employee or independent contractor. Some factors may indicate that the worker is an employee while other factors indicate that the worker is an independent contractor. There is no magic factor or factors that determines if a worker is an employee or an independent contractor. Also, factors that apply in one situation may not be applicable in another.

TAX TIP

Consider the following list when making a decision to classify workers as an independent contractor or as an employee. Determining a worker's status is the responsibility of the business. The checklist below considers many factors when making your determination. Each item below is used by the IRS and many states to establish the employee and employer relationship. Remember it is about financial and behavioral control.

> ➢ If the company provides worker training.
> ➢ Work completed at the company's facility.
> ➢ Company provides direct supervision.
> ➢ Worker is required to maintain a regular work hours.
> ➢ Work is salaried and not contracted.
> ➢ Company set hourly rate.
> ➢ Company provides tools and materials.
> ➢ Company restricts worker's ability to obtain other jobs.
> ➢ Company pays worker expenses.
> ➢ There is no written contract detailing job limits.
> ➢ Company and worker have long term relationship.
> ➢ Company furnishes vehicle and equipment.
> ➢ Does the worker have financial risk?
> ➢ Did the worker complete Form W-9?
> ➢ The subcontractor prohibited from hiring employees to complete the work.
> ➢ The independent contractor is performing the same type or even the same job.

TAX TIP

With millions of illegal aliens seeking work, it is tempting to hire these workers as independent contract labor. There are several Web Sites providing you information on how to hire an illegal alien and for the short term the IRS probably will not catch you. Paying sub-standard wages, not withholding and matching payroll taxes is a significant and attractive inducement. However, there are penalties and tax assessments that could wipe out your company and you personally as a business owner. The amounts, you pay illegal immigrants may not be a deductible expense, and you are subject to very high penalties and maybe you could be responsible for the illegals tax liability. The state of California is currently activity reviewing employers with large independent contractor deductions. Once the state has considered this deduction, the IRS is notified, and they will also take action.

TAX TIP

A few businesses incorrectly classify an individual as an independent contractor, and they have compounded this error by paying an independent contractor, under the table. They 'steal' unreported income from their company and use it to pay an independent contractor. They continue this deception by failing report the payments to the IRS on Form 1099. I'm not an attorney, but it appears that both individuals have committed a couple of felonies. Failure to report income and conspiracy to defraud the IRS are two serious crimes. Do not compound incorrectly classifying contract labor by committing tax fraud.

Dues and Subscriptions: Dues for a professional organization are deductible. Subscriptions for professionals are also deductible including books and magazines related to your profession. A subscription to an investment magazine is also deductible if related to the production of income. You may not deduct dues paid for membership in a social, business, or recreational organizations. Membership fees, and monthly dues for country clubs, athletic clubs, airline clubs and hotel clubs are not deductible.

TAX TIP

Dues paid to the Kiwanis Club, the Lions, the Rotary Club and other civic organizations are deductible as a business expense provided that their principal purpose was to help communities and not provide members with entertainment.

TAX TIP

I prefer that you use the words 'Trade Associations Membership Fees' when deducting dues on your tax return. Because many "Dues" are not deductible, the IRS may question your "Dues" expenses.

Educational Expenses: The IRS has educational tax deductions for both the employer and the employee. As an employee, you may be able to deduct education expenses in two locations different on your individual 1040 Tax Return. Contact your tax consultant for information about this deduction under the American Opportunity and Lifetime Learning Credits. Double check the deduction as it is set to expire in 2013.

Employers have several ways they can provide deductible educational benefits to their employees. As a proprietorship, you can deduct your expenses for qualifying work-related education directly from your self-employment income.

(www.irs.gov/publications/p17/ch27.) This deduction reduces both income tax liability and your Social Security Tax liability.

There are three educational programs employers can offer their employees.

> ➤ Tax-Free Scholarships: If an employee is seeking a degree at a qualified educational organization and uses the funds for tuition, fees, books and supplies. The scholarship must be for past, present or future employment services to the scholarship amount is taxable to the employee.
> ➤ $5,250 in Annual Educational Benefits: Employers can provide tax-free education assistance up to $5,250 annually, per employee. There must be an employer - employee relationship.
> ➤ Work Related Education: An employer can deduct the cost of work-related education provided; the employee maintains or improves job skills or meets requirements for an employee to remain in his or her current position.

TAX TIP
Small business owners can hire their children. As an employee, your child would be eligible for education assistance programs established for all employees.

Employee Awards and Bonuses and Gifts: Awards and Bonuses are deductible and are considered wages to your employee. Businesses gifts are limited to a maximum of up to $25.00 a year, per client. Gifts to customers are limited to $25.00 per year, per customer. Realtors often give 'Closing Gifts' when selling a home. Any gift exceeding $25.00 per year, per client, is deductible provide you prepare a Form 1099 at year's end notifying the IRS and the client? Treat cash certificates, cash or even a gift certificate from a restaurant given to an employee as taxable wages.

Employee Achievement Awards: Non-cash achievement awards such as an award for length of service or safety achievement can be excluded from the employee's income. The cost cannot exceed $1,600 for a planned award and $400 for an unplanned award. There must be a 'meaningful' presentation, and the employee must have five years of service to qualify for a length-of-service Award. There are other requirements, and you need to review IRS regulations before establishing Awards.

Safety Recognition Gifts or Prizes: Safety Awards in recognition of meeting safety goals are considered nontaxable by the Internal Revenue Service. Again these Awards must meet certain requirements.

Holiday Bonuses: Holiday bonuses given to employees are considered non-taxable if not in the form of cash or cash equivalent. Gift baskets, hams or turkeys are examples of nontaxable gifts. Include cash bonuses on the employees W-2 as wages and withhold the required payroll taxes.

TAX TIP

Gift items classified as entertainment are limited to a 50% deduction as opposed to a gift; that is limited to $25.00 per year and per client.

Example: Giving a client a food basket or liquor which is intended to be consumed at a later date is a gift and subject to a $25.00 limitation. Consider as W-2 wages.

Giving tickets to a sporting event or a cultural event can be considered a gift or entertainment. You can treat the cost of the tickets as either a gift or and expense. Whichever is to your advantage. However, if you go to the event with the client, the ticket price is entertainment.

TAX TIP

Realtors often present a buyer or seller with a house closing gift. Such gifts while very thoughtful are taxable to the client, and a 1099 is required from the realtor. You are limited to a maximum deduction of $25.00. Every sales individual has the same problem. You can only deduct a gift costing $25.00 of less.

However, you are allowed to cut your commission on the closing statement. You cannot collect a fee and then kick back a portion of the commission. Kickbacks are illegal as determined by real estate boards in every state. Disclose the discount on the closing documents by paying a part of the closing cost. Have the Title Company create a line item documenting the fact you are assisting the buyer or seller by a percent of the real estate purchase price or some other fixed amount.

Employee Benefits Plans: There are many different Fringe Benefits an organization can provide their employees. Fringe benefits, usually, are deductible by the employer and taxable to the employee. However, some benefits are tax deductible to the employer and not taxable to the employee. To cover the details of each benefit is beyond the scope of this Handbook. I have listed many of the benefits below as a reference. Contact a CPA or Tax Accountant for details.

- ➢ Accident and Health benefits subject to certain restrictions.
- ➢ Adoption Assistance benefits subject to dollar limits.
- ➢ Cafeteria Plans offer two or more benefits.
- ➢ Deferred compensation. May be taxable now or tax deferred.
- ➢ Dependent Care Assistance for qualified employee in order to work.
- ➢ De Minimis Fringe is minimal use of company equipment or office.
- ➢ Education Assistance offer three different programs.
- ➢ Employee Achievement Awards are tax-free but subject to limits.
- ➢ Employer provided vehicle is available, however, personal use taxable income to the employee.
- ➢ Group Life Insurance. You can provide up to $50,000 policy for your employees.

➤ Job Placement Assistance. Can be provided tax-free to an employee subject to conditions.
➤ Meals and lodging. Tax-free to an employee using an Accountable Plan for employer benefit.
➤ On-Premise Gym is tax-free to employee and family but not for public use.
➤ Qualified Employee Discounts. Subject to conditions but, usually, tax-free.
➤ Qualified Moving Expense is tax-free to an employee for qualified expenses.
➤ Qualified Retirement Plans. Tax deferred income to the employee until funds are drawn from the fund. There are many types of retirement plans. Please visit with your CPA, Financial Advisor or Tax Accountant.
➤ Qualified Transportation Benefit. Up to $125 per month is excluded for qualified transit pass for 2012.
➤ Retirement Planning Services is tax-free to employees.

Because different IRS codes apply to S-corporations, LLC's and even proprietorships for many different fringe benefits I suggest you contact your Tax Accountant for the deductibility of any fringe benefit. When dealing with employee benefits, most have restrictions. Employee Benefits plans are available to any size company; however, most small businesses do not have the capital to initiate a retirement plan.

TAX TIP
Review the benefits available above and select one idea for your company. Because there are many different benefits and plans, do not tackle employee benefits as a group. Solve a particular need by concentrating your efforts on cost, availability, limits, deductibility and qualifications for one single benefit at a time.

Employing Training: Training classes and seminars are fully deductible. Travel expense associated with the training or conference is also deductible.

Entertainment – Business: Entertainment expenses that are both ordinary and necessary in carrying on a trade or business may be deductible if they meet the Directly-Related Test or the Associated Test.

You expect to receive income or a business benefit at some future time, or you are currently involved in a business relationship with the person being entertained. Only 50% of meal and entertainment expenses are allowed as a deduction.

TAX TIP
Entertainment receipts are not required when the expense is under $75. However, you must reduce the event to writing being aware of the four-finger and thumb rule.

For years, I have suggested that my clients follow my 'Four Finger and Thumb Rule' when determining if the entertainment is deductible. Receipted or not, you must record:

➢ Pinky: Record the date.
➢ Ring: Record the location or restaurant
➢ Middle: Record the person or persons entertained.
➢ Index: Record the amount spent including the tip

➢ The most important; Thumb: Detail the business purpose, subject discussed and benefit expected.

TAX TIP

Many times you are out with a client and you pay for qualified entertainment expenses by using your personal credit card, personal check or even cash. Anytime you use your funds to pay business expenses create an 'Expense Report' and request your company to reimburse you.

TAX TIP

You Are Not the Company: Always treat yourself as an employee. We often talk about wearing different hats - you work for the company as an employee even if you are a proprietorship. You change hats to be the boss, owner, HR, bookkeeper, etc.

TAX TIP

Many times you will use a personal credit card to purchase a significant asset such as a computer of even a copy machine. Your company owes you for these expenses. Prepare an expense report documenting the purchase with receipts. If your business does not have the funds to pay you, you have become a creditor of your business. The company owes you for any businesses expenses you incurred personally on behalf of the enterprise. The computer or even business mileage is posted as an asset or as an expense, and the amount is a company liability payable to you.

TAX TIP

There are few areas where meals and entertainment expense are not subject to a 50% limitation and are 100% deductible:

➢ Meals provided to employees who are not highly compensated. The value of the meals is excluded from their gross pay.
➢ Directly related to business meetings onsite.

Home Office Expense: In order to deduct an Office in the Home, you must be able to demonstrate:

General Rules required to claim an Office in the Home
➢ The office space is your principal place of business
• You meet with client's in the ordinary course of business or
• You conduct normal business activities in your office.

- ➤ Must be a part of your home. Separate structure has different rules.
- ➤ Must use the office exclusively and regularly as your office.
- ➤ Can use storage space as part of your business office percent.
- ➤ You will use a percent of the home used for business.

Simplified Option

- ➤ Same qualifications.
- ➤ For proprietorships - Schedule C, with limits.
- ➤ Employee – Schedule A
- ➤ $5.00 per square foot – maximum of 300 Square Feet.
- ➤ No depreciation or depreciation recapture as income.

Regular Method

- ➤ Same Qualifications
- ➤ Include actual expenses of home. Mortgage interest, property taxes, insurance, utilities, repairs and depreciation.
- ➤ The deduction is based upon a percent of your home devoted to the office.
- ➤ Calculate office space Square Footage and divided the result by the total home square Footage for percentage of business use.

Proprietorship or Single Owner LLC

- ➤ Complete Form 8829 and transfer result to Schedule C.

C Corporation

- ➤ Create an Accountable Plan that reimburses employee out-of-pocket expense.
- ➤ Rent the office space to the Corporation. This plan is not practicable. A percent of Interest and taxes are the only expense deductible. You already deduct such cost as an Itemized Deduction.
- ➤ Deduct office in home expense as an Itemized Deduction. Again this plan is not practicable since it is subject to a 2% of Adjusted Gross Income limit.

TAX TIP

Use the Accountable Plan for out-of-pocket expenses only. You are o depreciation deduction. The IRS may take the position that this is a rental. Keep careful records and be prepared to back-up your deduction.

S Corporation, Partnerships, and LLCs

- ➤ As an employee, you can deduct office expense as an Itemized Deduction. Same problem as #2 C Corporations.
- ➤ The S Corporation reimbursements you're percent of office expense. No depreciation. The S-
- ➤ Corporation expenses the amount and such reimbursement is not taxable to you.
- ➤ You rent the office to the Corporation. Same problem as ##2, C Corporation.

INSURANCE EXPENSE: The IRS has different rules concerning insurance expense deductions. Create separate <u>Accounts</u> for the various business insurance costs. Some types of insurance are deductible, and some are not.

> - Fire, theft, flood is fully deductible when a business expense.
> - Credit insurance covering losses from business bad debts is deductible.
> - Deduct malpractice insurance for professional negligence.
> - Workers' compensation insurance as set by state law.
> - The cost of state and Federal Unemployment Insurance.
> - Insurance for business interruptions such as a disability, temporary government closures, and sickness or injury are deductible.
> - Car and other vehicle insurance that covers vehicles used in your business for liability, damages, and other losses. Check Vehicle Expense below to determine vehicle insurance deductibility.
> - Life insurance is covering your employees if you are not directly or indirectly a beneficiary under the contract. Limited to a $50.000 policy and amounts greater are taxable income to the individual.
> - Business interruption insurance pays for lost profits if the business is shut down due to fire or another insurable cause.

Insurance Expense – Medical: Health insurance as an employee benefit is deductible to the employer and nontaxable to the employee as a result of the payment of plan benefits, if the plan meets certain rules. Different business entities have special rules and regulations.

Self-employed Individual

Health insurance is not deductible on Schedule C as a business expense. 100% of the amount paid is deductible subject to profit limits, on page 1 of the individual tax return. Dental insurance long term insurance are also deductible as Health Insurance. Since the medical insurance is not deductible as a business expense, the amount of health insurance is paid using income subject to Social Security Taxes of a combined amount of 15.3%. Health insurance costing $10,000.00 a year is subject to $1,530.00 in Social Security taxes.

Sub Chapter S Corporation

If you own more than 2 percent of your S corporation, medical insurance is considered a taxable fringe benefit. The company makes a payment for the health insurance, and the cost is included in the shareholder and employees W-2 wages. The amount is not subject to Social Security Taxes. The medical insurance amount is also deductible on page 1 of the individual tax return.

TAX TIP

The S-Corporation includes the cost of medical insurance as W-2 wages. Unlike regular wages, payroll taxes such as Social Security and Medicare cost are not required. Of course, the company's profit is reduced by the amount of wages. Provided your company's profit is greater than the cost of the insurance, the amount is deductible on page 1 of your individual tax return.

You received a benefit that is not subject to payroll taxes. The cost of the insurance is included in your wages, but you are allowed to deduct the same amount on page 1 your individual tax return. The net effect for an S-Corporation is health Insurance for the owner/officer is not taxable.

Limited Liability Company

Members (Owners) of a company classified as a Partnership entity or as an LLC entity are considered self-employed. The partnership or LLC makes the payments for the medical insurance. The insurance expense is deducted on the Partnership tax return as a guarantee payment to the partner. The partnership deducts Guaranteed Partner Payments as a business expense that reduces your partnership income. Guaranteed payments are taxable income on your individual tax return and are subject to Social Security payroll taxes which are currently 15.3% of Self-employed income. Provide sufficient profit is generated by the partnership, the same amount is deducted on the partners (members) individual tax return.

TAX TIP

One additional advantage of an S Corporation is the treatment of medical insurance. Social Security is a government sponsored retirement plan funded by a 12.4% tax on earned income. I recommend Social Security as I have seen it benefit many entrepreneurs who failed to support other retirement plans. Anytime there is a saving of Social Security Tax it I suggested you use that money to increase your retirement plans.

Interest Expense – Lender Loans: The interest you pay lenders is reported to the IRS at the end of the year by your lender. The IRS compares the Lenders 1099 Interest report with the amount you report on your tax return. Recording interest paid in separate cost <u>Accounts</u> allows you the ability to check your numbers quickly against the yearly statement received from the lender.

TAX TIP

The IRS compares your interest deduction with the amount reported paid by your lender. If the amounts do not match, you could receive a tax bill plus interest and penalty for deducting excessive interest expense. This procedure by the IRS is not an audit only a program by the IRS to ensure you have reported the correct deductible interest.

Interest Expense – Credit Cards: Interest paid on business debts is deductible. If you do use a personal credit card for business and personal expenses, you need to compute the amount of interest that is business. If you have a business credit card and use it for personal purchases, you must prorate the interest between business and personal. Only the interest charges for business credit is allowable.

TAX TIP

There are a few mathematical geniuses that can correctly split a credit card interest expense between personal and business. Dividing the personal and

188

business cost is almost impossible to calculate because of new monthly personal and business charges and payments personal and business. Please do not co-mingle business and personal expenses on the same credit card. Obtain a business card for your company and use it only for business (No Personal charges).

TAX TIP

Using one credit card for 100% business is the first suggestion; do not co-mingle credit cards between personal and business. Using a credit card for purchases is only buying on credit, even if you pay off the card every month. See the example below:

Internet Fees: Prorate between business and personal internet cost for an office in the home. Maintain a record of the time you use the computer for business and personal. Prorating is the only way to take this deduction. There is no such thing as 100% business use of internet costs for office in the home. Companies that provide computers and internet service for their employees, usually, have strict rules concerning personal use of the employer-provided equipment. However, most businesses deduct 100% of these costs as a business expense. Any expense that is ordinary and regular for conducting business is deductible.

TAX TIP

For those employees who are not provided an office except a home office; you can either take your 'business Internet Cost' on Schedule A or request your employer to reimburse this cost under an Accountable Plan. See Office in the Home deduction.

Lease – Real Estate: See Office in the Home information. The lease expense paid for office, warehouse and storage space used for business is deductible. When using rental space for both business and personal you must pro-rate the cost and only deduct the business portion.

Lease – Equipment And Tools: Leasing equipment and tools for a short period is considered an operating expense. You have no expectation of ownership, and clearly this is an operating lease. Long term leases of equipment can be either an operating lease or a capital lease.

Operating Lease

In an average lease, the lessor retains ownership. The rental payment is fully deductible as a business operating expense. The lease may have the option to purchase the equipment at the end of the lease for Fair market value. Many operators prefer operating leases because the assets and the liability amounts are not on the company's balance sheet.

Capital Lease

A capital lease depends upon the agreement of the parties. If the ownership of the leased property is transferred to the lessee at the end of the lease, or if the lease contains a bargain purchase price, then the contract is considered a Capital Lease. The property leased is regarded as a Capital Asset. The lease payments are converted to principal and interest, and the property is subject to depreciation and 179 Depreciation.

TAX TIP

When negotiating an equipment lease, consider the benefits of a Capital Lease. Although the cost of the equipment and the related liability are recorded on your balance sheet as any other purchase, the benefits could be considerable because of the 179 depreciation available.

Miscellaneous Expense: Certain unreimbursed employee expenses are deductible as miscellaneous itemized deductions on Form 1040, Schedule A. The expense must be:

- ✓ Paid or incurred in the tax year
- ✓ For carrying on your trade or business of being an employee, and
- ✓ Ordinary and necessary

Office Supplies: Office supplies used for your business are deductible. Not only are the cost of office supplies and materials you have purchased deductible, the cost of stamps and postage used for business is also deductible. Some office supplies such as computers, copy machines, and furniture are considered capital equipment and are deductible over a period of years. See Capital Assets information.

Some materials, supplies, and postage may be considered Cost of Goods Sold. Cost of Goods Sold is that cost directly related to the production of income.

Operating Supplies: I use this category to those supplies not related to the direct production of revenue but are necessary for the operation of the company. Such things as towels, cleaning products or in a bar the CO_2 for keg beer would be an operating supply.

TAX TIP

We tend to forget the main purpose of bookkeeping is to produce a financial statement. Management uses Financial Statements to track income and expenses for determining the health of the business. The category called 'Operating Supplies' can be a catch-all and because of this many bookkeepers post a broad range of costs to this one Account. I suggest you post similar costs consistent month to month and year to year using the same Accounts so you can easily review and track your expenses.

Pest Control: Pest control cost for your office facility is a deductible expense. Pest control for Office in the Home would be part of the cost to maintain an office, and a prorated amount is deductible.

Postage, Freight & Delivery: Postage, freight & delivery cost are fully deductible. Product or manufacturing inventory cost includes the delivery cost to your facility. The cost of receiving inventory items is included as a cost of most inventory items. When paying delivery cost shipping finished inventory to the customer, the cost should be considered a Cost of Goods Sold not a postage expense under operating cost. Again for consistency similar cost should be posted to the same Account or category.

Printing and Reproduction: Many times printing cost is considered an advertising cost. For those businesses that make extensive use of printed material they may want to create a separate Account or category for such cost. Management uses separate Accounts as a method of controlling expenses.

Repairs and Maintenance: Classifying repair costs may be complicated since some repairs are Capital Assets and must be depreciated over its useful life. Incidental repairs do not add to the value of the property or extend its life may be deducted as an expense.

There are exceptions when determining classification of expenditures for major equipment repair. Court cases have determine that although the repair has increased the value of the asset, the useful life may not have increased. A repair expenditure may be classified as a capital improvement. Expensing a repair or capitalizing a repair is a complicated tax decision, and you need to consult your tax advisor.

Sanitation – Trash Removal: Trash removal cost should be considered as part of utility costs when deducting an office in the home. Trash removal expenses from your office or warehouse are fully deductible.

Salaries – Children: There are several benefits when hiring your child as an employee. As a proprietorship, you can engage your child, age 18 or less without deducting or matching the Social Security Tax.

Hiring your child in your corporation or LLC also provides considerable benefits. All wages are subject to payroll taxes. However, your child's income tax bracket is could be considerably less than yours. You may be in a 39% tax bracket, and your child may be in a zero tax bracket. Also, your child would be able to invest in an individual retirement fund if not provided by your company.

TAX TIP

If your company is unincorporated, (Sole Proprietorship or single-owner LLC) and your children are under the age of 18 you are allowed to hire them and receive special benefits.

- ➢ The work performed by your child must be essential to the operation of the business.
- ➢ The duties must be appropriate to both the child's age and his skills.
- ➢ Pay your child a reasonable wage for the work performed.
- ➢ Treat your child as you would any other employee.
- ➢ Benefits of hiring your kids as an employee

➢ No Social Security or Medicare taxes until the child turns 18.
➢ No federal, and probably state unemployment insurance taxes for your children.
➢ Social security taxes have a combined employer and employee amount of 15.3% of wages paid.

Salaries – Officers-Owners: Compensation received by owners of any entity are handled differently because of the entities legal status.

Sole Proprietorship or Single Owner LLC

The owners of either one of these entities are allowed to withdraw funds from the company at any time and in any amount. Draws from a Sole Proprietorship are recorded against the owner's <u>Account</u> and are not considered a deductible business expense. Proprietorship or single owned LLC use Schedule C. The profit on a Schedule C is subject to social security tax at the current rate of 15.3%. Profit generated on the Schedule C could be considered as 'Owners Income' of 'Owners Wages'.

TAX TIP

I suggest owners take a fixed draw each week or even once a month. Too often, the owner and their wife use the company checking account as a slush fund for running their personal life. Many times I have had clients who helped themselves to the cash register and I have had many restaurants feed not only their immediate family but also their extended family. Soon it is apparent the business cannot afford such expenditures. You must account for the cost of inventory that is consumed by you or anyone else if such use is not a valid business purpose.

Partnership and LLC

LLCs are not recognized by the IRS and are considered a partnership for tax purposes. LLC and a Partnership owner(s) receive guaranteed payments that are subject to payroll taxes when preparing your individual Tax Return. The guaranteed payments flow-through from the LLC/partnership tax return to the individual tax return. The guaranteed payments are subject to Social Security taxes at 15.3%, the same as a proprietorship.

TAX TIP

Treat regular payments to partners for performing work as Guaranteed Payments. Guaranteed payments are defined by the IRS as payments received by partners for services or the use of capital. The Guaranteed Payments can be made without regard to the income of the partnership. Your Guaranteed Payments are subject to social tax of 15.3%. Although Partnerships and LLC losses flow-through to the owner's individual tax return, the loss may or may not reduce your Social Security Tax liability depending upon ownership percentage.

S-Corporations

Owners of an S-Corporation are considered shareholders (Stock shares reflect ownership). Shareholders receive dividends, and dividends are earnings for their investment. If you owned stock in Ford or IBM, you would receive dividends as a return on investment. Millions of people invest in the stock market and many companies pay quarterly, semi-yearly or yearly dividends from Retained Earnings.

As a review; Retained Earnings are taxed profits from past years used for the benefit of the business operation. Remember, profits from an S-Corporation flow through to the shareholder's Individual Tax Return. Previous year's profits have been taxed, and the amount is recorded in the S-Corporation's books in an <u>Account</u> called Retained Earning. The term Dividends is used by C-Corporations and accountants have established the name Distribution of Profits for dividends from an S-Corporation. Both terms signify the distribution of profit, already tax and from an <u>Account</u> called Retained Earnings.

Retained Earnings are, usually, distributed to shareholders yearly or semi-yearly, and a few companies distribute dividends quarterly. The company Directors declare the distributions of profit and a payment date established. Distribution of Profits more often than this schedule and without proper documentation can lead the IRS to reclassify the distributions as wages or salary and subject to payroll taxes.

The second procedure for withdrawing money from your S-Corporation is wages or salaries subject to payroll taxes. Some owners prefer to make all withdraws as Distributions of Profits not subject to payroll taxes and not received as a salary. The S-Corporation regulation require that officers receive a wage commensurate with the position and experience.

This issue is a complex, and currently the Congress is considering applying a Social Security Tax on all withdraws for any S-Corporation with three or fewer shareholders/employees. An officer of a corporation is an employee of the company. Distributions and other payments by an S-Corporation to a corporate officer/shareholder must be treated as wages to the extent the amounts are reasonable compensation for services rendered to the corporation."

TAX TIP

Make sure that the salary you're paying yourself is reasonable for the work performed. If you're underpaying your salary or not paying yourself a salary to avoid payroll taxes, your distributions of profits could be reclassified as wages. Payroll taxes plus a penalty could be assessed. Pay Distributions of Profit from Retained Earnings on a schedule not less than quarterly and not without proper documentation.

If you follow these two rules and document each withdrawal, you should not have a problem with the IRS reclassifying any Distribution of Profit.

TAX TIP

Many times a husband and wife own an S-Corporation. Both are entitled to a share of the profits as investors, owners and shareholders. Both have paid taxes on their share of the profit. As with any corporation a distribution of profits from Retained Earnings is paid to the shareholders because of their

193

investment. If both work for the corporation both must receive wages commensurate to the work being performed and the wages are subject to payroll taxes. Many times one spouse is the only corporate employee and owner. The other may enjoy his or her share of the profits but is not considered an employee. The IRS may challenge an insufficient salary and convert a distribution of profits to salary. The spouse who is not employed by the corporation will not have their distribution challenged.

Section 1244 Stock

Not all attorneys are aware of Section 1244 of the IRS tax code. If you are investing in a small domestic corporation under section 1244 of the tax code, which includes S-Corporations, there are special tax benefits. Purchasing Section 1244 stock allows you to deduct stock losses as an 'ordinary loss' instead of capital loss. Under the code, capital losses are subject to a $3,000 limit. Section 1244 allows you to deduct the full amount in a single year provide special requirements are met. You can deduct up to $50,000 as an ordinary loss. Any amount over $50,000 is treated as a capital loss subject to a $3,000 limit per year. When forming your corporation ask your attorney if the stock will qualify under Section 1244.

TAX TIP

If your business cannot be classified as an S-Corporation because of IRS code, I suggest you chose an LLC entity for your company. All profits will be subject to payroll taxes, but you will not have the problem of double taxation. Double taxation can be devastating when you want to sell your business, and the buyer will not buy the stock and demands to purchase a business, from a C-Corporation. You will be stuck with double taxation. Corporate gains on the sale and individual tax on the dividends when passed to the shareholder. I do not like C-corporation for a Small Business because of this tax problem.

Salaries – Staff: Salaries or Wages and the employer share of payroll taxes are deductible.

TAX TIP

I prefer recording salaries paid to officers as a separate line-item Account. Wages paid to your staff can be divided into different Accounts that allows an easy comparison with wage reports. Because wages and the corresponding payroll taxes are reported to the state and Federal agencies, I suggest you maintain a line-item Account for Social Security and Medicare cost.

Security Systems: Security systems, guards and even security cameras are fully deductible for your business facility. Security systems protect the office in the home business and the home cost is prorated between personal and business use.

Taxes – Employer FICA and Medicare: This Account is for the cost of employer's share of employer FICA and Medicare taxes. The Total amount reflected in this Account should match with employees FICA and Medicare on your Quarterly 941s.

Taxes – Federal Unemployment: The current Federal Unemployment tax rate is 6% on the first $7,000.00 of wages paid. In some states, the rate is higher but the base rate is 6%. I set up a separate <u>Account</u> for Federal Unemployment taxes to ensure I did not forget to pay them.

Taxes – State Unemployment: Each state has a different unemployment insurance tax rate. As an example, one state's tax rate is a minimum of 5.5% too a maximum 8.95% based upon $12,900.00 in salary. In this state, an employer's cost for each employee is between $709.50 and $1,154.50. Many states have very low rates such as 3.5% on $10,000.00 in wages. A separate <u>Account</u> allows you to track your state, unemployment insurance cost.

Taxes – Property: Home property taxes can be deducted on Schedule A, Itemized deductions. Property taxes are also an expense for the Office in the Home calculation. Divide the office space square footage by the total house square footage and multiply this percent times the total property taxes. You can use the amount on your Schedule C – Office in the Home deduction or use the amount when computing office space charges in an Accountable Expense Report for your employer.

TAX TIP

Deducting part of your property taxes as office space can save you a minimum of 15.3 the amount of Social Security Payroll Taxes on net business profit. See Office In the Home Tax Tip above.

Telephone Expense: You cannot deduct the cost of basic local phone service (including any taxes) for the first telephone line you have in your home, even if you have an office in your home. You cannot divide the expense between business and personal. One-hundred percent of the primary phone line is non-deductible.

TAX TIP

Charges for business long-distance phone calls on your personal telephone are deductible. A second line into your home used exclusively for business is a deductible business expense.

Travel Expense – Motel, Transportation and Meals: Ordinary and necessary business related expenses are deductible and reimbursable. Meals, motels and hotels, transportation and entertainment expenses cannot be lavish or extravagant. This handbook suggests that your company reimburse employees and you (Officer or as an employee) for travel and entertainment expenses under an Accountable Plan.

The expenses for transportation, meals and lodging are deductible if the business trip is away from the taxpayer's tax home. The taxpayer home includes the entire city where business is conducted. Travel expense must include an overnight stay away from the company tax home. The tax home is the primary place of business and where most of the time income is earned. Many individuals work in another city where they daily commute and even

195

spend nights away from their residence. The other city is considered the tax home and the cost of travel back and forth is not deductible.

Travel – Special Considerations: There are many things to consider concerning deductible travel expense for you and your employees. Remember treat yourself as an employee by either having your business pay qualified travel expense directly or submit an expense report.

Travel - Temporary Versus Indefinite Assignment: Expenses for employment assignments for periods less than one year away from your tax home are deductible. If the job is temporary and the taxpayer intends to return to his tax home after the job ends, the lodging, meals, vehicle expense and even laundry expenses are deductible. There are a few major consideration when considering a temporary assignment. Again the tax law is complicated, and research is required.

Travel Expense – Business and Personal: If a business trip is 100% business the entire business expense is deductible. Travel expense to and from your business destination is 100% deductible. Lodging and meals are deductible as are another travel expense. Side trips not related to a business trip, are not deductible. If you spend three personal days on a 10-day business trip the cost of Lodging, meals, and even travel are a personal expense. Check IRS regulation to determine if a part of the travel expense is deductible.

Special Travel Rules: Luxury water travel, conventions and cruise ship conventions all have special rules and regulations. Travel outside the United States is 100% deductible if the trip is entirely business. If a trip is a combination of personal and business all travel cost including airfare are prorated by the number of days business, versus personal.

Maintain All Records of Proof of Business Travel: Travel expense is an area the IRS audits frequently because many taxpayers fail to keep adequate records. In this day and age of electronics, maintaining your records is much simpler. Your credit card company has at a minimum, a record of the date, where the funds were spent and maybe why the funds were spent. You are still required to provide proof that the travel was for business. As a side note, business entertainment still requires adequate proof using the four fingers and thumb rule detailed above.

Exceptions to maintaining copies of receipts: For travel and entertainment expense the receipt for an expense costing less than $75.00 is not required. (Not including lodging receipts). However, you must maintain a record of the Date, amount, location, name of the person entertained and business purpose. For travel expense only list the cost of meals, cabs and other costs less than $75.00.

Per-Diem Rates: Per diem rates are established by the IRS for meals, lodging, and other incidental expenses. The Per Diem rates are set depending on the travel location. Instead of deducting actual expense incurred for meals and lodging use Per Diem amounts plus documentation a proof the cost occurred.

The IRS has volumes written concerning deductible business travel expense and is beyond the scope of this book. The recommend what I feel is the best procedure for deducting business travel expenses for a Small Business. Owners with over 10% ownership and Sole Proprietors are not considered as employees for travel expense employee deductions. You can deduct travel expense but of course, you have to use a different method.

TAX TIP

I recommended that all business travel; meal cost and transportation expenses are paid from the company checking account only when an itemized expense report (an Accountable Plan) is received. Paying your employees a flat amount for any business expense (a Non-accountable plan) cost you as an employer and require your employee to pay extra taxes.

If the employer does not reimburse employees for business expense, such expense can be deducted on the employee's individual tax return as an itemized deduction

As a sole proprietor business expenses are deducted from income on Schedule C and therefore are not subject to Social Security Taxes. The worst tax scenario is when business expenses are deducted as an Itemized Deduction. Not only is the amount of the business expense deductible limited, the business expense is subject to Social Security taxes as wages.

Utilities: Utilities for your office, shop, store or any 100% business occupied facility is a deductible business expense. Maintain records of services for office in the home cost.

Vehicle Expense: Taxpayers can deduct the business use of the vehicle using the Actual Cost Method or the Standard Mileage method;

Basic Information Needed to Deduct Vehicle Expense

- ➢ Need the total mileage driven for the year.
- ➢ Need total business miles driven for the year.
- ➢ Need total personal miles driven for the year
- ➢ Date of purchase or date vehicle placed in service.
- ➢ Need the cost of the vehicle or Cost Basis.

Actual Cost Method

Step 1: Calculate the total vehicle operating cost. Including:

- ➢ Gas and oil.
- ➢ Repairs and maintenance.
- ➢ Lease payments

➤ Vehicle insurance.
➤ Registration, inspection & emissions testing and licensing.
➤ Tires, batteries and servicing.
➤ Washing and polishing cost.
➤ Depreciation.

Depreciate the cost of the vehicle over a period of years as allowed by the IRS code. The IRS considers Vehicle depreciation as the decline in value over a period. The amount of the reduction is an expense on the vehicles owner's tax return.

Step 2: Compute the percent of Business use: Divide the business miles driven for the year by the total mileage driven for the year to arrive at the percent of business use. 16,489 Total business miles/ 22,545 Total miles driven = 74%.

Step 3: Compute the Deduction: The total vehicle operating expense times the business use percentage, equals the amount of car expense deductible.

Note: Parking and Tolls for business are deductible as a separate line item. Parking and Tolls are ordinary and necessary and are reimbursable under an Accountable Plan.

Note: You can convert from the standard mileage method to the actual cost method any year.

Standard Mileage Rate Method.

The vehicle owner is allowed to deduct car expense using an IRS approved mileage rate. The rate in 2014 was 56.5 cents a mile. Using the example above, the deduction would be 16,489. Business miles times 56.5 Cents = $9,316.

Note: Businesses owning and operating five of more vehicles must use the Actual Cost Method for computing vehicle expense deduction.

Determining Business mileage

➤ Traveling from one work location to another within the taxpayer's tax home area. (Generally, the tax home is the entire city or general area where the taxpayer's main place of business is located, regardless of where he or she resides.)
➤ Visiting customers.
➤ Attending a business meeting away from the regular workplace.
➤ Getting from home to a temporary workplace when the taxpayer has one or more regular places of work. (These temporary workplaces can be either within or outside taxpayer's tax home area

> Mileage from your home to your place of business is commuting and not deductible.
> Mileage from your home to your first business stop is not deductible.
> Mileage from your last business stop to your home is not deductible.
> When using your vehicle for both personal and business trips the mileage from any business stop to a private stop or from the private stop to a business stop is not deductible.
> There are few exceptions when a vehicle could be considered 100% business use.
>   • Carrying business materials or equipment could qualify your vehicle as 100% business use.
>   • Leave your vehicle at your office. By leaving your car at the office and only using it for business, you can justify 100% business use.

TAX TIP

I always remind clients that stopping by the grocery store is personal mileage. The IRS realizes that few vehicle are use 100% for business and business audits always concentrate on this deduction. Without adequate mileage records the mileage deduction will be cut in half or the IRS may disallow the total deduction.

Leased Vehicles

You are allowed to use the standard mileage rate for a leased vehicle. You are not allowed to use the standard mileage method one year and actual expense method the next year for leased vehicles. Whatever method selected, you cannot change. If you do select the Actual Cost Method, lease payments are not deductible. Leased vehicles are not considered a capital asset and depreciation is not allowed. The lease payment is a deduction if the actual cost method is used.

TAX TIP

When using your personal vehicle for corporation business, record the business mileage and using the standard IRS mileage rate invoice your company as would any other employee. As the vehicle owner, you are responsible for 100% of the operating expenses. The only amounts that should be paid by your company is the standard mileage rate. This rate covers gas, oil, maintenance, tires, battery, and insurance and depreciation expense.

The operating expenses for a vehicle owned by an S-corporation can be deducted using the Actual Cost Method or the Business miles method. When a corporation owned vehicle is utilized by an employee for personal business, the employee is required to reimburse the company for such personal use. Because the company owns the vehicle, does not automatically make the vehicle 100% business use. Record must be kept of business and personal mileage.

199

TAX TIP

Vehicles owned by a C Corporation, S Corporation, a Partnership or an LLC should require employees to keep mileage records. Employees need to reimburse their company for any personal use. Use the standard mileage rate for this purpose. If you do not maintain mileage records, the minimum you should do is pay your corporation a monthly fee to account for such personal use.

Seperating yourself from your corporation is necessary. You are not the company. You must treat yourself as an employee.

© Randy Glasbergen.

"I can claim a 70-inch plasma TV as a business expense because my accountant said it's important to look at the big picture."

Chapter 8
Business Information, Observations and Rules For Success
SMALL BUSINESS HANDBOOK
The best and most complete handbook for the Small Business Entrepreneur.
Essential information for starting, buying, operating and succeeding.

Colonel Harland Sanders, of Kentucky Fried Chicken fame, was my first business hero. In the early 1950's Colonel Sanders lost his restaurant. The prospect of living on a Social Security check of $105.00 a month created a drive to achieve success. He decided to franchise his one remaining asset, his chicken recipe, and his basic cooking technique. For months, the Colonel called on restaurants and demonstrated his fried chicken method and entered into a handshake franchise agreement for five-cents a chicken. He made 1,006 calls before his first sale. If a 65-year-old man, wearing a white coat and sporting a beard can make 1,006 sales calls before his first sale; think what you can do. The key to success is a marketing strategy that results in sales. Colonel Sanders had faith in his marketing plan, and he did not stop when the 312th restaurant said no, nor did he stop at sales call 861; he kept going. With determination and perseverance, sales and success can be realized.

Entrepreneurs can and do succeed by studying and observing successful business operations. Although our government ignores history and continually throws money at a problem expecting different results; small entrepreneurs can study business success or failures and apply out of the box solutions with little or no extra funding. Critique every business you enter or visit. Look at the appearance, service, quality, prices, attitude and anything else you feel is important.

Successful entrepreneurs critique every element and detail of their business operation. Several years ago I coined the term **Inside Competition**, which defines all the facets within the control of management. Managers make notes of every detail requiring attention. They then develop a business, marketing and operating plan that leads to success. Nothing is left to chance. The observations below are a combination of thousands of business critiques I have made over the years. I still observe every business I visit paying careful attention to all phases of their operations starting with the outside appearance and I continuing my critique exiting the outlet. I love to engage owners or managers in an exchange of new and astute business management practices. Why mimic failure. Entrepreneurs succeed by copying successful operations and adding their personal vision and signature.

It is all about Sales: Your number one job is to produce sales. Wow, what dumb advice. Of course, I need sales to achieve success! Over and over I have watched start-ups totally oblivious to what it takes to become successful. Often new business owners spent most of their dollars and time creating the nuts and bolts of their business and very little time and money on marketing.

Copyright ©

We all gravitate to activities that we enjoy and provide a feeling of comfort and accomplishment. Conversely, we shy away from those activities that make us uncomfortable. Actively soliciting customers creates rejection, and most of us shy away from placing ourselves in awkward and embarrassing situations. Can you sell your products and services? In Chapter 1, I covered the many reasons why business do not achieve success and of course, each hurdle must be overcome for you to realize success. However, you must understand you. Do you have the capability, aptitude, talent and facility to succeed?

I particularly admire the article "The Top 10 Reasons Why People Don't Succeed" by Leslie Fieger and the article by Kevin Geary, "Change Your Tree." Both authors do an excellent job pinpointing why business failures may not be the result of a business problem, but may be more directly related to the entrepreneur themselves. Fieger points out that the fear, passion, lack of resolve and lack of action create failure and Geary tackles the problem by creating seven reasons people fail. I highly recommend both of these authors for a greater insight into what makes you tick.

I can bang your head against the wall over and over, stressing the need for sales in order to be successful. However, you must look inward and tackle all elements of <u>Inside Competition</u>. Read Fieger and Geary and know the attributes within you that need improvement to be successful. Both authors define the problem but are part of the solution. Fieger presents four clear and precise actions and Geary's conclusions clearly explains why you can achieve success by always looking at yourself for the solution.

© Randy Glasbergen / glasbergen.com

"When we pay women less, that's discrimination.
To make it fair, we should pay everyone less."

Understand the Basics of Sales

All professions require communication. We tend to associate a particular skill-set to different jobs when in fact, all jobs need the ability to communicate effectively.

A marketing plan is a guide for capturing your share of the market. Your primary problem is how to create enough product or service sales at a profit margin necessary to sustain your business model. Anyone can give away merchandise or service. The essential key to success is selling a product or service at a price that results in a Net Profit that supports your operation. Entrepreneurs must analysis their competitors, but the key to success is sales.

Spend your time developing your market. College professors, large corporations and our government measure success by the dollars invested into a problem. You must think outside of the box when creating sales. Money is not the answer. Be creative. I started my income tax preparation business with zero dollars for marketing. Out of necessity I went door to door in a new housing area visiting the same potential clients three times over several weeks. Secondly I talked about my expertise as a tax accountant to anyone who would listen, people on the street, restaurants and I even developed a client on an elevator. One time I received a telephone solicitation from a local insurance company and convinced the telemarketer to have me prepare her tax return. The third marketing technique involved rewarding my clients with a new dollar bill plus a thank-you note for any referral. The dollar did not create the referral. The process of acknowledging my clients contribution to my success was the key. The fourth action I took was keeping detail notes concerning my client's personal information. I remembered the names and ages of their children, the name of their dog and any particular hobbies or sports interest. I knew my clients, and when I saw them once a year, this knowledge of personal information always impressed them. My clients believed I was a whole lot smarter than I am. It is all about perception.

Use your imagination! Printing companies spend a great deal of money advertising Business Cards, and it is some of the best advice you will ever receive. Make things happen and never be without a business card. Trade business cards and follow-through with an email or even a phone call. There are thousands of sub-contractors and independent commission salesmen; daily contact a potential client by visiting your target market. If each customer generates $500.00 in sales income and your cold call rate of success is 10%; contacting 100 potential customers will result in sales income of $5,000.00. Too often, we measure our sales call results by the number of 'No's'. Look forward to receiving nine "no's" because the tenth response is $500.00 in your pocket.

Use your employees as an extension of your advertising plan. Give them business cards with customer discounts on the back and for every 5 or 10 cards returned, the employee receives a bonus. Set aside two hours per day for direct customer marketing. Talk to everyone, you never know who will be your next client. Standing in line at a restaurant or even waiting at the doctor's office should be productive. There are thousands of unique tactics that will result is a sale. If the strategy fails, try another. Remember, success is only 1006 sales calls away.

We live in a world of electronic messaging. Create interest in your products and services by using a Web site, tweeting, e-mailing and joining blogs. There are hundreds of young people who have the skill and knowledge to be helpful building an internet presence. A Web Site is passive adverting that customers stumble upon when surfing the Web.. You must be pro-active using all electronic media to ensure customers find your Web site and your business.

<u>Sales = Creating a Marketing Plan and Working your Plan</u>.

Cost of Goods Sold: Have you ever heard the statement: "I'm losing money for tax reasons" or 'I'm only taking on this job to keep my employees busy.' Businesses do not price their product or services to create a loss. Losses happen because companies lacked sales with adequate product and service margins. Pricing your product to create an acceptable Gross Profit margin is the second most important ingredient in your business operation. Don't let the competition dictate your prices. You have inside competition and outside competition. You cannot control your outside competition but can control your product, service, location, presentation, and price. What do you offer that will support a higher price? Grocery stores price many products at cost or even at a loss, however hundreds of other products are offered at a price that represents a larger markup to offset the 'loss leaders.'

When the economy started going crazy in 1990s, one of my clients continually increased his prices as demand increased. In 2007, our economy took a tumble, and he was forced to reduce his prices and his margins to compete. He paid attention to his market and competition. His product and services always demanded a higher price than his completers because he controlled his <u>Inside Competition</u>. His work product was outstanding; his service was first rate, but his market had changed, so did he. He cut expenses and discovered new ways of doing business by instituting more economical products and services. He was able to reduce his costs and maintain a lower, but acceptable margin that allowed him to maintain his market share.

<u>Sales and Sufficient Margins are the Two Keys to Success.</u>

Fixed Salary or Draw: Take a flat salary weekly, semi-monthly or monthly if you are a corporation. If you are a proprietorship or partnership (LLC) withdraw a flat weekly or monthly amount. If your company is unable to pay your salary or draw because of cash shortage, you will have to wait for your money just as if you were another creditor. Do not make a disbursement for yourself whenever you want. Many times the cash drawer becomes the cash box for the family. It's hard to maintain your records and of course without limits you end up living on whatever you take. Soon you will be broke.

Money Management: Personally manage the business checking account. If you are a single individual operation, there is no one else, so you are stuck with the job of making deposits and paying bills. However, I strongly suggest you always control your money. Maintain control over deposits and payments until time restraints prevent you from doing so. Once you hire employees split the bookkeeping functions between yourself and a bookkeeper. The individual that handles the deposits should never post the accounts receivable and the person who writes the checks should always be double-checked by a second person or yourself. Sign every check and monthly double check the disbursements against the Bank Statement. Set up procedures to streamline and protect your money.

Checking Account: As a Small Business Owner learn how to balance your checking account. I know it's hard to believe, but employees steal. Servicemen take on service appointments without going through the office and employees who post receivables take the money and record the customer's account as paid in full. My office has caught more than one bookkeeper forging the owner's signature on checks. Organize the access to receipts and payments and the access to checks and cash flow to prevent a thief. Anytime you are dealing with money the urge to participate in your profits becomes almost irresistible.

Organize Your Time: Each night or every morning organize your day. Rushing to the office or store to open the doors at 8:00am when it is already 8:15am creates confusion and disorganization. Arrive 30 minutes to an hour early to organization your day. Schedule to-do items and make your appointments. Plan your day – work your plan. I know that is an old cliché, but it is crucial. I once had a client who was a realtor, he always arrived at the office at 7am to plan his day and complete his to-do list. His earnings were three to four times greater than the average realtor.

Make Lunch Productive: Why do realtors, car salesman and salesman in general have lunch with each other? Business owners are salesmen, and they need to act as such by using every hour of the day, including lunch to interface with clients. Operating a small business requires you to be the top salesman in your company and eating lunch with your employees on a regular basis does not increase sales.

Marketing Plan: The marketing plan can be detailed or a general plan which summarizes your commitment in money and efforts for obtaining sales for your products and services. I never could understand why business owners used word-of-mouth as their only marketing activity. Word-of-mouth is not a marketing plan it is a plan for disaster. Your marketing plan is a written commitment of time and money. It does not have to be as extensive as a small book, but your plan must account for daily actions such as time set aside to contact local newspapers or an action item to personally contact potential customers. Schedule 5 hours a week for personal contact with potential customers. Go see clients if at all possible. Be proud of your abilities and blow your own horn.

Prepare A Budget: The budget is a financial document used to project future income and expenses. Prepare your budget using a scratch pad or for a more formal plan, use a computer spreadsheet program such as Excel. I think a yearly budget is necessary, but a revised monthly budget is indispensable. I had a client who consistently had good sales, but could not control his costs. He prepared his budgets but did not follow his projections and of course he now works for Home Depot. Make a budget and follow it in daily.

Know you're Daily Nut: Reduce your average monthly operating expenses to a daily average. Take your monthly expense budget and simply divide that amount by the number of days your business is open. If your monthly expenses average $12,000 and your business is open 22 days per month, you're need to generate $550 in Net Profit, (Sales Income – Cost of Goods Sold). Every day you open your doors. If your profit margin is 40%, you need $1,375 in sales each day to survive. Many times I ask clients to understand their hourly-nut. If you have to have $171.88 in sales every hour, you and your employees should know that amount. It is not a secret that you need to keep from your employees. They are part of your failure and your success.

Daily or Hourly Employee Incentives: I love daily, weekly or even monthly employee incentives. You do not do them every day, but you do them consistently. Make it a cash bonus and make a big deal out of it. Present the money at the end of the day or after the end of a shift and make sure every employee understands that next time it could be them. The only downside is the requirement of including the cash incentive into the workers' wages. Just add the incentive to the employees wages and deduct the same amount as already paid. All bonuses are subject to payroll taxes.

Employee Tips: Operating a business where employees receive Tips requires several actions on the part of the employee and the employer:

➢ Tips belong to the employee – it is illegal for a company to participate in any Tip.

➢ Tip pools are acceptable but must have a written agreement.

➢ Employees must report the amount of Tip Income received to Employer.

➢ Employer reports Tips as wages received and must withhold payroll taxes and matching FICA and Medicare.

➢ 100% of Tips are taxable.

➢ You cannot use a flat percentage to compute Tip income. Percent's such 8% or 10% of gross receipts are not acceptable. The 8% rule is a guide used by the IRS to determine if an employer is reporting Tips correctly. It is applied to the employee's gross revenue to determine if employees are reporting their tips income correctly.

➤ Employers are allowed to reduce the employee's wages per state and IRS mandates. Under federal law the employees who earn at least $30 per month in tips can be paid as little as $2.13 an hour. Calculate the wages and tips received to determine if the employee is receiving the minimum wage amount. If an employee's total earnings fall short of the minimum wage, you must make up the difference.

➤ Some states, including California, don't allow employers to pay tipped employees less than the minimum wage. And some states require employers to pay a higher hourly amount to tipped employees. Check your local laws for exceptions to distributing Tips and other local regulations.

As I stated above I'm addicted to observing business procedures and critiquing their operations. When visiting a local restaurant, the owner explained that he seized all the Tip money and each month he awarded the Tips to his employees as bonuses. He determined some nebulous procedure for allocating most of the money to those employees he thought had done an outstanding job. First off, once the Tip is received it belongs to the employee and secondly the employer cannot determine who should receive the bulk of the Tip money.

Share Information with your Employees: During crises it is best to share the fundamental business problems. Employees probably have a good idea what is happening and of course they have a vested interest in your success. I don't like secrets. Let your employees understand the daily nut, the amount of sales it takes to break-even and other information. Salaries and wages usually are a secret and guess what; everyone already knows. Why maintain a secret that is common knowledge? Don't advertize salaries but don't stick your head in the ground, and pretend employees don't know who deserves higher pay, and most will accept the differences. The one reason I don't like nepotism is sometimes the relative's wages are greater than other employees doing the same job.

Pay Your Federal Withholding Tax: Many companies have cash flow problems and sometimes these companies fail to deposit payroll taxes withheld from their employee's wages. It is easy to get in debt to the IRS. The IRS is not demanding payment when the companies pays the salaries. Unlike other creditors, withholding amounts could be payable monthly, and the IRS procedures take considerable time for enforcement. However, the IRS debt may become overwhelming and with interest and penalties impossible to pay. The IRS may accept a payment plan. However, on any payment plan the interest and penalty are paid first, the companies matching payroll tax amounts are collected next, and the payroll taxes withheld from employees' wages are collected last. The IRS understands the law and by applying payments as above, the IRS is in a position to receive as much as possible.

Once paid, the gross earnings belong to your employee. The IRS requires you to withhold Income Taxes, Social Security and Medicare taxes from the employee's wages. Amounts withheld are 'Trust Funds.' You are acting as a trustee for the IRS. The amounts belong to your employee and payable to the IRS or in some cases the state income tax. The owner, president or anyone responsible for transferring these funds to the IRS may be held personally liable. The IRS will take action by creating a 'Trust Fund recovery penalty' or just called a '100% penalty,' assessing the amounts against an individual responsible. The IRS files liens against an individual's personal property, and collection actions by the IRS are extensive.

Two important concepts:

 ➢ Amounts withheld from employees' wages, Trust Funds, cannot be included in bankruptcy filings. You can include most liabilities, including individual income taxes assessment and interest and penalties in your bankruptcy filing, but "Trust Funds" cannot be included. (Note: Contact your attorney for particulars and exceptions)

 ➢ As a proprietorship or a partner in a partnership, you can be personally responsible for the Trust funds and matching taxes. A corporate and LLC entity may limit your responsibility, and you need to meet with an attorney for advice. In general Trust Funds could create a personal liability from your LLC or corporation if you are responsible for payment.

There is considerable tax law, bankruptcy law, and IRS code concerning payroll tax liability. The IRS has ten years to collect this debt, and I strongly suggest you pay all withholding taxes. It is not an obligation to ignore.

Keep Records: There are no easy answers as to how length of time you need to keep your tax records. In general you need to keep tax records for taxable income items for a minimum of seven years and expense records (deductions), including receipts, check copies and invoices for three years. However, records concerning capital assets, equipment, real estate and fixtures must be held for seven years past the disposal of the property. Selling an asset is considered income and the IRS, by code can review income transactions for a seven-year period.

Many individuals have destroyed records related to their home because they falsely believe there will never be a tax on the sale. Tax on the profit generated from the disposal of a personal residence can occur, again contact your tax accountant for details. However, you will need your records to substantiate your position. Converting your personal residence to a rental property or gifting your property may also create a tax liability scenario. Again you will need all your records.

Basis of Property: The 'Adjusted Cost Basis' or 'Book Value' of capital assets, including equipment, residents, rental house or other property acquired either by purchasing or trading starts with the investment. The basis in the capital asset usually begins with the purchase cost and is adjusted for certain tax items as follows:

➢ The adjusted cost basis of the asset increases as follows:

   ✓ The purchase price – or the Book Value of an asset traded.

   ✓ The cost of improvements. Such as a new roof for a rental property.

   ✓ Legal costs related to the purchase or the use of the asset

   ✓ When selling the asset the cost of the sale such as realtor fees are an additional cost.

If you were buying a Rental Property, the cost of the property plus 100% of the closing cost would be your starting Adjusted Basis. If you remolded the property, the cost of the remodel would increase the Adjusted Basis.

Tax Tip

Many times taxpayers borrow money against a rental property and unless the borrowed funds are used to improve the property, the amount of the loan does not increase the adjusted cost basis. Taxpayers are sometimes surprised when a rental property sells, little cash is received, yet thousands of dollars in tax liability may be due.

This scenario occurs many times with rental property ownership. If the property was a rental the depreciation taken each year reduces the cost basis. On a $200,000 property, the depreciation deduction is $7,300.00 each year. Although the depreciation deduction reduces the taxes on the rental income and may be other revenues, landlords may not be aware that the depreciation will be taxable as capital gain income, in the year of sale. If the depreciation is recaptured in the year of sale and you owned the property ten years, $73,000.00 is taxable income. Many times the rental property owners borrow money against a rental and a few years later sale the property and the tax liability could be greater that the cash received from the sale.

Many clients request that depreciation not be deducted if it becomes taxable income in the year of sale. However, for straight-line depreciation the deduction reduces taxable income. As an example, if I have wages of $25,000.00 and depreciation on a rental creates a $5,000.00 loss, the taxable income would be $20,000.00. If the tax bracket is 30%, the $5,000.00 loss saves $1,500.00. When selling the property you may have to pay taxes on the $5,000.00 because of the gain on the sale. However, the $5,000.00 would be taxed as a Capital Gain, and the tax could be as low as 10% or $500.00. Taking depreciation could save thousands of dollars. The example above is simple, and taxes can be more complicated, so please contact your Tax Accountant.

The other reason you must take depreciation is Depreciation is Allowed or Allowable. If you do not claim the depreciation allowed, the IRS code requires that your gain is determine as if you took the depreciation. In the example below the depreciation for ten years is $73,000. This amount could have saved $21,900.00 at 30%. However, if the taxpayer failed or refused to deduct the depreciation it would be considered taxable income.

Cost of the rental	$200,000	
Depreciation for ten years.	73,000	
Cost Basis		$127,000
Loan at purchase current amount due	$125,000	
Second Mortgage	100,000	
Total amount payable at date of sale		$225,000
Net sales price	$250,000	
Cost Basis	127,000	
Profit		$127,000
Taxes Due at 20%		$31,750
Actual cash received at sale		25,000

Again contact your tax accountant before making a property sale or trade. The gain on personal property such as a vacation home is taxable income in the year of sale. Losses may not be deductible for personal property.

➢ The adjusted cost basis is reduced as follows:

✓ Depreciation. Each year a portion of the cost is allowed as a Business Tax Deduction.

✓ Losses are due to a casualty or theft. A portion or all of the asset cost could be reduced by deducting the cost of a casualty or thief.

✓ Any other tax-related costs and loss.

Basis of property received as a gift: The adjusted cost basis of property you receive as a gift maintains the same adjusted cost basis as the donor's cost basis in the property. As an example if parents give a house to a child, the child cost is the same as the parents cost. The amount of gift tax paid increases the cost basis. Many times it is difficult or impossible to determine the Cost Basis of a gifted property because the donor (giver) purchased the property years ago and cost basis information is not available. Parents give their children stock certificates, the child holds the stock for many years and then decides to sell. Many times it is impossible determine the price the parents paid for the stock. When receiving a gift of property attempt to establish the cost basis at the date of the gift. Both State and Federal taxes apply to the profit if the gift is sold.

Some parent's gift their home to their children in an attempt to create the illusion of poverty. Older people become concerned that a debilitating illness may force them into a nursing home, and Medicare will force a home sale to use the funds to pay nursing home care. Secondly many taxpayers believe the IRS will take their property at their death to satisfy inherence taxes, commonly known as the death-tax and therefore deny their children of this asset. Usually, most people do not have taxable estates. Check the Federal and State inherence tax rates before making a decision concerning gifting property. See your Tax accountant before transferring any property.

Basis of inherited property: The cost basis of inherited property is the Fair Market Value at the date of death. (Or at six months after death) Because Federal Estate Taxes start when the estate value exceeds $5,340,000 for 2014, most inherited property is passed to the heirs without out any Federal Inheritance Tax. However, inherited property should be appraised correctly because the Fair Market Value establishes the Cost in the hands of the heirs. Many times estate attorneys are only concerned about inheritance tax and ignore establishing a correct value. An incorrect low appraised value can cost thousands of dollars in capital gains tax when and if the heir sells the property.

Don't Work For Money: I worked for Lockheed-Lockheed when it was called Martins. I hated the job, the company, the work, the bosses and the little pay. I guess I would have died many years ago if I would have continued my career at Martins. Many people thrived in that atmosphere, but it was a slow death for me. I fell in love with preparing income taxes and interfacing with tax clients. I would have done it for free if I had figured out how to feed my family. I make money to survive – I work because I loved what I did. You need to find a professional who works because he loves his job.

Open and Close On-time – Get Your Ass out of Bed: Get your butt out of bed and begin your business on time. I have had clients borrow money from their parents or create a second mortgage on their home to start a business but treat that opportunity with little respect. They sleep-in and open their business late and even close early. Their bad habits seem to intensify when they are not under the guidance of the employer.

Answer the Phone: Businesses today incorrectly believe they are saving money by replacing personal contact with an answering machine. Many phone messages are extensive, and you never can talk with an agent. Companies spend millions on advertising but do not take advantage of the opportunity to market their product or service when a customer is on the phone. The marketing plans objective is to convince you to buy, but only if you don't bother them. Give me your money but please don't call me. I purchase many audible books from Audible.com. Several times I have had difficulties with my account or purchase and Audible not only answers their phone or uses a direct on-line contact, they handle the problem in a timely fashion. Microsoft is on the other end of the scale. It is hard finding a phone number, let alone speak with anyone. They do have good customers service during the sale but within a few seconds after the purchase they no longer wish to talk to you. You can quickly determine the companies respect for their customers by the volume of their customer service Web Site. Microsoft has spent millions to eliminate any contact with consumers. Got your money - now go-a-way.

Use direct phone contact to secure business. It is an opportunity for you to make a sale. They called you! It doesn't take a mental giant to understand that an opportunity exist when you speak directly to your customer.

Negative Advertising: I was at a self-serve car wash in Littleton, Colorado many years ago before swiping a credit card was available as a payment option. The coin changer was empty, so I walked forty feet to the next business, a fast lube outlet. A sign attached to their front door warned quarter less individual that 'We are not a Bank – We do not make change.' What is wrong with this picture?

Many strip-malls allow their tenants to place a sign that denies parking unless you are their customer. A cleaners next to a fast food sandwich shop in Austin, TX felt this was the only way to cope with a parking problem. What is wrong with this picture?

Both of these businesses designed customer barriers that offend consumers. Turn these problems into an opportunity. The fast lube outlet should have an employee at the carwash handing out five quarters for a dollar for the first dollar of change and a coupon offering a 10% discount. They had customers within 40 feet of their business but chose to insult them because it was inconvenient. Think about the parking problem. A shopper can't find a parking place, so you piss him off further by denying him a place to park. He is at your door, take advantage of your opportunity to get a new customer. Have an employee invite customers to park during busy hours and they give them a discount coupon. You can also have an assistant ready to deliver and pick-up cleaning from the customer's car. Does the solution have problems? Of course, it does but logistically my solution develops new customers, it does not drive customers away.

Think about your business, and the negative actions your take each day that create a barrier to new customers.

Dumb Business Decisions: Historically many businesses fail because they do not understand their market. In a small town exist a dumpy bar which serves the greatest greasy burgers in the area. Nothing is better than beer and a hamburger. How about some fries? Not only do they not offer French Fries they actually advertise that you cannot buy fries and don't ask. I have eaten there many times, and it is possible that this Bar serves 200 to 300 customers a day. If 50% of the customers wanted French Fries and we use 200 customer visits, the Bar could sell 100 orders of fries a day. Open six days a week or 600 orders a week times 52 weeks is 31,200 orders of fries a year. Using a sales price of $3.50 and cost of 88 cents they are losing $81,744.00 a year in gross profit. Tell me again why you don't sell fries?

Customer demand may not create an opportunity. The example above is simple however many times a small business cannot be all things to all people. When you cannot provide a product or service make sure, you provide information directing your customer toward their mission. Many times employees take great glee in saying No. The customer is in your store; you may not be able to fulfill his needs, but his visit is an opportunity for you to make a future sale. When visited in my accounting office by a drop-in stranger or even a door-to-door sales person, it was always an opportunity for me to secure a new client.

Treat Your Employees Right: Although we have seen it on TV a thousand times, employee mistreatment is real and not just some story line. These last five years jobs have been difficult to obtain with unemployment hitting over 10% in many states. This shift of power to management has created bosses who manage by intimidation. Yelling and disrespect may be the standard operating procedure but being an ass will back-fire. Job performance declines and if you are not on site I assure you that your employees do not have your best interest in mind. Your employees are an integral and essential part of your success. You will not succeed without the help of trusted employees. Treat them accordingly.

Lease or Buy Business Vehicle: Probably the most asked question in my business. Dealing with the problem is as simple as a mathematical event - it is cheaper to purchase a car than lease a car. There are many positive reasons to lease; a small down payment, always drive a new car, protect your equity position and of course lower payments. Leasing has many negatives. Most of the time the lease is for the full MSRP with no discounts, the contract documents are often vague, and the extras for additional mileage or excessive wear and tear are not clearly defined. The difficulty of getting out of a lease versus selling your car is another negative.

However, if you cannot manage an acceptable down payment or the payment is unacceptable you may be forced to lease. I have been through all the figures on many car leases and leasing cost more. There are far too many uncontrollable variables when leasing. The price, the residual value and the interest rate may be hidden. Excessive mileage is another problem. I have had clients park their leased vehicle for several months before the end of the lease because excessive mileage cost were 15 to 25 cents a mile. Build equity and buy.

What Motives Your Employees: Employees are motivated by different rewards. Many managers use negative motivation such as fear of being fired or even of being demoted. We have seen fear motivation on TV as comedy, but I assure you that fear motivation is not funny. I have seen fear motivation, and often employees respond by negative job performance.

Money is not the motivation for all employees. Some employee's value flexible work schedule, titles, making a difference in their jobs and many would rather have challenging work. Some employees want education benefits, retirement benefits, and many want an office. Peer recognition is also a great motivator but some employees thrive on independence and many employees just want a job with a livable wage to support their family. Learn what motivates your employees and your profit will increases.

Dress Code: A dress code creates a positive image of your company and instills confidence in your customers and employees. A professionally dressed employee is usually more productive. A dress code is imperative to prevent your employees from dressing in a manner that is unacceptable and defies common sense. Some workers have been known to wear pajamas, tank tops or even shorts to work. A more practical dress code clearly identifies employees in the workplace. Many companies furnish uniforms or smocks if appropriate.

Nepotism: Nepotism is the term for employers, managers or anyone in a position of power granting favoritism to a family member or a friend without merit. Nepotism can have damaging effects on the internal operations by eroding employee morale. In many small businesses, nepotism can be viewed as a synonym for succession. Many companies avoid nepotism by forbidding relatives from working in the same departments or the same company.

In a small business, nepotism can be a short track to failure. The words Father and Son on the company can be a source of pride and success. We all want our children to follow in our footsteps however many times your kids do not have the same abilities or work ethic as you do. I have seen companies in dire financial shape layoff key employees and retain a relative. Employers overlook the capacities of a spouse or child because they are family.

"Can you think of any others?"

The many Hats of an Entrepreneur: When failure occurs most entrepreneurs blame competitors. In fact, most failures are because the owner failed to understand he could not wear all the hats necessary for a successful operation. Small business owners need to delegate many tasks. If you do not have the ability in accounting, marketing or any other aspect of your business, hire a professional. There are many reasons for failure.

1. **Failing to change with the times:** The ability to recognize opportunities and be flexible enough to adapt is crucial to surviving and thriving. Learn how to wear multiple hats, respond nimbly, and develop new areas of expertise.

2. **Ineffective marketing:** Customers can't do business with you if they don't know you're there. It doesn't cost a lot to advertise and promote your business through online marketing, social media, email, local search, and more.

3. **Underestimating the competition:** Customer loyalty doesn't just happen — you have to earn it. Watch your competition and stay one step ahead of them. If you don't take care of your customers, your competition will.

In America we have equal opportunity, not equal results. No one owes you a living. If you fail, try again. Some great men have filed for bankruptcy. Abe Lincoln and Henry Ford are a couple who failed and tried again. Sitting all day drinking beer is not the road to success. Start again and if that does not work start again.

Never make pre-payments: Almost every contractor wants a cash deposit for 'materials' before starting a job. Many are such poor managers that they need to pay expenses for old jobs before they can begin a new job. They may lack the capital to operate their business or pay day to day cost. This is not your problem. Think about it. If your contractor does not have money to run his company, how is he going to pay for screw-ups? Whatever the reason, don't pay in advance. Companies never pay an employee in advance, why should you pay a stranger a large sum of money so he can do his job. I have heard every story there is, and paying in advance is foolish. There are three actions you can take to ensure you are protected.

➤ Hire a bank to inspect the progress and pay completed work. The contractor is protected, and you are protected. You can also request an attorney to hold the money and make payments based upon pre-determined completion commitments.

➤ Pay for the materials directly or make the payee on your check the contractor and the supplier. The contractor can begin your job and receive payment as work is completed. You need to make sure materials delivered to your job site are paid. You can be held liable if the contractor does not pay for materials. Always pay the supplier directly for any materials delivered to your job. If the contractor insist that he pays his bills, call the material provider and ask.

➤ Pay your contractor daily, or every three days as the job is completed. Write the terms on the contract. Pay as different segments of the work is finished or as agreed. Also check to make sure workers are paid. They have the right to take legal action against you if the contractor skips without payment.

Workman's Compensation: Many employers fail to obtain Workers Compensation. In most states, it is a requirement. However, many states don't requirement this insurance. If one of your employees, a sub-contractor or even an employee of a contractor you hired, is hurt on your job you could be held responsible for medical expenses and maybe lost pay. Before hiring any contractor request a copy of his Workers Compensation Certificate. My home state of Colorado requires anyone hiring an employee, contractor or a sub-contractor to either provide worker's compensation insurance or require coverage. Cover all contacts with your attorney and request workers compensation.

2% Error Rate: I prepared a tax return for a client who I admired for his work ethic and the detailed preparation. Each year I looked forward to seeing him and his wife. We shared stories about our hobbies and his job as a police officer. Everything was great until one year I made a mistake on his return. It was a simple error and easily fixed and of course I paid any interest or penalty assessed by the IRS. But it wasn't simple for him. He was offended that I could make any error. I never saw him or his wife again. His perfect world was shattered, and he had no tolerance for mistakes. You and your employees will make errors. Get over it! It is not the mistake that is the problem; it is the way you handle the problem that is important. Always get on top of the problem and correct the error if possible.

Employment of Your Child if Under 18 Years of Age: A sole proprietor can engage the services of his/her child under the age 18, pay the child a tax deductible wage amount, pay no employment taxes on the wages, and the child will not have to pay income taxes on the wages unless the amount exceeds the IRS minimum deduction on the child's tax return. The wages need to be paid for work actually performed by the child for the business, payments need to be actually made to the child, wages must be reasonable in relationship to the services rendered, and records need to be maintained. This is one of the better income-shifting tax strategies. As an example, a sole proprietor parent in the 39.6% tax bracket pays his/her child $6,300 for services rendered, saving $2,495 in federal income taxes. The child puts $2,000 of the earnings in a tax-deductible IRA, and has no income tax on the entire $6,300 received. You also may be able to claim the child as a dependent. Check with your CPA or Tax Accountant.

Tax Tip:
As a sole proprietorship you can hire your children as an employee. You are not required to withhold Social Security and Medicare taxes on payments made to the child, as long as the child is under 18 years of age.

Paid Tax Preparers: Several years ago I corrected three years of tax returns for a small contractor. The returns were prepared by a national tax firm by the owner or manager of the franchise outlet. The net result was a refund of over $27,000. The tax preparation fees were over $2,500.00 and even when the taxpayer pointed out the errors the company refused to refund the fees. This example does not reflect all the tax preparers in this company but even my contacts with the franchisor yielded no results for a refund in fees charged. Not only was the tax preparer incompetent he was dishonest.

If you pay someone to prepare your tax return, the IRS urges you to choose that preparer wisely. Taxpayers are legally responsible for what's on their tax return even if it is prepared by someone else. So, it is important to choose carefully when hiring an individual or firm to prepare your return. Most return preparers are professional, honest and provide excellent service to their clients.

Here are a few points to keep in mind when someone else prepares your return:

Check the Person's Qualifications: New regulations require all paid tax return preparers to have a Preparer Tax Identification Number (PTIN). In addition to making sure they have a PTIN, ask if the preparer is affiliated with a professional organization and attends continuing education classes. The IRS also had required tax preparers to take a qualifying preparer test, however in January 2013 the court over turned this requirement. Enrolled agents and CPAs are required to obtain continuing education each year.

Check the preparer's history. Check to see if the preparer has a questionable history with the Better Business Bureau and check for any disciplinary actions and licensure status through the state boards of accountancy for certified public accountants; the state bar associations for attorneys; and the IRS Office of Enrollment for enrolled agents.

Find out about their service fees. Avoid preparers who base their fee on a percentage of your refund or those who claim they can obtain larger refunds than other preparers. Also, always make sure any refund due is sent to you or deposited directly into an account in your name. Under no circumstances should all or part of your refund be directly deposited into a preparer's bank account.

Ask if they offer electronic filing. Any paid preparer who prepares and files more than 10 returns for clients must file the returns electronically, unless the client opts to file a paper return. More than 1 billion individual tax returns have been safely and securely processed since the debut of electronic filing in 1990. Make sure your preparer offers IRS e-file.

Make sure the tax preparer is accessible. Make sure you will be able to contact the tax preparer after the return has been filed, even after the April due date, in case questions arise.

Provide all records and receipts needed to prepare your return. Reputable preparers will request to see your records and receipts and will ask you multiple questions to determine your total income and your qualifications for expenses, deductions and other items. Do not use a preparer who is willing to electronically file your tax return if you have not received your W-2. Using your last pay stub is against IRS e-file rules.

Never sign a blank return. Avoid tax preparers that ask you to sign a blank tax form.

Review the entire return before signing it. Before you sign your tax return, review it and asked questions. Make sure you understand everything and are comfortable with the accuracy of the return before you sign it.

Make sure the preparer signs the form and includes his or her preparer tax identification number (PTIN). A paid preparer must sign the return and include his or her PTIN as required by law. Although the preparer signs the return, you are responsible for the accuracy of every item on your return. The preparer must also give you a copy of the return.

The IRS can help many taxpayers prepare their own returns without the assistance of a paid preparer. Before seeking a paid preparer, taxpayers might consider how much information is available directly from the IRS through the IRS Web site. Check out these helpful links:

Elevator Deductions: I coined this term when I over-heard a tax payer explaining to his friend he could deduct the cost of his swimming pool as a medical expense. Could be true but just because you deduct an outrageous expense and the IRS does not audit your return, does not make the deduction legal or acceptable. Have fun by typing "Weird and illegal tax deduction" into your browser. The resulting list of creative tax deductions is amazing.

Tracking Your Self-Employed Income: Although companies are required to file Form 1099 for monies paid to contract laborers or independent individual contractors, many do not. Just because the payer failed to follow the law by reporting your income on a 1099 does not make the income received non-taxable, you are required to claim that income. When a payer snubs the law by failing to file 1099s, it does not create Non-Taxable income for the independent contractor. As a self-employed person you are required to maintain a record of your income and report all your income.

Home Office Deduction: If you use part of your home for business, you may be able to deduct expenses for the business use of your home. The home office deduction is available for homeowners and renters, and applies to all types of homes. Regular and Exclusive Use.

> **Regular Use:** You must regularly use part of your home exclusively for conducting business. For example, if you use an extra room to run your business, you can take a home office deduction for that extra room.

> **Principal Place of Your Business:** You must show that you use your home as your principal place of business. If you conduct business at a location outside of your home, but also use your home substantially and regularly to conduct business, you may qualify for a home office deduction. For example, if you have in-person meetings with patients, clients, or customers in your home in the normal course of your business, even though you also carry on business at another location, you can deduct your expenses for the part of your home used exclusively and regularly for business. You can deduct expenses for a separate free-standing structure, such as a studio, garage, or barn, if you use it exclusively and regularly for your business. The structure does not have to be your principal place of business or the only place where you meet patients, clients, or customers.

Dealing with the Internal Revenue Service: The IRS is responsible for enforcing tax laws and regulations. Filing and <u>paying income tax</u> is "voluntary," meaning the IRS allows individuals and businesses to calculate what they owe. But paying taxes isn't optional. If you don't pay your taxes, the IRS will initiate a collection process. The process starts with a bill in the mail. If you fail to pay or file for an extension or installment plan, the IRS will send collection agents to seize your assets. If the IRS finds irregularities in your tax filings, it will issue an audit of your financial records. Taxpayers have the right to fight any decision by the IRS and file a petition in U.S. Tax Court.

After years of dealing with the IRS I have discovered IRS agents are just like any other government employee, city, state or federal. Some are great to work with and a few are power happy bureaucrats. Most IRS agents are well trained and understand the problems facing the average tax payer deciphering 72,000 pages of IRS code. I cannot over emphasis the need to be represented by a qualified tax professional at any audit. No one individual understands all the IRS codes or the thousands of pages of regulations written for each income item or deductible item and you need your professional for support.

Select for an Audit: If you have been selected for audit don't become paranoid and assume the IRS is out to get you. Usually audits are selected by an IRS computer what has been programmed to analysis averages and create a numerical score for each return filed. These averages are available but the numerical score the IRS uses to select a particular tax return is a secret. We do know that business returns that have high automobile expenses deductions, high travel expenses and with little or no profit are audited more frequently.

CORRESPONDENCE AUDIT: The Correspondence Audit is a request from the IRS to send in copies of checks or receipts verifying one or two deductions. Usually this audit is limited to a small number of tax returns and your business probably will not be audited completely unless you cannot support the deductions in question.

If an income item or a deduction on your return does not match information the information the IRS received on a 1099 form, you will be notified that you owe additional tax and interest. Dividends, interest income, sales of stock and real estate sales are reported to the IRS on Form 1099. If you failed to report income or you reported a deduction item incorrectly the IRS will sent you a request for additional taxes or an explanation of the item. This is not an audit and is only the IRS system of checking many income items and deduction automatically.

Office Audit: An Office Audit is a more comprehensive and requests that you bring checks and receipts for several deductions to a local IRS office. Sole Proprietorships using a Schedule C and having receipts of less than a half a million dollars are audited more frequently. Many times the IRS couples a Schedule C audit with an audit of Itemized Deductions.

IRS Field Audit: Can be difficult and I suggest you obtain a CPA or accountant to represent you. Usually the audit is conducted at the Taxpayers business because the IRS agent is instructed to view the business facility. Many times your representative can change the location to his/her office. The auditor will interview the taxpayer and of course your representative should be present so he can protect you from questions that are considered fishing expeditions. IRS agents are trained to conduct the audit in such a manner as to probe areas where your business may be vulnerable such as areas where records are limited.

A TCMP Audit: TCMP means Taxpayer Compliance Measurement Program. I would prefer someone beat me with a stick and then ask me to fight a Bear naked than represent a client at a TCMP audit. Every line item on the return is reviewed down to the smallest detail. Pages and pages of notes are recorded by the auditor and a simple audit turns into a marathon of boredom and accusations. If you believe the IRS considers you guilty until you prove your innocent you should sit through a TCMP audit you may want to go to jail just to get away from the harassment.

Professional Representation: Sooner or later every small business will need an Attorney, a Public Accountant and/or a CPA and a Bookkeeper. Hiring any of these professionals presents many problems. I'm convinced that many professionals are not passionate about their profession and are more interested in your money than they are about your Business. If I could hire the perfect professional the following attributes are on top of my list.

Knowledge, Experience and Proficiency in his Profession

Passion for Her Profession

Imagination and Creatively To Foresee the Problems

Ability to explain and clarify who, what and why

Communication Skills with Client – Maintain Contact of Work Status

Timely Professional Service - Return Phone Calls and Emails in a Timely Manner

Does the Professional Provide Cost Estimates – Charge by the Hour or Provide Bids

There is no easy answer when hiring an attorney, CPA, Doctor or any other professional. You must get a referral. If you need a business attorney ask a small businessman that you know and respect. Ask a friend or even a relative. You are in charge when hiring any professional. List your questions, get an estimate and demand information about your problem and get answers. Demand weekly contact and a periodic up-date. If hire a bookkeeper or accountant read Chapter 5 and Chapter 6 in this handbook and request in writing what is included in the engagement. As an example you want a balanced set of books, bank statement balances and each month a meeting reviewing your business financial statements, include these requirements in your engagement agreement.

© 2007 by Randy Glasbergen.
www.glasbergen.com

"I can't talk right now. I tried to be more passionate about my job and my tongue is swollen from French kissing my coffee cup."

Notes

_____

_____

_____

_____

_____

_____

_____

_____

_____

_____

_____

_____

_____

_____

_____

_____

_____

_____

_____

_____

_____

_____

_____

_____

_____

41933500R00134

Made in the USA
Lexington, KY
02 June 2015